Globalization and Changes in China's Governance

Issues in Contemporary Chinese Thought and Culture

Edited by

Arif Dirlik
Yu Keping

VOLUME 1

The titles published in this series are listed at brill.com/icct

Globalization and Changes in China's Governance

By

Yu Keping

BRILL

LEIDEN • BOSTON
2013

This volume is also published in Chinese by Chongqing Publishing House as part of a special agreement between Chongqing Publishing House and Koninklijke Brill NV.

This book is printed on acid-free paper.

Library of Congress Cataloging-in-Publication Data

Yu, Keping.
    Globalization and changes in China's governance / by Yu Keping.
       p. cm. — (Issues in contemporary Chinese thought and culture ; v. 1)
      ISBN 978-90-04-15682-1 (hardback : alk. paper) 1. China—Politics
and government—1976-2002. 2. China—Politics and government—2002-
3. Globalization. I. Title.

    JQ1510.Y9 2008
    320.951—dc22

                                                                    2008011286

ISSN   1874-0588
ISBN   978-90-04-25030-7

This paperback was originally published in hardback under ISBN 978-90-04-15682-1.

Printed by Printforce, the Netherlands

CONTENTS

CHAPTER ONE

INTRODUCTION
CHANGES IN GOVERNANCE AND POLITICAL DEVELOPMENT IN CHINA UNDER THE IMPACT OF GLOBALIZATION

There is an intensifying awareness globally of globalization as the creation of an integrated global market place, signaling a high degree of interdependence of the global economy. But, globalization goes well beyond the merely economic. Political and cultural factors have, in fact, become the main bone of contention, as well as the aspirations implied by the term. Rather than compartmentalizing globalization into facets of political, economic, and cultural integration, it is important to spell out its essential contradictions, such as between integration and fragmentation, uniformity and diversity, centralization and decentralization, internationalization and also localization.

The impact of globalization on political life speaks for itself. In international politics, traditional concepts of sovereignty and governance are undergoing far-reaching transformations. Economic globalization has also changed important political structures and processes, as well as concepts, challenging traditional assumptions, thus injecting new life into the political process.

Nation states have served as the core of political life in modern times. Nation states have been established as the center-piece of political modernity along the principles of territory, sovereignty, and citizenship. [For any independent political entity to become a country it must have a certain expanse of territory that is independent and inviolable. This independent and fixed territory must have a sovereign organ that represents the will of the state. State sovereignty cannot be divided, nor be imposed by way of intervention by any other country. Within a certain territory there must be a sufficient number of citizens, whose responsibilities and rights are protected only by the laws and government of this territory. Such citizens can only express their wills and use their rights when they belong to a territorial country. Therefore, citizens (*gongmin*) are usually identical to nationals (*guomin*).]

The traditional nation state has been seriously challenged in its three main components, namely of territory, sovereignty, and citizenship, thus unsettling people's minds around the world. As Ulrich Beck notes:

> People can either deny and attack globalization or applaud it. But no matter how people evaluate globalization, a [certain] popular theory will be involved, which is to say, that the use of territories to characterize and define social realms, which has attracted and inspired political, social, and scientific imagination in every way for [the past] two centuries, is now disintegrating. Global capitalism is accompanied by processes of cultural and political globalization that cause the collapse of the self-images with which people have been familiar and the [collapse of the] picture of the world based on territorial socialization and cultural and intellectual systems.[1]

Economic globalization is prevalent in the flows of capital, products, and communication, breaking through national barriers, demanding free movement throughout the world. Without the free flow of capital, products, and communication there is no globalization to speak of. This global flow also requires global organizations, as organs of coordination. International organizations, and multinational corporations in particular, are thus given enhanced status.

The global market and multinational organizations of necessity conflict with the concept of state territory. Wherever boundaries restrict the requirements of global economic circulation, multinational corporations and organizations will strive to overcome these boundaries which they regard as being artificial. Where economic globalization conflicts with state territory, the territory gives way to the imperative of economic globalization. As Ralph Dahrendorf has stated: "Globalization points out a direction, and only a direction. The space of economic activities is expanding and it goes beyond the boundaries of nation states. And the important thing is that the space for political adjustment and control is also expanding."[2]

Territory is closely connected with sovereignty. In the words of Smith and Naim, in *Altered States*:

> In this aspect, globalization has a powerful and complex impact: the regulations of globalization concerning human rights and democratic governance are penetrating national boundaries and reshaping the tra-

---

[1] Ulrich Beck, "How feasible is democracy in the age of globalization?" *Globalization and Politics* (Beijing: Zhongyang Bianyi Chubanshe, 2000), p. 14.

[2] Ralph Dahrendorf, "On Globalization," *Globalization and Politics* (Beijing: Zhongyang Bianyi Chubanshe, 2000), p. 212.

ditional concepts of sovereignty and autonomy…these regulations have been formed, are developing, and are making legitimate international intervention which prevents serious violations of human rights and collective security.[3]

The influence of economic globalization on state sovereignty can be illustrated by three points. First, global economic activities such as multinational investment inevitably require appropriate political environments. When the demands of the former conflict with political structures, it is now taken for granted that the political structures need to compromise. Consequently, the original processes of political and economic decision-making in nation states have undergone greater or lesser degrees of change. Such systemic changes, directly or indirectly, challenge sovereignty.

Second, economic globalization has resulted in the generalization of certain political values, such as freedom, democracy, human rights, and peace in particular. Instances of genocide, for instance, invariably trigger international calls for intervention—although power politics invariably enter into such decisions. Finally, domestic phenomena, such as the environment, resources, poverty, crime, drug abuse, or overpopulation, have become internationalized, as problems of this nature rarely stop at borders and therefore require multilateral and international cooperation. Welcomed or not, such international cooperation often weakens a state's sovereignty.

Economic globalization also challenges both the nation state and concepts of citizenship and nationality. The generally recognized consequences of financial globalization have their equivalent in the labor market. Heads of multinational corporations, their senior managers, technicians, and even general laborers, increasingly travel to the branches of multinationals established around the globe. Loyalty is first and foremost to their corporation rather than to their own country or nation. Immigration is rising in tandem. According to statistics published by international immigration organizations, the number of new immigrants totaled over 100 million in the early 1990s. Most were legal immigrants, although a small number were illegal. These immigrants find their sense of national identity challenged by spatial relocation. Even for common citizens who remain at home, traditional notions of

---

[3] Gordon Smith and Mois Naim, *Altered States: Globalization, Sovereignty, and Governance* (IDRC, 1999), p. 27.

political identity are being tested. Economic globalization, the Internet, and the internationalization of the ecological and environmental awareness have made the sense of national identity among citizens less important than global awareness. So-called new identity politics have appeared, and some among the pioneering parties, such as those who see themselves protecting the international environment, have even called themselves "global citizens."

These changes have inspired some scholars to define globalization as "de-statification," eliminating the unity between economic and political space. As Dittgen has noted, "it is impossible for the Western World to go back to the age of the nation state." "The trend of de-statification in various societies means that the connections and roles of the economic, ecological, cultural, and military behavior are quickly developing, so the creation of a multinational political administrative organ is of critical practical importance but develops only very slowly."[4] Some scholars have even hypothesized that globalization has damaged national autonomy, and that a "social world" is replacing the "national world," rendering the nation state obsolete and leading to its destruction.[5]

This, however, may well be exaggerated. Nation states and sovereign governments will continue to play essential roles in the political life of mankind for the foreseeable future. Nor can their continued importance be denied. But we cannot deny that the role of the state is gradually being reduced, and governance formed by citizens and civilian organizations is gaining in importance. The age-old dream of "governing without government" and "stateless governance" seems to be becoming a reality in many realms of political life. Democracy, human rights, and legal justice have gradually become universal values, while autocracy is losing ground.

Global governance has become one of the most prominent issues of the post-Cold War era. In 1992, the United Nations established a "Commission on Global Governance" at the initiative of veteran German politician Willy Brandt; Ivar Carlsson, former Swedish prime minister, served as its first chairman. In 1995, the commission published a study entitled *Our Global Partnership*, which has influenced international rela-

---

[4] Mitchell Zen and others, "The Reactive Mode of Black, Green, and Brown Concerning the Trend of Anti-Nation State," in Ulrich Beck, *Globalization and Politics* (Beijing: Zhongyang Bianyi Chubanshe, 2000) pp. 162 and 171.

[5] Herbert Dittgen, "World without borders? Reflections on the future of the nation-state," *Government and Opposition* 2.34 (1999).

tions until the present day. In the same year, the committee created the magazine *Global Governance*.

Global Governance postulates that the end of the Cold War does not mean the end of conflicts among regions and countries and that, on the contrary, conflicts have become more widespread, sometimes escalating to regional catastrophes. Such conflicts remain a major threat to livelihood, peace, and human rights. Violence and conflict cannot be ignored and need to be eliminated by concerted international action. Meanwhile, international cooperation in political, economic, cultural, scientific and technological issues has increased in an unprecedented way. Such cooperation calls for a common regulatory system to which each country adheres in order to respect and preserve values taken to be universal. Third, every country is called upon to protect the environment, eliminate poverty, contain international terrorism, and eliminate multinational crimes, so that the order within the international community is maintained.

In order to promote the common good, global governance requires that we seek democratic consultation and cooperation among all governments, international organizations, as well as individual citizens. In essence, it requires the enhancing of a new, worldwide political and economic order, leading to security, peace, development, welfare, equality, and human rights. In a sense, global governance is the extension of domestic governance into the international. As Pierre Sanerkellens has argued:

> In the field of international relations, global governance is first of all the product of agreements and practices among countries, particularly, among powers. The regulations and systems cover not only governments, but also the non-governmental mechanism that depends on its own means to realize its will and achieve its goals. Governance is regarded as a regulatory system formed by major agreements. It can implement certain collective projects without the authorization and approval of governments. The informal process promoted by various organizations of governments, non-governmental organizations, and multinational corporations, is also included in governance. Therefore, it is not only the product of international negotiations in which each country participates, but also, it is the result of combinations of individuals, collectives, organizations of governments, and non-governmental organizations.[6]

---

[6] Pierre De Sanerkellens, "The Crisis of Administration and the Mechanism of International Regulation," *International Social Science* (Chinese edition) (February, 1999), p. 91.

In the post-Cold War age of economic globalization, there is a need to maintain a new global political and economic order, as well fulfilling the promise of existing international and governmental organizations, as nation states are unable to govern the world. Under such conditions, some people wish to see the United Nations strengthened, until it can take on the functions of a national government—a "world government," so to speak. For the foreseeable future this is obviously utopian.

In its history of over fifty years, the United Nations has played an important role in maintaining international security and in promoting common policies (such as for health, culture or crime prevention). It will continue to play this essential role for a long time into the future. Nonetheless, it is as impossible for the United Nations to become the sole seat of global governance as it is for individual state governments to substitute this role. Global governance should be shared by the individual governments, international organizations, and worldwide civil society. As the Commission on Global Governance has stated, "At the global level, governance basically refers to the relations among governments. However, we must understand now that it also includes non-governmental organizations, civil movements, multilateral cooperation, and the global capital market."[7]

"Worldwide civil society" is an umbrella term for, inter alia, international non-governmental organizations, global civil networks, and civil movements. In the age of economic globalization, its role cannot be overemphasized. In quantity and relevance, non-governmental organizations are increasing at a daily rate. According to *The Yearbook of International Organizations*, of the existing 48,350 international organizations, non-governmental international civil organizations constitute 95%, i.e., totaling in excess of 46,000. To cite another example, in 1972 there were fewer than 300 non-governmental organizations participating in the United Nations' Environmental Conference, whereas by 1992 the number of registered non-governmental organizations in the Environmental Conference had risen to 1,400. Those participating in the Forum of Non-Governmental Organizations had transcended 18,000. In 1968, at the Tehran International Human Rights Conference, non-governmental organizations which had gained the status of official observers numbered fifty-three, and there were no more than four attending its

---

[7] "The Commission on Global Governance": *Our Global Partnership*, chapter 1 (Oxford University Press, 1995), p. 3.

preliminary meetings. In contrast, at the 1993 Vienna International Human Rights Conference there were 248 similar organizations with observer status, while 593 non-governmental organizations attended the conference. At the 1976 Non-Governmental Forum of the World Women Conference in Mexico there were only six thousand attendees, with 114 non-governmental organizations attending the formal meetings. However, the 1995 Non-Governmental Forum of the World Women Conference in Beijing counted 300,000 attendees and three thousand non-governmental organizations.[8]

A new development in worldwide civil society is the formation of global civil networks established on the basis of the internet and other technological communications. It is impossible to calculate accurately the number of global civil networks in existence, though it is certain that such networks are being generated on a daily basis throughout the world—with problematic political consequences, we might add. The number of global civil networks is much higher than that of global civil and social organizations. As of the present, governments and multinational organizations (such as the United Nations) have played predominant roles in global governance. Their roles are increasingly being shared by global civil society.

A recent trend that has emerged in Western theories of global governance provides a new challenge; namely that multinational corporations, alongside individual countries, may intervene in the internal affairs of other countries in the hope of establishing international hegemony. By emphasizing the multinational and global nature of governance, at the expense of government national sovereignty, and of international boundaries, theoretical ammunition is being provided to multinational corporations to intervene in the internal affairs of other countries in order to implement policies of international hegemony. This certainly constitutes a highly destabilizing trend within the theoretical framework of global governance.

The influence of economic globalization on the domestic politics of nation states is proving to be equally pervasive. In addition to challenges that can be summarized as 'anti-nation state' economic globalization is also transforming established domestic processes and systems of politics and culture. Values such as democracy, freedom, equality, human rights

---

[8] Ann Marie Clark, E.J. Friedman and K. Hochsterler, "The Sovereign Limits of Global Civil Society," *World Politics* (October, 1998), pp. 1–35.

are becoming universal political values and standards. With the rise of satellite television, the internet, and electronic publications domestic monopolies over political information are quickly losing ground. Moreover, since economic globalization mainly consists of bilateral or multilateral communication and interaction, we see that domestic political processes are gradually changing from the traditional form of vertical interaction (top to bottom) to a more horizontal type. That is to say, mandatory governmental action lessens as consultative and cooperative action increases. In terms of political systems, we see that economic globalization directly or indirectly promotes countries that, by participating in international economic life, establish a set of more democratic and effective political mechanisms to ensure a stable and peaceful environment for economic development. This brings prosperity not only in economic terms, but also in a concrete political sense.

To sum up, in terms of domestic politics, globalization is transforming the traditional operational mechanisms of power, the way in which politics are conveyed, the organizational structure of politics, and political culture. Globalization is transforming governments from traditional "good government" (*shanzheng*), to modern "good governance" (*shanzhi*). This globalization of political life does not only occur in developed countries, but also in the developing world. The recent far-reaching transformations in Chinese political life amply demonstrate this.

China's process of reform and opening to the outside world is as much an expression of the desire to end self-isolation as of a willingness to actively participate in globalization. As the chief architect of China's reform program, Deng Xiaoping decided to interweave domestic reforms with international liberalization. Deng Xiaoping thus had a good understanding of the key characteristics of our age, namely that against the imperative of economic globalization, domestic life is inextricably entwined with international affairs, constituting two sides of the same coin. The great accomplishments of the past twenty-odd years, and here all leading academics agree, have been mostly limited to the economic sector, without fundamental changes in the political realm. Some scholars go further, attributing the good fortune of the Chinese reforms with failed policy programs in the late Soviet Union, theorizing that the very emphasis on economic rather than political reform provided the recipe for success.

It is a fact that Chinese political reform has lagged behind economic reform. The assumption, however, that China has merely experienced economic transformation without any political changes is not accurate. Historical hindsight stipulates that any immersion into economic globalization will sooner or later change domestic politics—regardless of popular rhetoric or state policies, China being no exception.

Since the beginning of the reforms, the Chinese government has signed up to a series of international human rights accords, particularly *The Treaty of International Human and Civil Rights* or the *The International Treaty of Economic, Cultural, and Social Rights*. Generally speaking, such measures should promote the systematic and international protection of civil rights. But it is not merely a reason to rejoice for China's citizens. The mere fact that the Chinese government has decided to adopt such international legislation indicates that the political and ideological culture governing Chinese society since 1949 has been greatly affected by globalization. The only elements of China's recent political culture to transcend its borders were those of international communism. Beyond the realm of economic and commercial treaties, no international or bilateral civil rights treaties with universally binding force were ratified. China's participation in the above treaties shows that, to a certain extent, the Chinese government has begun to acknowledge the existence of political values that transcend national borders, political systems and ideologies. Realizing universal political values requires the concerted efforts of the international community, including the cooperation of countries with different political systems.

The existence of universal political values, as a concept within civil political culture, has become increasingly acknowledged within China. This may be regarded as a consequence of the reform policies. Indeed, the terrible era of so-called speech crimes, the period of brutal oppression and struggles that the Chinese people have had to endure seem to belong to the past. And yet, Chinese intellectuals still criticize the government and the current political system in a tone unprecedented since the rise to power of the Chinese Communist Party. How to interpret such a contradictory phenomenon?

One factor is that political reform is lagging behind economic development. Negative political realities are evident in political corruption, social inequity, violation of democratic rights. On the other hand, this may also be due to the transformation of the standards of evaluating politics. During the chaos of the Cultural Revolution, devoid of law and tolerance, those who did not criticize the political system and instead resorted to worshipping it did so because of the dogmatic positions of the extreme left. Ever since, people have gradually come to express their dissatisfactions with the political situation openly, sometimes even criticizing sharply. This is due to the fact that modern, democratic values have become the standard by which people interpret politics.

This "new democracy" incorporates components from every major democracy, and encompasses universal values that transcend national boundaries. As a result, the evaluation of politics has changed from an emphasis on hierarchical political structures (vertical perspectives) to the corruptions of everyday life (horizontal perspectives). Among young intellectuals we hardly hear the comment that China is doing much better compared to the past. Instead, we hear mantras of how backwards China is compared to other countries. No matter what the development materially, China still suffers from negative evaluations, no matter what the changes!

Such transformations constitute radical changes in political values, political culture and the standards for evaluating politics. In other dimensions of political culture, such as attitude and ideology, we see obvious changes as well. An increasing number of China's citizens, especially, among the young, no longer submit to government oppression, or social pressure to conform. They have begun to hold relatively independent attitudes and reactions to government policies. The slogans such as "We will fight wherever the Party directs us!" or "We will follow the Superior's directives whether or not we understand them!" belong to the past now. On the contrary, civic awareness and self-protection have increased greatly. Attitudes are gradually departing from Chinese traditions, instead approaching universal political values. There can be no doubt that without the reforms and without foreign influence China's relative isolation would have continued. Economic globalization has accelerated processes of political and cultural transformations. Without the globalization of the 1980s, such great changes would have been difficult within such a short time.

Civic values, ideology and attitudes determine civil conduct. The transformation of China's civic culture has inevitably resulted in changes in social and political life, which in turn reflect the transformation of the Chinese political culture. It is due to this changing political culture since the 1980s that China's politics has, directly and indirectly, reflected globalizing trends.

The Beginning Separation of Party and State

The PRC's traditional politics have been characterized by the integration of Party, state, and government. When Mao Zedong referred to this political system as "the absolute and centralized leadership of the Party" he meant a highly centralized mode of leadership. Thus, the Communist Party as the sole powerbroker controls all aspects of administration, legislation, and judiciary, even economic and ideological management. The Party thus equals both state and government.

At the very start of the reforms, the leaders of the Chinese Communist Party had propagated "the separation of Party and administration." After twenty years of political effort, the Party has not attained this goal. This is partly because in reality it is impossible to completely separate the Party from the government in a one-party state. Nevertheless, there has been important ideological progress. The Chinese Communist Party has formally declared that it is not above the law, and that it must abide by PRC laws. The new Party constitution stipulates that "the Party must act within the scope of the constitution and laws." From the Central Committee to the grassroots, Party organizations and members have been instructed not to transgress against the state's constitution and laws.[9]

Secondly, the Party no longer can take over the government's administrative roles. The political report of the Thirteenth Central Committee of the Party made particular reference to the separation of Party and government, stipulating that the Party was not to replace the government as the administrative organ. The key to such political system reform is to define the functions of the Party as distinct from those of the government: "The Party leads the people and establishes national authority, by organizing the people, the economy and cultural life. The Party should ensure that authorized organizations play their roles to the fullest, and it should respect the work of enterprises and institutions rather than seeking to replace their roles." The report also reiterated that the Party's authority over the state should not constitute administrative but rather "political" leadership, namely in terms of guidance concerning political principles and direction, critical decision-making, and the recommending of cadres to positions within the government.[10]

---

[9] The Central Committee of the Chinese Communist Party, "The Announcement of the Central Committee Concerning the Firm Safeguarding of the Socialist Legal System" (July 10, 1986). See *Selected Documents of the People's Congress by* the Research Office of the Standing Committee of the People's Congress (China Democratic and Legal System Press, 1992), p. 166.

[10] See "Advancing Along the Socialist Road which Features Chinese Characteristics," and "The Political Report of the Central Committee of the Chinese Communist Party," *Selected Documents of the People's Congress by* the Research Office of the Standing Committee of the People's Congress (China Democratic and Legal System Press, October 25, 1987), p. 185.

The Emergence of Civil Society

China under Mao Zedong witnessed not only a high degree of integration between Party and state, but also between state and society. There was virtually no independent civil society. However, a relatively independent civil society has gradually developed, with the following four characteristics: 1) Rapid increase in the number of civic organizations; 2) Diversification of types of civic organizations; 3) Enhanced independence of civil organizations; and 4) Increased legitimacy of civic organizations. Pre-reform period organizations, such as trade unions, the Communist Youth League, and the Women's Federation, were without exception subordinate to the Party and government. These were deeply integrated with Party and government, and had no independent features. This began to change with the emergence of civil society as a by-product of the reform period.

Since the 1980s, civic and social organizations have undergone dramatic developments. Between the 1950s to the 1970s, the number of independent associations and mass organizations was negligible. During the 1950s, there were merely forty-four nationwide associations. During the 1960s there were fewer than one hundred national organizations, and only about six thousand local associations. In contrast, in 1989, the number of nationwide associations had dramatically increased to 1,600 and local ones to 200,000. In 1997, associations and organizations above county level numbered 180,000, those at provincial level numbered 21,404, while nationwide associations and organizations numbered 1,848.[11] Although we do not have any formal statistics for the number of all civic organizations, a conservative estimate would put these at above three million.[12] Among these, we find some 730,950 village committees, and 510,000 union organizations at grassroots level.[13]

---

[11] *Zhongguo Minzheng Gongzuo Nianjian 1998 (Yearbook of China's Civil Work: 1998)* (Beijing: Zhongguo Shehui Chubanshe, 1999), p. 274.

[12] Since the 1990s, many civil organizations have been developed in villages and towns. Usually, there are 3 or 4 civil organizations in each village, such as villager's self-governing committee, women's association and elder's association. China has a total of 2,135 counties, 44,689 towns, and approximately 740,000 villages. According to a conservative estimate, registered and unregistered civil organizations number up to at least 3 million or more.

[13] *Zhongguo Tongji Nianjian 1998 (Yearbook of China's Statistics: 1998)* (Zhongguo Tongji Chubanshe, 1999), p. 385.

In addition to community organizations, China has developed another type of special civic organization, the so-called civic non-enterprise unit [Minban Feiqiyi Danwei].[14] Civic non-enterprise units are civil service units. Based on initial estimates, in 1998 this type of organization numbered more than 700,000.[15] These civil organizations are playing important roles in Chinese democracy and administration.[16]

Rule of Law

The roots of the political tragedy unfolding with the Cultural Revolution lie in the lack of rule of law at the time. The state depended on being ruled by one man, rather than by legal principles. Because of a traditional propensity to place individuals above the law, Chinese leaders and intellectuals have particularly emphasized the construction of a legal system, with the long-term goal of establishing an immutable legal system. In September 1997, the Fifteenth Central Committee of the Chinese Communist Party formally announced that its political aim was to "rule the country by law and to establish a socialist state under the rule of law." This goal was included in the report from the meeting. In March 1999, the Second Meeting of the People's Congress revised the existing constitution and formally included the stipulation of "ruling the country by law and establishing a socialist state with rule of law" into the constitution. It also promoted the stipulation "ruling the country by law," as a principle in the state constitution. From 1979 to 1999, the People's Congress and its standing committee passed 351 laws and related resolutions, while the State Council established more than 800 administrative legal regulations. The local People's Congresses and their standing committees established over 6,000 local legal regulations.[17] From 1994 to 1996, the national People's Congress and its

---

[14] Concerning the definition of civil non-enterprise units, see *The Temporary Regulation of the Registration of Civil Non-Enterprise Units* ("Instruction of the State Council of the People's Republic of China, No. 251" passed by the Eighth Standing Committee of the State Council on September 25, 1998).

[15] *Zhongguo Minzheng Gongzuo Nianjian 1998 (Yearbook of China's Civil Work: 1998)* (Beijing: Zhongguo Shehui Chubanshe, 1999), p. 274.

[16] About the rise of Chinese civil society and its impacts on political life, see "The Rise of Chinese Civil Society and Its Impacts on Governance," Yu Keping, *China Social Science Quarterly*, Hong Kong, Fall, 1999.

[17] See *Renming Ribao (People's Daily)*, April 14, 1999, p. 3.

standing committee promulgated a law almost every thirteen days. The State Council established one administrative law every six days. The expressed aim of the Chinese government is to establish a functioning legal system before 2010.[18]

Direct Elections and Local Autonomy

China's leaders during the reform period have paid close attention to implementing democracy at grassroots level and have stressed grassroots democracy. Accordingly, *The Election Law of the National and Local People's Congresses of the People's Republic of China* stipulates that county level delegates and local representatives should be directly elected by general vote. Even though party and government functionaries at any levels of government are not directly elected by citizens, one administrative village (*xiang*) head and one town (*zhen*) head were directly elected by voters in Sichuan Province in 1989, and in the Shenzhen Special Economic Zone in 1999. This indicates that the scope of direct elections at municipal level may be expanding gradually. In terms of grassroots democracy, the most remarkable development can be seen in the implementation of village autonomy. *The Organization Law of Village Committees of the People's Republic of China* passed by the Standing Committee of the People's Congress in December 1989 stipulates that an autonomous system for villages will be gradually implemented. State authorities no longer administer village affairs and village head and cadres will be freely elected by villagers. At the end of 1997, about 60% of China's rural areas had begun to implement village self-governance and had elected more than 900,000 village committees. The rate of participation of villagers in elections rose to 90%. Village self-governance rests on four main principles:

1) *The Principle of Village Election*
   The village head and members of the village committee are elected by villagers in direct, free, and secret ballots.

---

[18] Jiang Zemin: "Holding High the Great Flag of Deng Xiaoping's Theory and Promoting the Socialist that has the Chinese Characteristics Into the 21st Century," *The Collected Documents of the Fifteenth Central Committee of the Chinese Communist Party*, People's Press (Beijing: Renmin Chubanshe), p. 33.

2) *The Principle of Discussions Concerning Village Affairs*
   Any large village event, including plans for economic and social
   development, public welfare issues, and "hot" topics, with which
   the majority of the village is concerned, must be discussed during
   a consultation of village representatives and the village meeting,
   pursuant to the relevant regulations.
3) *The Principle of Openness in Village Affairs*
   Any issues of interest to the entire village should regularly be
   publicized and supervised by members of the village.
4) *The Principle of Village Regulations and Agreements*
   Village affairs are administered autonomously and in agreements
   with the village population.

Of China's population of roughly 1.3 billion people, more than 800
million are peasants. The implementation of village autonomy has
played an important role in developing Chinese democratic politics.

The Separation of Government and Private Economy

Government ownership and direct management of enterprises constituted one of the characteristics of traditional socialism. Under such a
system, the state held a monopoly and operated all important enterprises. The leaders of the enterprises were appointed by the Party and
the government. These leaders enjoyed the attention of administrative
officials. These enterprises were characterized by strict hierarchies identical to those within the civil service. The most important enterprises
enjoyed political and economic attention from the ministries. At ministe-
rial level officials served as the main managers. The integration of the
government and enterprises formed the basis of the traditional command economy and was the inevitable result of a planned economy.

The implementation of a market economy requires the establishment
of a system of modern enterprises. The prerequisite of such a system
is that an enterprise must be an independent legal entity. The new
generation of China's leaders has regarded the separation of government and enterprises as a major reform aim. The twenty-year reform,
in a certain sense, has been a process of separating government from
private enterprise. The Fourth Plenary Session of the Fifteenth Central
Committee of the Chinese Communist Party centered on reforming
state enterprises. The plenary session passed a resolution that formally

decided to establish the system of modern enterprises adapted to a market economy.

The separation of government and private enterprise is a complex process, and it is far from finished. Nevertheless, there have been remarkable accomplishments. All enterprises, including those hitherto under state management, have been completely separated from the administrative system. The government no longer manages enterprises directly. The majority of state-owned enterprises has transformed, or is in the process of transforming, their form of ownership and mode of management. Leaders of enterprises will no longer enjoy the attention of party and government officials.

The integration of administration and the economy serves as the basis of absolute, centralized politics. Since this foundation is now extinct, absolute and centralized politics have been fundamentally shaken.

Local Government Innovations

With recent changes in the political ideology and culture, local governments, particularly those at grassroots level, have proven to be a powerful force for system innovation. Innovation has become a conscious act for many organs of the Party and the administration. We can discern the following characteristics:

1) *Political Transparency*

    a. Openness in Administrative Affairs
Before making important policy decisions, Party and state organs are urged to accept advice and suggestions from the population and experts. Wherever possible, persons affected are able to participate in the decision-making process, to avoid "operating in a black box."
Policy is made public before it is issued and implemented.

    b. Openness in Police Affairs
On issues of interest to citizens, such as public security, registrations of residence, detainment, authorities inform the affected population, and allow them to give their feedback.

    c. Openness in Judicial Affairs
Trials are conducted openly and citizens are allowed to attend and listen to trials.

    d. Openness in Procuratorial Affairs
       In order to maintain public scrutiny in procuratorial affairs, lawyers are allowed to prepare in advance against criminal suspects.

    e. Openness in Making Appointment
       The authorities publish a candidate list before part and administrative leaders within Party and administration, while listening to the opinions of the public within a set period of time.

    f. Government by Internet ("e-government")
       The government issues administrative messages, conducts other government business, handles public affairs and accepts virtual visits by citizens.

2) *Administrative Services*

    a. Mayor's Hotline
       A 24-hour Mayor's Hotline is set up. Citizens can make direct phone calls and put forth criticism, opinion, and suggestions concerning government policies and actions. The government maintains responsibility for handling such calls.

    b. Leader Visits
       Public leaders such as mayors, county or township heads, and Party secretaries make regular visits at the grassroots level accompanied by leaders of Party organs and local government leaders, to solve problems "on the spot," by listening to citizens' complaints, requests, and suggestions. When an issue can be solved immediately each organ makes an effort. If a resolution is not forthcoming, such problems are to be resolved within a determined period of time, otherwise a response and explanation is issued to the concerning party.

    c. "Government Affairs Supermarket"
       Village governments concentrate their administrative organs on doing business in order to provide convenience to residents who live in that administrative area.

    d. Assistance to the Poor
       The government issues concrete plans and policies to help the poor or disadvantaged to rid themselves of poverty within a certain period of time.

e. Public Security and Joint Defense
A patrol system within communities has been established, including the 110 Emergency Phone Call System, preventing a further rise in criminal activities.

f. Universal Education
The government runs compulsory schools in rural districts and urban communities in order to provide free education to residents.

3) *Cadre Selection and Power Restriction*

a. Appointing Cadres through Competition
Authorities publish information concerning official openings, encouraging qualified citizens to apply and participate in fair competitions. Candidates are selected and employed according to merit. Currently, open competitions for the highest official position depend on the departmental head.

b. Direct Election of Town Heads
In recent years, some provinces and towns have implemented direct elections, as an offshoot of elections of village committee directors, and mayors. For example, direct mayoral election occurred in Buyun Town in Sichuan Province, and Dapeng Township in Shenzhen.

c. Public Recommendation and Selection, or the "Two Votes System."
In some grassroots areas, outside pressure can now influence the decision of the Party branch secretary at elections within the Party.

d. Administrative Lawsuit ("citizens sue officials")
Citizens may lodge suits against any illegal government conduct in court. If the court decides that a government has acted illegally, citizens have the right of remuneration of damages.

e. Financial Audit at the Time of Leaving Post
Before cadres of the Party and the administration leave their posts, they are required to undergo a financial government audit in order to determine if they have violated state and Party rules during their time of service.

f. Supervision of Public Opinion
Some local governments have made special legal regulations to ensure that the media can supervise government actions, and to allow the media to expose and criticize illegal actions of government officials.

4) *Administrative Efficiency and Honesty*

    a. Simplification of Administrative Approval Processes
    Many local governments provide "a package" of administrative services in order to reduce approval times and administrative costs.

    b. Focus on Administrative Responsibilities
    The government implements various types of duty systems in order to prevent bureaucracy and (a "ball game" situation) corruption.

    c. Handling Emergencies
    The government should deviate from regular administrative processes in order to handle public service emergencies.

The political developments in China discussed above have different characteristics. Some of these characteristics are universal, others local; some have developed from the elite level to the grassroots level, and some have developed from "bottom" to "top." Some pertain to systems and some to policy. Some are mere formalities and some have had real impact. Yet there exist common aspects underlying these political developments. First, all of the above developments and changes were products of the reform period, related to domestic politics. However, China's political realities have been closely connected to the policy of opening up to the outside world. In this sense, political reforms have been the outcome of economic globalization. Without the active participation in economic globalization, it would have been very difficult to achieve such political developments.

Secondly, the above developments have emerged out of China, as a creation of the Chinese people, thus deeply integrated with China's national characteristics. At the same time, they manifest universal political values: freedom, democracy, equality, and human rights.

Thirdly, the basic aim of political change has been to establish a modern, democratic administrative system, and to ensure the enjoyment of democratic rights such as freedom, equality, dignity.

China's participation in globalization as a developing country is not a matter of whether it is willing to participate, but rather how to seize this opportunity, choose its own way of participation, and avoid as much as possible any negative influences. The Chinese government has actively implemented the policy of opening up to the world, has developed economic and commercial ties throughout the world, and has made great efforts to join the WTO. This shows that China is actively participating in economic globalization. China ought to bravely face the challenges of globalization, outbalancing negative influences by positive ones. This is the correct attitude needed to face economic globalization.

In brief, economic globalization will inevitably bring important changes not only to China's economy, but also to its society and political life, both in terms of global and domestic governance. In terms of global governance, China has actively undertaken important responsibilities in international peace and security, and it has played an important role in the United Nations and other international organizations. It has been dedicated to establishing a new international political and economic order, and promoting peace and development. In terms of domestic governance, China has gradually established political values such as democracy and a legal system, emphasizing values such as efficiency, honesty, responsibility, cooperation, participation and fairness. Such are the political requirements of economic globalization.

CHAPTER TWO

GLOBALIZATION AND CAPACITY OF PUBLIC SECTORS: A CASE STUDY OF CHINA

Introduction

We have entered a new historical period, characterized by economic globalization, multi-polarization, cultural diversification, and information networking. Globalization of capital, markets, production, information, science, technology, and labor not only intensifies interaction and communication between states, but also greatly affects the economic and political realities within. This became evident in the aftermath of the South-East Asian financial crisis and the September 11th terrorist attack on the USA, directly influencing the entire world.

Globalization is shaping the history of all nations, including China. The most recent stage in the modernization of China, initiated in 1978 and characterized by reform and opening to the outside world, is a process of active participation in globalization. This modernization strategy has created an economic miracle. From 1978 to 2003, the Chinese gross national product has increased from RMB 362.4 billion (US$44.2 billion) to RMB 11,690 billion (US$1,425.6 billion). Ignoring the price index, it has increased 8.4 times, with an average annual growth rate exceeding 9%. This growth rate is much higher than the 2.5% average GNP growth rate of developed countries, the 5% growth rate of developing countries, and the 3% average world growth rate during the same period, when China has registered the fastest economic growth in the world. At current foreign exchange rates, per capita GNP in 2003 was US$1,090, catapulting China from one of the "low income countries of the world" to the rank of "medium-low income countries." In the past twenty-five years, China has solved the problem of providing adequate food and clothing for people below the poverty line, which in its rural areas has been reduced from 30.3% to 3.1%. The chasm in economic performance between China and the major developed countries has been reduced. According to World Bank statistics, in 2002 already, the domestic national product in China was ranked sixth only after the USA, Japan, Germany, France, and the United Kingdom.[1]

This economic miracle is a product of Deng Xiaoping's policy of domestic reform and external liberalization, two dimensions of the same modernization process. Inadvertently, Deng Xiaoping demonstrated that he regarded globalization as the historical condition for China's development strategy. In his view, economic, political and cultural interactions have become so important that "no country can develop by isolating itself from the outside world."[2] Attempting to do the opposite would result in political suicide. As the biggest developing country, China is no exception. The new generation of Chinese leaders is clearly aware of the historical objectivity of globalization, and seeks to meet its challenges, participating actively in its processes.

The Chinese government is determined to seize the opportunities brought by globalization to hasten modernization. The vision of modernization as "fully developing a prosperous (*xiaokang*) society," was announced even earlier than the United Nations proposition of Millennium Development Goals (MDGs). The Chinese government first formulated the concept of social prosperity as early as in 1980, but the term itself entered official Party policy only with the sixteenth session of its Central Committee in 2002.

Creating prosperity within twenty years presupposes continued and rapid economic growth, leading to improvements in the quality of life for the population as a whole, to enhanced environmental protection, democracy, a legal system and cultural development. According to this long-range plan, by the year 2020, the gross economic output will reach thirty-six trillion RMB (four trillion US dollars). This means that on the basis of a 9% yearly average economic growth rate of the past twenty-five years, the average yearly economic growth rate in the next fourteen years will have to be sustained at around 7–8% per year.

In addition, the quality of life in both urban and rural areas will need to be improved, environmental degradation checked, political

---

[1] China Statistics Bureau: *Zhongguo Tongji Nianjian (China Statistical Yearbook, 2003)*, China Statistics Press (Beijing: Zhongguo Tongji Chubanshe); World Bank: World Development Report, 2004, China Financial and Economic Press (Beijing: Zhongguo Caizheng Jingji Chubanshe, 2004).

[2] Deng Xiaoping: *Selected Works by Deng Xiaoping*, volume 3, People's Publishing House (Beijing: Renmin Chubanshe, 1996), p. 117.

participation widened, and the legal system rendered compatible with the market economy and democratic practices. Moreover, the nine-year compulsory education system will need to be fully realized, a social security system established all over China, and extreme poverty made a thing of the past.

During the first six years of the new century, the Chinese government has made smooth progress in achieving planned targets, and moving toward the long-range goal of constructing a "prosperous society." This is illustrated in the Human Development Report of the United Nations Development Program, which evaluates China's implementation of the Millennium Development Goals of the UN (see tables 1 and 2).[3]

Table 1   China Development Context

Indicator	Value	Year	High prov/region	Low prov/region
Population size (10,000,000)	1,276	2002	95.55	2.63
Population growth rate (‰)	6.95	2001	−0.95	12.62
Life expectancy at birth	71.4	2000	78.9	65.7
Real GDP per capita (US$)	912.5	2001	4522	350
Poverty per capita ratio (%) of rural China of US$1 per day	11.5	1998		
Percentage of population below international poverty line	8	2000		
Estimated HIV prevalence range from 800,000 to 1.5 million	0.06 to 0.11	2002		
Percentage of population with access to safe water supply	75	1999		
Percentage of population with under-weight children	10	1998		

---

[3] UNDP: *Millennium Development Goals in China*, UNDP coordination office in China, 2003, pp. 2, 40–41.

Table 1 (*cont.*)

Indicator	Value	Year	High prov/region	Low prov/region
Net primary enrollment ratio (%)	98.6	2002	100	94.6
Ratio of girls to boys in primary education (%)	90	2002		
Under-five mortality rate (per 100,000 live births)	36	2001		
Maternal mortality ratio (per 100,000 live births)	53	2000	10	466

Table 2   China MDGs Status

Goals and Targets	Status (Achievement)	Status (Supportive Environment)
Eradicate extreme poverty & hunger by 2015		
Halve the proportion of population below minimum level of dietary energy consumption.	On track	Well developed
Halve the proportion of underweight children under five years old by 2015.	On track	In place
Universal primary education by 2015		
Achieve universal primary education by 2015.	On track	In place
Gender equality		
Achieve equal access for boys and girls to primary and lower secondary schooling by 2015.	(Maybe not on track)	In place
Achieve equal access for boys and girls to upper secondary education by 2015.	Problems	In place
Under-five mortality		
Reduce under-five mortality by two-thirds by 2015.	On track	In place

Table 2 (*cont.*)

Goals and Targets	Status (Achievement)	Status (Supportive Environment)
Reproductive health		
Reduce maternal mortality ratio by three-quarters by 2015.	On track	In place
Universal access to safe/ reliable reproductive health services (contraceptive methods) by 2015.	On track	Well developed
Combat disease (HIV/ AIDS, TB & Malaria)		
Halt and reverse the spread of HIVS/AIDS by 2015.	Maybe not on track	Maybe not on track
Halve the prevalence of TB by 2015.	Maybe not on track	In place
Reduce the incidence of malaria.	On track	In place
Environment		
Implement national strategies for sustainable development by 2005 so as to reverse the loss of environmental resources by 2015.	Maybe not on track	Well developed
Basic amenities		
Halve the proportion of people unable to reach or afford safe drinking water by 2015.	On track	Well developed
Improve the proportion of rural people with access to improved sanitation.	On track	In place

While globalization provides China with opportunities for development, it also brings challenges and pressures with it. Globalization has both positive and negative effects. On the positive side, it is beneficial to effectively allocating resources from around the world, improving the quality of international cooperation, sharing information, the advancement of science and technology, the dissemination of internationally accepted human values, and for resolving global problems such as air pollution, the decreasing of the ozone layer, the rampant spread of drugs and illegal immigration.

On the negative side, globalization has strengthened the hegemony of developed countries over international economic and political life, increased the risk of crises in international finance, enlarged the north-south gap, and made it much easier for the developing economies to be controlled by international capital.

For China, globalization provides good opportunities: it helps to attract foreign capital as well as advanced science and technology, administrative and organizational experience. It is also beneficial in propagating Chinese products throughout the world and encouraging participation in international cooperation. Globalization can, however, also bring negative consequences, which were emphasized in academic publications after the economic and financial crisis in Southeast Asia, and which can be broadly analyzed in three categories. Firstly as a threat to economic security. Foreign control of share markets and their monopoly on advanced technology threatens independent advance. Excessive foreign debt may entail potential risks, while increased reliance on foreign capital and trade may weaken the capability to protect the country from fluctuations in the world economy, due to the unfettered liberalization of financial markets.

Secondly, globalization weakens state sovereignty. One of the basic conditions for participating in globalization is to abide by existing international rules, international treaties and agreements. Most of these international regimes have been established in accordance with the interests and standards of advanced countries, they reflect the interests of the West (i.e., North). In order to gain economically from globalization, developing countries have to make concessions in administrative jurisdiction, thus weakening their sovereignty.

Thirdly, globalization has been interpreted as a menace to domestic political values and culture, leading to the possible loss of control over social order, and increased risks to domestic governance. With advanced Western countries controlling the course of globalization and dictating the terms of globality, it is inevitable that they will also seek to export their world views and value systems along with their capital, technology and products. These world views and value systems may clash with Chinese traditions of culture and political order, creating a potential for social and political instability.

In order to realize the Millennium Development Goals and those for erecting a "prosperous society," the Chinese government has developed a set of development strategies and models of governance that scholars increasingly refer to as a "China Model" or "Beijing Consensus." These may be relevant to other developing countries seeking social modernization under globalization. More will be said about this later.

Government and Globalization

China has emerged as one of the big winners of globalization. It successfully protected itself from the shocks of the Asian financial crisis, and has realized its goal of entering the WTO after ten years of assiduous effort. High-speed economic growth has been accompanied by expansion of the scale of foreign trade twenty-two-fold over the past twenty-two years. China's position in terms of total foreign trade volume jumped to the current sixth position from the previous thirty-second at the beginning of the reforms.

China has achieved new progress in diversifying its world market. While continuously consolidating and expanding exports to European, American and Asian markets, China has been actively developing markets in Africa and Latin America. The number of countries and regions where the volume of China's export exceeds one hundred million US dollars has increased from 67 in 1995 to 82 in 2000. Since 1993, China has been ranked as the second recipient country for attracting foreign investment, just behind the USA, and the first among developing countries, receiving a total foreign investment of up to four hundred and fifty billion US dollars.

With the continuous growth of foreign trade volume, China has also been gradually improving the quality and structure of trade. The average foreign investment scale per program has been gradually increased from US$1.2 million in the beginning of the 1980s, and US$1.3 million in the beginning of the 1990s, to more than three million by the end of the 1990s. An ever-increasing number of companies and financial corporations are investing in China—more than four hundred out of the five hundred global Fortune companies have investments in China. Foreign reserves have reached a higher level, with the exchange rate between Chinese currency RMB and foreign currencies remaining stable. By the end of 2002, foreign reserves had already reached US$286.4 billion, which is 14.7 times the 1992 level, ranking second in the world.[4] Due to the Asian financial crisis and large-scale currency

---

[4] China Statistics Bureau: *Zhongguo Tongji Nianjian (China Statistical Yearbook, 2003)*, China Statistics Press (Beijing: Zhongguo Tongji Chubanshe, 2003), pp. 653–654.

devaluation in neighboring countries, China insisted on the policy of non-devaluation, and the exchange rate between Chinese and foreign currencies has remained stable since 1997.

While participating actively in the process of globalization, China has benefited not only economically, but also by improving the quality of the national economy, and reducing the economic and social gap with developed countries. Through foreign investment, trade and international economic cooperation China has learned from developed countries not only in terms of science and technology, but also in the conduct of economic transactions and modern administrative practices. Through a process of active participation in globalization China introduced a market economy, and gradually established modern business, finance and administrative systems. International cooperation and division of labor have forcefully facilitated the transformation of China's traditional industries, hastened the pace of structural economic adjustment, and enhanced the position of Chinese products on the international market. Active participation in globalization has enhanced national power, and has therefore brought China into the ranks of the major economic powers.

The primary reason for China to become one of the big winners of globalization has been the ability of its government to deal with the challenges of globalization. With a good understanding of the processes of globalization, China has adopted an active and independent globalization strategy. China is still a country with its politics highly influenced by ideology, but ideological considerations have been consciously put aside in the pursuit of globalization. While many Chinese scholars doubted whether globalization was an inevitable historical process, whether it was positive or negative, or whether it equaled Westernization or convergence with capitalism, Chinese leaders have made their own independent judgments about the nature, advantages and disadvantages of globalization. They have decided that:

> economic globalization is an objective requirement and necessary consequence in the development of social productivity, science and technology; it is an irreversible trend. Both the increase of economic and trade activities among various countries and regions, and the rapid spread of knowledge and technology are beneficial to facilitating the gradual optimization of economic factors all over the world, and it is thus beneficial to enhancing economic efficiency.[5]

---

[5] Jiang Zeming: *"Zai Dibajie APEC Lingdaoren Feizhengshi Huiyi shang de Jianghua (Speech*

Also, as an objective process, economic globalization had a dual aspect. It was beneficial, but owing to the dominating roles of Western developed countries in leading economic globalization, developing countries [were] in a disadvantaged and passive position and, without a right strategy, will be put in a more disadvantaged position.[6]

With this positive yet critical attitude toward globalization, the Chinese government adopted an active globalization strategy and took appropriate actions. For example, China has joined the World Trade Organization, expanded international cooperation and exchange, promoted global governance and international anti-terrorism efforts. It has developed the Shanghai Cooperation Organization, and pushed forth negotiations for eliminating nuclear weapons on the Korean peninsula.

The second measure is to improve the qualifications of government officials, to select and promote knowledgeable elites favorable to globalization, and to train officials in the knowledge economy and in matters of globalization. Currently there are 672,531 officials above county level, and 90% of these have academic degrees equivalent to or above associate college level, up from 16% in 1981. In 2003, on the basis of two existing national institutions for training high-ranking officials, another three institutions were set up to train officials in Shanghai, Jiangxi and Shanxi respectively, bringing the total number to five.

China has also strengthened its capacity to train local government officials. Currently there are more than three thousand institutions of public administration and Party schools above the county level. According to the training plan of the central government, twenty-five thousand officials above the rank of county or division will be trained from 2001 to 2005, among them two thousand officials at provincial and central government level. In addition, in cooperation with international organizations and developed countries, the Chinese government has also conducted technical training programs. A successful example is the Training Program for High-Ranking Officials, authorized by the Central Organization Department of the CCP and jointly conducted by the Development Research Center of the State Council at Qinghua University and the Kennedy School of Government at Harvard

---

on the Eighth Unofficial Meeting of the Leaders of APEC), Nov. 16th, 2000, Bandar Seri Begawan, Brunei)," *Renmin Ribao (People's Daily)*, Nov. 17th, 2000.

[6] Jiang Zeming: *Accelerating the nurturing of middle aged and young leaders who are able to manage the new century* (Speech at national conference on work of party school, June 9th, 2000) in Lun Sange Daibiao (*On the Three Represents*), Central Archive Press (Beijing: Zhongyang Wenxian Chubanshe, 2001), p. 28.

University. Fifty-nine high-ranking officials received training in the first phase of this program, which has now entered its second phase. This new group of professionally competent leaders has been trained in international cooperation and exchange activities. They are to become the pivotal forces of the Chinese government in dealing with the process of globalization.

The Chinese government has developed a flexible system and mechanisms with strong adaptive capability. Participation in the global game means abiding by global rules, which may contradict local ones. How to deal with such potential contradictions is an issue that the Chinese government must face. After a careful assessment of the advantages and disadvantages of globalization, Chinese leaders made a painful but correct choice: to adapt Chinese domestic rules to international norms, and to revise domestic regimes if necessary. Consequently, the government bypassed traditional forbidden zones and signed a series of international treaties that cover a wide range of issues from political rights to international security, international trade, and environmental protection. They also revised relevant domestic laws in accordance with these international treaties.

In joining the WTO, for example, government leaders clearly stated that:

> for the laws that are not consistent with international trade regimes and China's goals, we will revise these rules to make them compatible; for those that are in contradiction with world trade regimes and China's goals, we will eliminate them; where laws are lacking or inadequate, we will make new laws.[7]

In the process of negotiating WTO participation, and subsequent to joining the WTO, the State Council had approximately thirty ministries and departments clean up about twenty-three hundred relevant laws and regulations in 2002. About half of the laws and regulations were eliminated or revised as a result. Local laws and regulations revised or eliminated by various provinces and autonomous regions amount to more than 100,000 instances.[8]

---

[7] *Ibid.*

[8] Institute of International Trade and Economic Cooperation, Ministry of Commerce: *A One Year Review on China's Entry to WTO*, in Zhongguo Duiwai Jingji Guanxi Baipishu (White Book of China's Foreign Economic Relations), CITIC Press (Beijing: Zhongxin Chubanshe, 2003), p. 68.

The Chinese government has been striving for international cooperation and the creation of a favorable international environment. China needs a peaceful international environment for focusing on development, and this is especially important in an era of globalization. In adapting to the challenges of globalization, the Chinese government proposed an international strategy of "peacefully arising." The main points of this strategy are to insist on the diplomatic principles of independence, self-reliance, and peaceful co-existence, to abide by the guiding ideology of "being peaceful and different," and strive for a new notion of security with "mutual trust, mutual benefits, equality, and cooperation." With these core principles, the government promotes global democratic governance, actively participates in all aspects of international cooperation, develops itself and pursues reciprocal benefits in peaceful co-existence and cooperation.

According to this strategic policy, the Chinese government overlooked ideological differences and developed bilateral and multilateral relations in the fields of politics, economy and culture. Within just five years, between 1998 and 2002, it signed more than 1,056 bilateral and multilateral treaties. At the same time, the Chinese government encouraged foreign exchange and cooperative activities conducted by local governments, individuals and groups in civil society. In 2002, the number of foreign citizens entering China was 13.44 million, while departures by Chinese citizens numbered 16.3 million. In the past five years, the number of entries and departures increased by more than 10% per year on average. As of 2002, 296 Chinese cities had established friendship and partnership relationships with 847 foreign cities.[9]

China constitutes a comparatively stable social and political environment. Globalization has increased the risks for domestic economy and politics; in a certain sense, the era of globalization ushers in the end to an era of stability. Maintaining domestic social and political stability is especially significant for realizing the goal of constructing a "prosperous society" and the Millennium Development Goals. With its experience of internal turmoil, the Chinese government has a good understanding of the importance of maintaining social and political stability. Therefore, from Deng Xiaoping to Jiang Zemin and Hu Jintao,

---

[9] *China Society of Urban Development*, see Zhongguo Chengshi Nianjian (*China City Yearbook*, 2003), China City Yearbook Press (Beijing: Zhongguo Chengshi Nianjian She, 2003).

China's leaders have emphasized incrementalism and gradualism, aiming for a "soft landing" in both politics and economics. In addition, while instituting economic reform, the government has taken a cautious attitude toward political reform, and adhered to a reform philosophy emphasizing the priority of political reform at local government level over central reforms, of technical problems over those concerning the political system, of government change over social change, of easy issues over difficult ones. During the twenty-five years between the end of the Cultural Revolution to the present, large-scale social turmoil has been almost absent, providing a favorable atmosphere for rapid social development.

The Chinese government possesses strong capabilities of macroeconomic control. The market economy in China is actually a kind of government-led market economy, and the government has powerful macroeconomic control mechanisms at its disposal. Through a series of policies governing areas such as industry, investment, finance, tax, banks, land and export, the government imposes forceful macroeconomic controls. At the same time, by using coercive legal means to eliminate obstacles to the market economy, the government has normalized commercial behavior, stabilizing the national economy. In the domestic sphere, the government has successfully managed several occasions of economic overheating in the 1980s and 1990s, demonstrating the efficacy of its macroeconomic controls. Similar observations could be made about external economic risks and pressures, when the Chinese government successfully evaded the shocks of the Asian financial crisis in the 1990s and, more recently, resisted considerable external pressure to appreciate the RMB. In the area of social control, the best example is China's success in fighting SARS which spread throughout the country in 2003. The government not only effectively controlled SARS, but also kept up rapid economic growth.

In spite of the achievements by the Chinese government and its public sector in dealing with the challenges of globalization, there are still many problems. Chief among them are the high cost of government, corruption among government officials, inadequate transparency in policy, persistent mistakes in policy making, low quality of public services, and local protectionism.

The high cost of government has two aspects. First, the government machinery is too big, and too many people are employed in the public sector, leading to high public payroll expenditures and operating costs. The burgeoning public sector is a familiar problem for China; All administrations since the early 1980s have tried to streamline government organization but achieved little progress.

By the end of 2002, 71.63 million people worked in state-owned and 11.22 million in collective-owned units; 10.75 millions of these work for Party, government and other official organizations. According to official statistics, in 2002, the salary expenditures on Party and government employees came to RMB 47.4 billion (US$5.78 billion), equal to 36% of the total expenditures on government administration.[10] However, the actual cost is much higher than this figure. According to some estimates, the "gray" income that these people receive is about 50% of their formal incomes. The operating cost in the public sector of Chinese government has also been high for a number of years and has received severe criticism from different social strata.

Taking procurement and transportation costs as an example, it is estimated that procurement costs governments over RMB two hundred billion yuan (US$24.4 billion) in 2002, which is equal to the total investment in the Three Gorges Project, while the total education budget for 1999 measured only RMB 334.9 billion yuan (US$40.8 billion).[11] According to the *Daily Electronic Bulletin* of the Xinhua News Agency, in 2000, there were three hundred and fifty million public automobiles used by party and government officials, and the total expenditure including the salaries of drivers amounted to RMB three hundred billion (US$36.6 billion), three times the national defense budget of 1998,[12] and transportation costs were over two hundred billion yuan (US$24.4 billion). The expenditures on these two items came to 38.7%[13] of the total government expenditure of 2002, which was RMB 1,383.3 billion (US$168.7 billion), averaging RMB 3.79 billion per day.

China's perennial corruption in the public sector is also a headache for the government. It has taken serious measures in fighting corruption, but the situation has not improved fundamentally. In fact, the scope of embezzlement and corruption has expanded, with increasingly greater amounts of embezzled money and larger numbers of high-ranking

---

[10] China Statistics Bureau: Zhongguo Tongji Nianjian (*China Statistical Yearbook*, 2003), China Statistics Press (Beijing: Zhongguo Tongji Chubanshe, 2003), p. 153, p. 285.

[11] Zhou Shaojin: "*Qianyi Quxiao Yewu Zhaodaifei de Haochu ji Banfa (A Brief Discussion on the Benefits and methods of Canceling Expenditure on Recreation)*," http://www.xslx.com/htm/szrp/shts.

[12] See: *Dangdai Qiche Bao* (Contemporary Automobile), Nov. 2003, volume 552.

[13] China Statistics Bureau: Zhongguo Tongji Nianjian (*China Statistical Yearbook*, 2003), China Statistics Press (Beijing: Zhongguo Tongji Chubanshe, 2003), p. 25.

officials involved. In the past five years, more and more officials above county and division levels have been punished for embezzlement and corruption. In 2002, registered law suits against embezzlement and corruption committed by public servants in all the procuratorate organs numbered 34,716 cases, of which 16,826 were large cases involving 38,022 persons, or 53.7% of the total.[14] This represents an annual increase of 4.5%. The 123 most severe cases measured each over RMB ten million (US$1.22 million) of embezzled money. 2,728 Officials above county level were punished for corruption. The severe corruption in the public sector has caused heavy economic losses to the country. It also undermines the legitimacy of the government and public trust.[15]

There are still major policy mistakes in the public sector. One reason for this is that there is inadequate continuity in government policy. Government policies change with changes in administration, confusing citizens, and shaking their trust and confidence in the government. Such mistakes cause enormous economic losses. According to information revealed from the recent "auditing storm" in 2003, the National Electric Power Company suffered direct economic losses of RMB 7.8 billion (US$0.95 billion) because of policy-making mistakes. Some estimates state that the economic losses caused by policy mistakes tops RMB 100 billion (US$12.2 billion) per year.[16]

The low quality of public services is another striking problem. Such problems often occur because of embezzlement, corruption, inadequate regulation and weak implementation. Examples include public construction works, disaster and poverty relief, and migrant placement programs. One of the most notorious phenomena is the so-called "stinking bean residue works" referred to by former premier Zhu Rongji. Targeted at low quality services caused by stinting on both labor and material and fake and bad-quality products, such "bean residue" is rampant in the construction of public buildings, river dykes, and roads. Low quality workmanship on the Yangtze River dykes caused disastrous floods, and relevant officials were severely punished. However, according to recent

---

[14] *Ibid.* p. 833.

[15] Operation office of National People's Congress: *Second Collection of Archives on the Tenth National People's Congress in People's Republic of China*, People's Publishing House (Beijing: Renmin Chubanshe, 2004), p. 148.

[16] See: *Liaowang Dongfang Zhoukan* (Oversee Orient Weekly), June, 2004, No. 6, p. 24.

auditing results, "stinking bean residue works" on the Yangtze River dykes are still commonplace.[17]

Some government agencies and local governments are seriously lacking in honesty and credibility. Many government officials vaunt achievements to attain promotion in their careers. This at times leads to "publicity projects," with no regard for cost. Some government officials even fabricate performance records and cheat citizens and governments at superior levels. Some local governments go back on public promises, contradict their own policies, and violate contracts and promises. The result of such activity is reduced confidence in government.

In recent years, local protectionism has been rampant, severely weakening government capacity. Some local governments publicly violate national laws and market economy standards for protecting their narrow regional interests thereby inflicting harm. Local protectionism is mainly to be found in regional industry protection policies, discriminatory practices in local markets and concerning migration. In some extreme cases, local governments directly intervene in the equity and independence of the local administration of justice and take advantage of local laws and local legal authorities for partial interests. A survey of the Ministry of Commerce shows that there are still twenty provinces, municipalities and autonomous regions where non-local products and services are blocked in spite of the State Council "Announcement of Prohibiting Local Protectionism" of 2002.[18]

Adding to problems in the public sector are problems threatening government capacity. First of all, the efficiency of state-owned enterprises is still not on a par with private enterprises. Secondly, there is still inadequate coordination in economic, political and social development. Some local governments and officials still stress pure economic growth, worshipping GDP figures while ignoring other aspects of development. Thirdly, there are still many uncertainties in economic and political development that the government feels are difficult to control. Fourth, in some localities, the antagonistic mood between government and citizens is severe, and complaints reflecting citizens' dissatisfaction with government behavior show an annually rising trend. Fifth, there

---

[17] Cong Yuhua: *Changjiang Difang Doufuzha Gongcheng cong Xinghui Shouhui Kaishi* (Poor-done Embankment Project at Yangzi River Starts from Bribery), *Zhongguo Qingnian (China Youth)*, July 1st, 2004, p. A1.

[18] Zhang Hua: Difang Baohuzhuyi yiran Yanzhong 20 Sheng you Fengsuo (Local Protectionism is still Severe, it is Found in 20 Provinces), http://www.zeronews.com/news.

are severe regional imbalances in development, the gap between East Coast Area and Northwest Area is becoming sharper. Sixth, the Gini coefficient, reflecting income inequality, is gradually increasing and according to expert estimates, it exceeded the critical point of 0.4 in 1994. Since then, there has been an increase of 0.1 percentage with 0.456 in 1998, 0.457 in 1999 and 0.458 in 2000.[19]

In order to overcome problems existing in the public sector and enhance the governing capabilities of the government, the Chinese government emphatically stresses government-related innovations, regarding it as an important part of political regime reform. The goals of these innovations may be generally summarized as constructing: a government with the rule of law, a service government, an accountable government, a quality government, a transparent government, a professional government, an efficient government, and a government of integrity. China has conducted many experiments in government innovations, and accumulated experiences that deserve praise for their results and achievements. In the following we shall be concentrating on only some of these efforts.

Constructing Service Government and Improving Quality of Public Service

In China, civil society and private enterprise are not as developed as in Western countries; therefore, government and state-owned organizations occupy a dominating place in providing public services. For a long time the state sector has had a reputation of providing low-quality service, with limited choice and bad service attitude, which has been an important cause of citizen dissatisfaction. Every administration has tried to change this situation. The administration that came to power recently has put forward the requirement of constructing a "service government" and adopted many pertinent measures.

The Chinese government is making great efforts to enhance the scope of service provision. In addition to improving public services in terms of an extension of compulsory education to nine years, family

---

[19] Yang Yiyong, Xin Xiaobai: *Zhongguo Dangqian de Shouru Fenpei Geju ji Fazhan Qushi* (Income Distribution in China today and its Changing Tendency), in Zhongguo Shehui: Qingkuang Fenxi yu Yuce (*China Society: Situation Analysis and Prediction*), edited by Ru Xin, 2002, Social Science and Documentation Press (Beijing: Zhongguo Shehui Kexue Chubanshe, 2002), p. 144.

planning, the prevention of epidemic diseases, eradication of poverty, protection of the environment, maintenance of social security, construction of public facilities such as roads and social welfare services, the Chinese government has been striving to incorporate globalization into the provision of public services. Such efforts are visible in the following five areas: development of a social security system to minimize the impact of market fluctuations, to specify (and improve conditions for) those living along the poverty line, and to provide unemployment benefits for redundant workers; improvement of the public health system by providing medical help for peasants; construction of a national mechanism for the prevention of epidemic disease; to provide the necessary medical, legal and financial protection for all citizens, but especially the disadvantaged; a poverty eradication plan leading to a rapid reduction of the percentage of the population living in extreme poverty. The following table summarizes the development of social services in recent years.[20]

Table 3   Status of Social Services Facilities

Year	Community service facilities in cities/towns	Service points in cities/towns	Community service centers	Social welfare units	Legal assistance organizations	Public health institutions
1998	148,042	345,075	6,154	105,000	500	314,097
1999	157,339	405,740	7,623	98,000	1,235	310,996
2000	181,444	451,567	6,444	101,000	1,890	324,771
2001	195,579	539,544	6,179	95,000	2,274	330,348
2002	198,845	622,986	7,898	94,000	2,418	306,038

One of the best examples of expanding public services is the government's guarantee payment of salaries to migrant laborers from the countryside who enter cities in the hope of finding work. As they do not enjoy the same living security as city workers, they become one of the most disadvantaged groups. Some private enterprises and government agencies do not comply with the legal formalities when hiring rural laborers, and thus their working times, compensation and welfare treatment are usually not guaranteed. What's more, it is commonplace for their already low wages to be subjected to deductions or delays.

---

[20] Zhongguo Tongji Nianjian (*China Statistical Yearbook*, 2003); Zhongguo Sifa Xingzheng Nianjian (*China Judicatory Administration Yearbook*), 2003, Law Press (Beijing, 2003).

Some peasant workers have reacted violently or committed suicide when they were unable to collect their salaries at the end of the Chinese year in order to return home.

When newly elected Premier Wen Jiabao visited a peasant family in Sichuan during the Spring Festival of 2003, one married woman complained to him about her experience of not being able to collect her salary for her hard work. The premier immediately ordered local government officials to use all possible measures to have the wages paid to the woman. Consequently, the central government issued administrative orders requiring local governments at various levels to take coercive measures which forced employers to pay out salaries or wages held in arrears. Payments not honored roughly add up to RMB 336 billion (US$41 billion) in construction alone. Owing to the government's intervention, between December 2003 and January 2004, circa RMB 21.5 billion (US$2.62 billion) were paid to peasant workers. Reports about official demands for the payment of overdue salaries were widely circulated among the Chinese public.[21]

With the rapid rise in the general economic performance, government expenditures on public services have increased concomitantly. For example, in 1978, expenditures on social relief measured RMB 1.891 billion (US$0.23 billion), while in 1990 it reached 5.504 billion (US$0.675 billion), and in 2002 RMB 37.297 billion (US$4.55 billion). This is an increase of 678% in the past twelve years.

Expenditure on culture, education and health was RMB 11.266 billion (US$1.37 billion) in 1978, RMB 61.729 billion (US$7.5 billion) in 1990, reaching RMB 397.908 billion (US$48.5 billion) in 2002; a 645% increase over twelve years. The following table shows the growth in government public service expenditures.[22]

Simplifying administrative investigation and approval procedures is an effective means for improving public services. A legacy of central planning and of the command economy is that the government exercises universal control over public affairs from the birth of children to the establishment of enterprises to travel abroad, all of which require approval by various levels of government. To gain permission to open a hotel or to build, application forms must be stamped by several dozen

---

[21] Ruan Yilin [for Xinhua News Agency]: *Hu Jingtao, Wen Jiabao: Preventing new delayed payment to peasants*, January 18th, 2004, http://www.china.com.cn.

[22] China Statistics Bureau: Zhongguo Tongji Nianjian 2003 (*China Statistical Yearbook, 2003*), China Statistics Press (Beijing: Zhongguo Tongji Chubanshe, 2003), p. 284.

Table 4   Growth in Public Service Expenditures unit: RMB 100 million

Year	Public infrastructures	Rural Service	Culture and education	Social Benefits
1978	451.92	76.95	112.66	18.09
1990	547.39	221.76	617.29	55.04
1996	907.44	510.07	1704.25	128.03
1997	1019.50	560.77	1903.59	142.14
1998	1387.74	626.02	2154.38	171.26
1999	2116.57	677.46	2408.06	179.88
2000	2094.89	766.89	2736.88	213.03
2001	2510.64	917.96	3361.02	266.68
2002	3142.98	1102.70	3979.08	372.97

to several hundred authorities. In order to overcome this situation, the central government initiated a program to simplify administrative investigation and approval procedures, beginning in 2001. The State Council specifically set up a special agency called the "National Executive Team for Simplifying Administrative Investigation and Approval" and took the lead in abolishing several thousands of outdated and complicated administrative procedures and approval criteria. By the end of 2002, the numbers of administrative regulations in Beijing Municipality were reduced from the previous 1,304 to 454 items, a reduction of 41.7%. In Henan Province, administrative procedures were reduced from 2,706 to 1,764, a reduction of 65.2%.[23]

The change of public sector service attitude is critically significant for constructing a service government. Traditional political culture put government officials at the center of political life, which was reinforced by the socialist command economy. Government officials still take a commanding attitude toward citizens. The metaphor of "doors difficult to enter, and faces not good to look at" vividly describes the image citizens face when they seek government services. In order to effectively change this situation, the central government put forward a

---

[23] Tian Qin: *Cujin Zhongguo Zhengfu Zhineng Zhuanbian de Xingzheng Shenpi Zhidu Gaige Zhengce* (Reform Policy on Administrative Investigation and Approval that is Promoting Government Function Transformation in China), in *Zhongguo Gonggong Zhengce Fenxi* (China Public Policy Analysis), edited by Center for Public Policy Research, China Academy of Social Sciences and Asia Center for Regulation Research, Hong Kong City. University, 2004, China Social Sciences Press (Beijing: Zhongguo Shehui Kexue Chubanshe, 2004), pp. 27–28.

service doctrine of "putting citizens first" and "providing convenience and benefits for citizens" for the public sector. The central government also requires governments at various levels to reform government services along the principle of "providing convenience and benefits for citizens." In recent years, "one stop shops" have been praised for improving government services.

The "supermarket of government services" in Xiaguang District (Nanjin, Jiangsu Province) is an outstanding representative in this regard. In October 2000, Xiaguan District decided to apply the advantages of supermarkets to government administration by changing the closed pattern of doing administrative work to an open one similar to people shopping in a supermarket. The district government transferred forty kinds of administrative work which are closely related to people's daily lives such as community service, helping army families and the handicapped, city planning, street cleaning, re-employment programs, business license issuing, tax collection, household registration, Party cell activities, and the provision of administrative information to an administrative hall. Local people can get related tasks done in an open environment; they can easily determine which desk to go to, who to ask, and what to prepare.

This project also requires that civil servants retain case files until these can be closed. Non-compliant civil servants are faced with concrete consequences. In the public administration hall, advice from representatives of the People's Congress can be sought as well as from lawyers and supervisors.

Within this project, administrative work can also be done on weekends. This project requires that everything asked by local residents should be done within a short deadline; things cannot be delayed for any reason. Citizens benefit greatly from this project. The public relations of the civil service and the effectiveness of the government have been greatly improved.

This project of transforming administration to the supermarket model has been highly praised by the municipal and provincial leaderships and has attracted tremendous attention in the mass media. The *People's Daily, Guangming Daily, Economy Daily, Xinhua Daily, Nanjing Daily*, and *Yangzi Evening Post* have covered this project prominently. More than one hundred governmental delegations from places as far afield as Guangzhou, Chongqing, Shanghai, and Shanxi have flocked to Xiaguan District in order to find out more. So far, the cities of Quanzhou

(Fujian), Shenyang (Liaoning), Jiaozuo (Anhui), and Xuzhou (Jiangsu) have implemented this project.

Accompanying the introduction of the market economy and the process of globalization, the Chinese government began to change its attitude to civil society organizations (CSOs), encouraging rather than prohibiting their existence. This change has contributed to the gradual formation of a comparatively independent civil society. In 2002, there were 1,330,000 registered civil organizations above county level. There are no formal statistics on civic organizations registered below this level, but by a conservative estimate there should be at least three million civic organizations at this level. Furthermore, as a result of the reform process, another special group of civil society organizations emerged, called civil non-enterprise units. Civil non-enterprise units are enterprises which provide civil services but do not have financial support from the government and maintain their operations by charging for the services they provide. Pursuant to the relevant regulations, these organizations are not primarily intended to produce. According to some rough estimates, this group of organizations numbered more than 700,000 in the year 1998.[24]

The major function of civil organizations is to provide public services and to compensate for the inadequacies in the government public sector. They focus largely on areas of environmental protection, aid to the poor, preventing and curing disease, developing education, and other public interests.

The most influential example of the provision of public services by civil society organizations is the "Hope Project." The Chinese Youth Fund initiating the "Hope Project" is a non-governmental organization. Its main goal is to help children who have dropped out of school due to poverty to continue their education. The Chinese Youth Fund raises funds from various social sources and then establishes "Hope Primary Schools" at locations where dropout rates are high in order to allow children to attend school at no cost.

Between its start on October 30, 1989, and December 31, 2000, the funds raised by both domestic and overseas sources added up to RMB 1.94 billion (US$0.236 billion). The total accumulated expenditure of

---

[24] Yu Keping: *Zhongguo Gongmin Shehui Xingqi yu Zhili de Bianqian* (The Emergence of Civil society in China and the Change of its Governance), Social Science and Documentation Press (Beijing: Zhongguo Shhui Kexue Wenxian Chubanshe, 2001), p. 14.

support funds reached RMB 1.688 billion (US\$ 210 billion). Across China, the national "Hope Project" has supported 8,355 "Hope Primary Schools" and funded up to 2.3 million dropouts.[25]

Participation in the market economy and globalization is accompanied by the emergence of private enterprises and organizations. These private enterprises and organizations occupy critical positions in China's economic development, accounting for 60% of total economic growth. However, the role they play in providing social services is very small. The main reason is that the government severely limits the private sector in entering areas of public service provision such as education, health and environmental protection. But it is also related to the fact that the private sector in China is not strong enough and is still at an early stage of development.

Since the government has not encouraged private organizations to provide social services, the relevant legal framework is also lacking or inadequate. It was not until recently that the government began to issue necessary laws, such as the *Laws on improving civil education*, or the *Administrative law on funding organizations*. These laws played outstanding roles in pushing the private sector to provide social services. So far, the area where the private sector provides the most service is in education. Education in China, whether primary, secondary or higher, has been a service area dominated by the government. It was not until the 1990s that the private sector began to enter this area. The educational services provided by the private sector have developed very fast. By the end of 2002, the number of private schools reached 61,300 with 11,479,500 registered students. Among these schools, 48,400 are private kindergartens, 5,122 are primary schools, 6,447 are secondary schools, 133 are private colleges and universities, and 1,202 are other higher educational institutions.[26]

The change from one-dimensional service to comprehensive multi-dimensional service creates practical conditions for providing comprehensive services. For example, the "platform of community service" in Beijing municipality is a successful model that effectively integrates

---

[25] Li Shiyang: Anli 13: Zhongguo Qingshaonian Fazhan Jijinhui (Case 13: China Youth Development Foundation), http://www.help-poverty.org.cn.

[26] See: *Zhonghua Renmin Gongheguo Nianjian 2003 (People's Republic of China Yearbook, 2003)*, People's Republic of China Yearbook Press (Beijing: Zhonghua Renmin Gongheguo Nianjian Chubanshe, 2003), p. 781.

e-government and e-commerce, community service and social service, public and private sector service.

A "platform of community services" consists of a community services network, a hotline system, and a software of community management website. The three-level community services information network (municipality, district and street) was established in December 2001. The hotline, using the most recent software, became operational in December 2002.

The platform is different from e-communities of other cities in three aspects: 1) The e-community platform has been established at a municipal level. Relying on information technologies, it can integrate various services from around the whole municipality and promote industrialization of community services. 2) The platform covers both community services and management information systems. It incorporates the two functions of e-governance and e-commerce. Consequently, it provides an interactive mechanism for community residents, service providers and governments. 3) Relying on community services centers, governmental departments and NPOs, the platform mobilizes a variety of resources effectively and can finance itself by providing services. Although it is dominated governmentally, a cooperative relationship between the governmental sector and the third sector is forming.

The "platform of community services" performs well. Firstly, the residents' requirements are basically met. Since the website of community service was established over two years ago, it has publicized over two million pieces of information on its website and has 47,000 registered social workers. The website was visited over 1,200,000 times. As for the hotline, the telephone number 96156 has been dialed 194,000 times. Over 95% of requirements for services are met and over 80% of services enjoy high appraisal.

Secondly, new management methods are provided for community committees to reduce their labor input. The management software has been installed and run in computers for 2,400 community committees. Staff spends less time in collecting, updating and reporting data, and information is processed routinely and efficiently.

Lastly, community services have been industrialized. The platform is a channel for governmental sectors, habitants and private sectors to interact. Since the hotline was opened, 68,147 service requirements have been sent to private service providers. Many providers enlarge their size or increase services to meet the growing requirements by habitants. Habitants are served with greater speed and ease.

Advanced science and technology also provide means for improving service quality. The "Agricultural Technology 110" project in Quzhou (Zhejiang) is a good example. Established on November 20, 1998, with branches in all thirty-nine urban districts, information providers were employed in all communities. Thus, a network for providing agricultural technology in the city was established. A telephone service (facilitated by dialing 110) linked to the internet was created so farmers can get access to the latest information on domestic and international markets. The service center also provides concrete help on the spot, displays examples of utilizing advanced agricultural technology, provides training, and collects and issues information. By August 2001, the Service Center had provided 252,000 consultations to farmers, and its website was visited 333,000 times, collecting 147,000 pieces of information, and issuing 57,000. Furthermore, the Service Center displays the prices of main agricultural products at twenty different urban markets. For Quzhou farmers this entailed an income increase of more than RMB 90 million (US$11.25 million). Projects such as Agricultural Technology 110 are in essence information highways utilizing telecommunications, television, and the internet. Institutes, colleges and universities offer information about agricultural technology and markets effectively to small-scale agrarian businesses.

Another imperative is decentralization. Through more localized and market-oriented measures traditionally public services have by all measures been privatized. An example of the reform of public services with market-orientation is Shenzhen (Guangdong), which embarked upon a market reform plan for enterprises in public utilities. The local government initiated a policy of "Further Reforming Investment and Financing System" in September 2001, starting the reform of public utilities. These market reforms were divided into two stages. During the first stage, investors flocked in, attracted by newly opened infrastructure, such as ports, roads and airports. The second stage already started in 2001, with emphasis on water, gas, and power supplies as well as public transportation. Strategic investors were encouraged to invest and laws and rules were issued to strengthen regulations. After a handful of years of practical experience, the market-oriented reforms of the public utilities have helped establish a solid basis for large and medium-sized SOEs to reform their property system.

The Shenzhen example is illustrative in more than one respect. Firstly the traditional investment and operation system of utility services has been changed by opening the monopolized infrastructure to private capital. The governmental burden of investing and operating has been reduced, and enterprises have become more dynamic and competitive. Secondly, legal regulations have been modified in order to monitor. Thirdly, the state-owned property system has been changed, its natural monopoly broken. Finally, financial consultation agencies have been hired by the government to attract strategic investors globally, according to international norms.

By reforming its public utility services, the Shenzhen government has accelerated the transformation of large state-owned utility companies. Strategic shares purchasing by multinational groups in energy, water, gas, public transportation and food supplies increased the Shenzhen Government total assets of SOEs (State-Owned Enterprises). Meanwhile, regulations on utility services have become streamlined. By the end of December 2003, total investment in five experimental SOEs exceeded seven billion RMB, in share value. Domestic private capital has been competing with multinationals, increasing their own performance and competitiveness. International companies engaging in finance, law, accounting and performance evaluation participate in SOE reforms by competing with domestic ones. Local government, large and medium-sized SOEs, investors and customers benefit from these reforms in equal measure.

Cooperation between the public and private sectors is an effective way to further good governance. The county government of Hefeng, (Hubei), for instance, cooperates with the private sector to establish projects aimed at helping the poor. Anti-poverty funds are made available to comparatively profitable private enterprises, requiring these to buy agricultural products at fair prices, thereby enabling the poor to escape from poverty. Alternatively, they can be asked to employ a certain number of villagers. The local government thus helped to end poverty more efficiently than earlier experiments, which directly distributed funds to the poor. Since its implementation in 1993, the "Company plus Production Bases plus Agrarian Households" initiative has been highly praised by the provincial and central leadership as the "Hefeng Model."

The link of anti-poverty projects with private enterprise enabled local governments to build up infrastructure and create a good environment for developing business. Large-scale private investment helps to tackle the unemployment problem and provide stability by purchasing agricultural products on a fair-trade basis. The "Hefeng Model" has thus proved to be a sustainable anti-poverty project. By lending money to profitable enterprises for poverty eradication programs, local governments have more money to invest. Private enterprises organize their agricultural investments based on their market judgments, benefiting both the enterprises and the agrarian households. Owing to this success, some 70% of all agricultural households in the county have been linked to this project. The number of people living in poverty has been reduced from forty thousand in 1995 to three thousand nine hundred in 2000.

Local governments are pivotal in providing public services. Local governments—especially governments at the grassroots level—know best their citizens' requirements for public services, and they face greater pressures to provide those services. At the same time, local governments possess richer resources in providing public services. In 2002, the central government spent RMB 125.314 billion (US$15.28 billion) on infrastructure provision while local governments spent RMB 188.984 billion (US$23.0 billion). For agricultural services, the central government spent RMB 11.974 billion (US$1.46 billion) while local governments spent RMB 98.296 billion (US$12.0 billion). In the areas of culture, education and health, the central government's expenditures amounted to RMB 44.79 billion (US$5.46 billion) as opposed to RMB 353.159 billion (US$43 billion). On social relief, the central government spent RMB 0.268 billion (US$0.033 billion) while local governments spent RMB 37.029 billion (US$4.5 billion). Finally, in order to support underdeveloped regions, the central government spent RMB 0.809 billion yuan (US$100 million) while local governments spent RMB 14.101 billion (US$1.72 billion).[27]

It is precisely because of the important role of local governments that big differences between regions exist, in terms of quality and type of services. Cities fare better than rural areas, and the same goes for the economically developed east. Based on figures for 2002, comparing Beijing with its 14.23 million residents and Gansu province with a population of 25.93 million, the public finance expenditure of the former was RMB 62.835 billion (US$7.66 billion) while the latter registered RMB 0.583 billion (US$0.071 billion). Eastern Zhejiang Province, population 46.47 million, compared with western Guangxi, population 48.22 million, spent RMB 7.499 billion (US$0.91 billion) while the

---

[27] China Statistics Bureau: Zhongguo Tongji Nianjian 2003 (*China Statistical Yearbook, 2003*), China Statistics Press (Beijing: Zhongguo Tongji Chubanshe, 2003), p. 292.

latter a mere RMB 4.199 billion (US$0.51 billion). The expenditure on education in the former was RMB 13.694 billion (US$1.67 billion) while for the latter it was 7.217 billion (US$0.88 billion). Health expenditures confirm this trend: RMB 3.723 billion (US$0.45 billion) compared to RMB 1.786 billion (US$0.22 billion). Social relief investments in Zhejiang amounted to RMB 1.387 billion (US$0.17 billion) while Guangxi enjoyed only RMB 0.871 billion (US$0.11 billion).[28]

Promoting Accountable Government, Increasing Participation, Accountability, and Transparency in Public Sectors

The SARS crisis in 2003 made the Chinese government aware of the necessity of an accountable government. When SARS was just beginning to spread, central authorities could not tackle the problem efficiently because officials in the health care sector and local governments hid information, which eventually led to the spread of the SARS virus. By June 14, 2003, twenty-five provinces, autonomous regions, and municipalities were affected by SARS. The number of cases rose to 5,327, and 346 people were to die from the virus.[29] Apart from the severe loss of life, the direct and indirect economic losses were also considerable. According to some estimates, these amounted to dozens of billions of RMB.

In an accountable government, officials in the public sector have to take responsibility for their decisions, which means that they may be subject to punishment if they are negligent. While tackling the SARS crisis, central authorities took serious measures against the Minister of Public Health and the mayor of Beijing who had direct responsibility for the exacerbation of the crisis. Both were dismissed from their positions.

Following the example of the central government, local administrations took similar measures to punish irresponsible officials. A preliminary

---

[28] *Ibid.*, pp. 296, 297.

[29] Guo Weiqing et al.: "*SARS Weiji Yingdui Zhengce: Cong Zainan zhong Xuexi* (Tackling SARS crisis: learning from disaster)," in Zhongguo Gonggong Zhengce Fenxi (China Public Policy Analysis), edited by Center for Public Policy Research, China Academy of Social Sciences and Asia Center for Regulation Research, Hong Kong City University, 2004, China Social Sciences Press (Beijing: Zhongguo Shehui Kexue Chubanshe, 2004), pp. 208–209.

investigation shows that more than two thousand officials were dismissed or punished for mistakes made during the SARS crisis. After the crisis, it became regular practice to punish government officials responsible for serious accidents. For example, Ma Fucai, CEO and chairperson of the board of directors of the China Natural Gas Group, who held the rank of minister, was dismissed due to a serious natural gas leak in Chongqing.

Table 5   Number of Local Officials Punished during the SARS Crisis

Province Autonomous region, Municipality	Number of punished officials	Province Autonomous region, Municipality	Number of punished officials
Henan	344	Heibei	145
Shanxi	319	Hunan	207
Jiangsu	122	Liaoning	83
Inner Mongolia	69	Sichuan	50
Jilin	51	Hubei	46
Chongqing	38	Gansu	38
Beijing	31	Shandong	11
Guizhou	13	Ningxia	9
Guangdong	5	Heilongjiang	13
Xinjiang	3	Hainan	2
Shaanxi	98	Jiangxi	18
Anhui	26	Guangxi	2
Total	1743		

Transparency of administrative information is a basic requirement for accountable governance. One of the lessons learned from the SARS crisis was that information should be allowed to flow freely and be disseminated in a timely fashion, and that policies should be as transparent as possible. Due to the fact that relevant officials did not report the real situation, central authorities failed to tackle SARS at its early stages when panic was already spreading among the people. To change the situation, central authorities ordered all relevant officials to report SARS cases quickly and truthfully or face punishment. At the same time, central authorities initiated the "Zero Report" system that aimed to publicize SARS cases. This was a breakthrough in the development of political transparency in China. Subsequently, conveying information truthfully to the public became a responsibility of government at all levels. For the first time the institution of government spokesperson was established to publicize information.

Globalization increases natural, financial, and social risks. The SARS crisis was a test of the Chinese government's capacity for tackling emergencies. An important reason why the SARS crisis was not managed effectively from the start was that an efficient emergency management mechanism was absent in China. As a lesson of the SARS crisis, governments at all levels developed mechanisms to deal with public crises.

First, a crisis management system consists of components such as leadership, information, telecommunications, supply, coordination, and accountability. Secondly, a crisis management system needs to efficiently coordinate government and military, center and periphery, Party and state, as well as state and society. The result ought to be an enhanced management capacity by both Party and state.

Political transparency is a citizen's right to relevant political information. This right should be protected by laws. The Chinese government realizes this and has begun to establish a legal safeguarding system to this effect. The central government has even established a special institution—the "National Leading Group on Publicity of Political Affairs." Such efforts have stimulated provincial and local administrations to issue laws and regulations aimed at protecting citizens' rights to information.

Apart from the legal system, governments also make use of information technology to publicize political affairs—e-government. By the end of 2002, internet users in China numbered 59.1 million. China is second only to the USA in the number of internet users. Thus, it is especially important for e-government to develop in China.

Already since the mid-1990s, e-governments became regulated under the "National Information Work Leading Group." Between 2000 and 2002, the annual growth rate of the demand for e-government in China was more than 20%. Investment in e-government in 2000 was RMB 23.3 billion (US$2.84 billion), and in 2002, RMB 34.4 billion (US$4.2 billion). The growth rate of the market for information services in e-government was significantly higher than that of the IT market as a whole. Its average annual growth rate since 2003 has been above 25%.

Most governments at county level and above have official websites. By 2002, internet addresses registered as .CN amounted to 179,544, 14,300 of which were initiated by governments and organizations.

These public websites became one of the most important channels for citizens to access government information.[30]

Political transparency not only requires governments to publicize information on the political decision-making process, but also demands open communication between the public and private sectors, as well as between the government and its citizens. Transparency should be ensured not only with regard to the political process, but also in the provision of social services. A number of recent events have shown that transparency helps prevent corruption of the public sector, and also enhances mutual understanding between the government and citizens. Transparency in the public as well as in the private social services sector simply leads to better results. This is clearly demonstrated in the case of the "Sunshine Salvation Project" initiated by the Social Security System in Qingdao, Shangdon.

Qingdao was among the first cities to establish the urban social security system, initiated in June 1994 before the State Council issued "Regulations on Urban Social Security" in 1999. Limited funds and unfair distribution in some localities resulted in complaints and protests. In order to make the Regulations work well, the Qingdao government systematically reviewed systems, procedures and methods, eventually propagating a system referred to as the "Sunshine Salvation Project."

Its five operational mechanisms were as follows: 1) A "Four-level Administrative Mechanism" embracing municipality, district (city), street (township/town), and community (village). 2) An "Evaluation Mechanism" that investigated pensioners' incomes and living conditions. This consisted of an evaluation group from a community committee, an evaluation committee from a "street affairs" agency, and an approval committee from the district government. 3) A "Standardized Procedure Mechanism" where every link, including application, investigation, evaluation, approval, publicizing and reviewing, had its own specific requirements. 4) A "Mechanism of Classification" providing different services according to the different needs of individual pensioners and their families. And 5) a "Supervision Mechanism" consisting of citizens, supervisors and the media. Supervisors are district congress representatives and members of the political consultation confederation. All

---

[30] China Information Association: *Zhongguo Xinxi Nianjian 2003* (*China Information Yearbook*, 2003), China Information Yearbook Periodicals Press (Zhongguo Xinxi Nianjian Qikanshe), pp. 99, 560.

phone numbers are available to the public. Publication boards were established in every community in order to inform the residents of the details of pension payments.

An urban social security system was completed in 2002 in Qingdao. By the end of 2003, a total of 15,348 households, and over thirty-six thousand individuals received social security. This is about 1.5% of the urban population. In the first half of 2003, 868 households, or 2,173 persons, opted out of social security due to re-employment.

The legal regulation of government behavior is crucial for strengthening accountability. In recent years, while pursuing the goal of accountable governance, the Chinese government also has committed itself to the rule of law. While trying to establish a legal system that is consistent with the market economy and globalization, the government has particularly emphasized the legal route. After putting into effect an "Administration Procedure Law" and "State Compensation Law" that enables citizens to sue officials, the "Law of Administrative Licensing" was put into effect on July 1st, 2004. According to this law, neither the government nor the public sectors are allowed to take administrative measures against any citizen without legal justification. According to Premier Wen Jiabao, the enforcement of the "Law of Administrative Licensing" in China, where authoritarianism and obedience to officials have deep roots, is a revolution in the administrative apparatus. An article entitled "We are Witnessing the Government Revolutionizing itself" summarized "eight significant changes in citizens' lives" that were brought about by the Law.[31]

1) "Citizens enjoy more legal autonomy."
[Case] The working committees of the party, management committees at the Longbao and Wuqiao migrants' development zones within Wanzhou District in Chongqing Municipality issued regulations one after another, stipulating "Xiongying" mineral water to be the only legal mineral water within the zones.

[Comment] It is the consumers' free choice to drink mineral water with whatever trademark. It is in fact a deprival of consumers' right to choose and a violation on consumers' sovereignty for the governments

---

[31] Zhang Xiaosong, "Du Yu: Xingzhengxukefa gei Baixing Shenghuo Dailai Ba Da Bianhua" (Eight Big Changes in Citizens Life Brought by Law of Administrative Licensing), *Zhongguo Qingnian (China Youth)*, July 1st, 2004, p. A3.

to force some particular trademark on consumers through governmental documents.

[Change] The "Law of Administrative Licensing" requires that governments at all levels exercise their power according to existing laws and legal procedures. The administration should refrain from intervening in those areas that could be autonomously decided by citizens, legal persons, or other organizations, or that could be adjusted through market mechanisms.

2) "Simplifying the procedures of application for governments."

[Case] Before starting its business, a joint venture in Henan had to visit the Industry and Business Bureau, the Foreign Trade and Economy Commission, and the Planning Commission repeatedly on several occasions without any outcome. To finally receive a certificate, the people in question had to visit governmental institutions eleven times.

[Comment] Red tape makes ordinary people feel powerless.

[Change] The "Law of Administrative Licensing" ensures the principle of helping people, which requires administrations to simplify licensing processes and to decrease relevant costs so as to promote efficiency and to provide high quality service. Institutions such as one stop shop service or one stop shop for getting license were established.

3) Farewell to lengthy administrative investigation and approval times.

[Case] It took at least six months for a high-tech company in Southern China already approved for business to go through the process of finalizing the approval. The process required thirteen administrative investigations, the presentation of fifteen reports, and the collection of fifty-four stamps.

[Comment] There used to be no time limits for the administrations to handle applications. In some cases, applicants bribed administrators in order to obtain licenses sooner.

[Change] The "Law of Administrative Licensing" makes clear regulations on time limits for processing applications. For example, the National Industry and Business Bureau amended its procedures for the registration of companies. An applicant can now register by sending an email while the National Industry and Business Bureau can inform the applicant of all the necessary materials in one reply. Once all materials have been submitted, the investigation and approval process could be done in one day.

4) "I have right to speak for all things related to my interests."

[Case] According to the Commerce Commission in Shanghai, it should hold a hearing into establishing any supermarket outside the ring road and larger than ten thousand square meters. The Industry and Business Bureau should issue approvals based on the outcome of the hearing.

[Comment] In January 2002, the first public hearing on national administrative policy-making—a hearing into train ticket prices—was held in our country. The hearings system allows citizens to participate in the decision of their governments.

[Change] The "Law of Administrative Licensing" clearly stipulates what must hold a hearing into getting licenses.

5) The investigation and approval procedure has become quite affordable.

[Case] According to an investigation in Shanghai in 2000, an automobile company spent RMB 191 million before being able to start business.

[Comment] Some administrations use license issuing to make money. To tackle the problem, the National Taxation Bureau stipulated that for their activities, administrations were not allowed to impose any fee on companies.

[Change] The "Law of Administrative Licensing" stipulates that fees cannot be collected pending approval. In the rare cases when this is allowed by law, the collected fees can only be used for fiscal purposes and handed over to the pertinent bureaus.

6) Disturbance of citizens' lives by law enforcement shall be reduced.

[Case] A manager of a pastry manufacturer complained to the correspondent: "What bothers me most is to deal with all those investigations. As soon as one load of paperwork has been done, another investigation comes along. Officials are like lords who cannot be offended."

[Comment] Many companies are seriously disrupted by endless inspections and investigations. Inspections on most administrative licenses could actually be done in writing simply to vouchsafe legal procedures. For example, production licenses and quality control certificates can be issued after inspecting the written materials submitted by a company.

[Change] The Law on Administrative Licensing stipulates that administrations should mainly rely on written materials instead of sending inspectors, since such visits to companies and organizations can be highly disruptive.

7) Cost of enforcing government policy is increasingly covered by the state.

[Case] In tackling bird flu, the state offers RMB 10 in compensation for each destroyed chicken. Xuan Lipu, chicken farmer of Chaixing village in Dongsheng (Jingyuan district, Gansu) commented: "1,780 chickens of mine were killed. But the government quickly gave me part of the compensation."

[Comment] To enforce the vaccination and killing of chickens is government policy and supported by current legislation. Nevertheless, it also incurs big financial losses. Governments should offer at least partial compensation.

[Change] According to the Law on Administrative Licensing, officials should not charge for issuing licenses arbitrarily. If substantial charges are necessary, the government should offer compensation.

8) The legal defense position of citizens is improving.

[Case] Law suit by farmers Ni Dengcai, Zhu Zhengzhu of Jiangxia District, Wuhan, against the municipal government of Husi over a land contract.

[Comment] In recent years, cases of citizens suing governments are increasing. The enforcement of Law of Administrative Licensing will create a platform for citizens and governments to communicate with each other on an equal basis.

[Change] The Law on Administrative Licensing guarantees the right to legal defense in three ways: firstly, by defining the responsibilities and duties of administrations; secondly, by adding rights, for example the right to demand hearings and compensation; thirdly, by defining standards on law suits and on verdicts.

An accountable government should involve citizens in policy making. It is not only a requirement of political transparency, but also a democratic principle. The new leadership in China has pronounced that governments at all levels should consult as many citizens as possible in its policy making. Moreover, this mass participation should be institutionalized, namely 1) by publicizing policy intentions and content so that citizens are informed about the aims of the government; 2) by consulting with scholars and experts on specific policies, thus allowing policy-making to become more scientific and rational; 3) by implementing policy hearings before making a particular policy; and 4) through a policy reviewing system, based on objective reviewing procedures and standards, to independently review policy enforcement. The hearing system is of special importance to citizens' political participation and democratic decision-making. It was introduced in the late 1990s. An early test case was the Public Meeting and Hearing of the Standing

Committee of the People's Congress of Guiyang City, Guizhou Province. In January 1999, the standing committee of the People's Congress of the city of Guiyang passed the resolution that henceforth all meetings of the standing committee be opened to the public. Citizens could come to listen to the debate and discussion at the meetings, and they would also be allowed to express their own ideas on the issues. By September 2001, all of the twenty-one meetings of the standing committee were open to the public, and more than two hundred citizens had been attending the meetings on average. This project is announced twice a year in the local newspapers and on TV and radio, with the topics of each debate being given half a year in advance, in order to cater for specific interests.

Four results of this project have become discernable. Firstly, the ideas and interests of ordinary citizens are being heard. Citizens now have a new channel to articulate themselves. Secondly, with rising public attendance figures, members of the standing committee have become more serious and active during meetings, improving the quality of their work. Thirdly, the supervision of the People's Congress stipulated by law has strengthened. At the thirty-second meeting of the standing committee held recently, two appointments of local cadres to local government positions were rejected. Last but not least, citizens have become more experienced in participating in the political process. They now have a better understanding of the laws, rights, powers, structures and operations of the government, and therefore have become more capable of taking part in politics.

To promote the development of grassroots democracy is crucial to increasing citizens' political participation. In the past twenty years, China focused on grassroots democracy in village elections, which is no doubt the right choice for a country in which 80% of the population lived in rural areas. It is equally important that democracy at township level should also be taken into serious consideration, since democracy is a precondition both for government accountability and public service quality. A number of challenging political experiments have been initiated in recent years that are likely to lead to breakthroughs in democratic governance at grassroots level. One prominent example is direct elections and/or semi-competitive elections for township governors. The first case of such direct elections is the experiment at Buyun Township in Sichuan Province.

In December 1998, Buyun Township elected its mayor through direct elections, gaining fame as the first township in mainland China to hold direct elections. In December 2001, Buyun Township successfully conducted elections for township leaders after re-adjusting voting methods in accordance with the Constitution of the People's Republic of China and the "Organization Law for Local People's Congresses and Local Governments at All Levels." This time citizens selected all nominees for township leader by direct vote, and these nominees were later submitted to the Township's People's Congress for final approval.

In both instances, Buyun Township acted in the spirit of direct citizen voting, though the specific circumstances were different, in two respects. Firstly, at a systemic level, the first elections were carried out through direct voting, which was a breakthrough in current township election systems, whereas in the second elections nominees were directly elected, in compliance with the current election law. Secondly, the two elections differed in procedural terms. Compared with the first elections, the second elections were conducted along more refined procedures, improving procedural fairness. This manifested itself as follows: 1) candidates' photos were printed on the ballots for the convenience of illiterate voters; 2) proxy voting was prohibited: one person, one vote; 3) separate booths (small rooms) became mandatory so that ballots could be cast in secret; 4) when candidates gave speeches in the same place, the order of speaking was decided by drawing lots; 5) all candidates were allowed to send representatives to monitor the counting of ballots. Moreover, the second election also increased fair competition by eliminating the nomination of candidates by organizations.

Buyun Township's two elections have had an obvious influence on local social, political and economic life. First of all, through voting, village citizens have clearly formulated their democratic rights, have familiarized themselves with election procedures, and have strengthened their confidence in direct election and their trust in government. Secondly, the township leadership, having been elected through direct election, has a much-improved sense of responsibility and accountability. Promises made by the successful candidate when running for election had largely been realized by the time of the second election. Every month there is a "Township Leader Reception Day," and every year at the eve of the lunar New Year, the township leader gives a work report to the citizens of the whole town. The township leaders have also tried to change their methods and attitudes to improve their standing among the citizens. Finally, local economic development has been relatively reasonable and coordinated. The township government has given full consideration to practical conditions and the interests of citizens, has reduced mistakes in decision-making, and has tried not to impose its will regardless of popular opinion. In the past six years, development has concentrated on the construction of basic infrastructure and structural adjustments in agriculture.

China has a political system in which the CCP is the *de facto* core of power. Therefore, democratic orientation, service orientation, legal orientation and accountability orientation within the Party are decisive. Government innovations aimed at building up rule of law, accountability, service and transparency reflect fundamental changes within the Party. Simply speaking, this change is a conscious change of the CCP from a revolutionary to a ruling party. This is illustrated by a redirection of Party ideology from class struggle to economic development, changes in the composition of leadership from the military elite to a knowledge elite, in social affairs away from reliance on command to reliance on laws and regulations, greater restraint by abiding to the law, and changes within the Party's social basis away from the proletariat to the whole body of citizens.

At the sixteenth Party's congress in 2002, a road map toward political democracy in China was drawn up to promote social democracy through promoting inner party democracy. Therefore, inner party democracy is vitally important to democracy in China. This democratization strategy has led to direct elections at certain Party Congresses.

From October to December 2002, the Organizational Department of Yaan City took advantage of the end of the term of the county and district level Party Congresses to conduct an experiment by holding direct elections for Party delegates in Yucheng District and Yingjing County, and by establishing the Party Congress as a standing body. A number of features distinguished Yaan City's methods from other local governments that have established the Party Congress as a standing body. 1) The party delegates were elected through direct election. All Party members could register to run for office, and candidates meeting the qualifications were required to give speeches to "lay out" a platform. Party members voted by secret ballot. Election results were published on the spot immediately after the election, and a "Certificate of Election" was issued to the winning candidate. All county and township leaders had to participate in the election as common Party members. 2) The Party Congress was established as a standing body so as to guarantee that Party delegates exercise their rights and duties. Party delegates have a special budget for activities and conduct delegate activities on a regular basis. Party delegates can raise proposals at the Party Congress, and present opinions and suggestions to the Central Committee and Standing Committee of the Party Congress. Party delegates must evaluate the job performance of members of the County CPC Committee and the Commission for Discipline. They must also submit an annual work report to the organizations from which they are elected. Party delegates can attend meetings of the Standing Committee and Central Committee of the County CPC Committee as observers.

3) New methods were being explored to strengthen democracy within the Party and enhance the influence of intra-Party democracy on society. For example, during the January 2004 Party Congress, Yucheng District set up a Supervisory Committee and a Consultative Committee for Decision Making. The function of the Supervisory Committee was to oversee the District CPC Committee and members of the Commission for Discipline. The function of the Consultative Committee for Decision Making was to guarantee that decision making procedures of the CPC Committee were scientific and democratic. Party delegates were allocated to fixed positions to avoid vacancies in the delegation when a Party delegate moved out of the represented region. Yingjing County invited members of the Political Consultative Committee to attend the Party Congress as observers, and thus improve communication and strengthen the relationship between the CPC, the other constitutional parties and non-CPC members.

After more than one year in operation, the direct election of Party delegates and the establishment of the Party Congress as a standing body in Yaan City have achieved clear results. First, the sense of cohesion and identification within the Party have been greatly enhanced. Now every Party member, whether a common CPC member or a delegate, can participate in Party life effectively, and communications among Party members and between members and their leaders have been strengthened. Secondly, the direct election of Party delegates and the establishment of the Party Congress as a standing body have achieved a rational distribution of power within the Party, and enhanced the transparency of decision making. Decision-making power has been returned to the Party Congress and the CPC Central Committee. Major issues are decided by vote and the power of the Standing Committee of the CPC is effectively checked. the Party is no longer "speaking with one voice." Finally, it has provided powerful institutional support for the realization of democracy. While advancing the institutionalization of the Party Congress, Yaan City also promoted the public election and public nomination of township leaders and leaders of government divisions and bureaus. Leaders chosen through direct elections within the Party can better withstand the test of direct elections.

Such transformations, though incomplete, are the result of globalization and democratization. A considerable number of policies have yet to be addressed. Many high-ranking Party officials still rely on edicts rather than laws in managing society. The relationship between Party and state is far from rational. The huge Party apparatus and the overlapping functions of the Party and government lead to high costs of administration and low efficiency. Inner Party democratization is lagging behind the democratization of society. Inner party corruption is severe. Further progress is mandatory.

Conclusion: "China Model" and "Beijing Consensus"
as Alternative Strategies Toward Modernization in the Global Age

Since the 1980s, China has put forward the goal of "constructing Socialist modernization with Chinese characteristics," as a strategic alternative to modernization in the global age. This has been known as the "China Model" or "Beijing Consensus." Joshua Cooper Ram, an advocate of the "Beijing Consensus," challenges the "Washington Consensus" as a development mode. For him, the "China Model" is already reshaping the international order and revealing a new alternative for development, especially in developing countries.

The Chinese government has had both successful and bitter globalization experiences over the past twenty-five years. The following features of the so-called "China Model" or "Beijing Consensus" as a successful experience are noteworthy.

Internal reform and international engagement are two sides of the same coin. From the perspective of China's experience, there would have been no genuine internal reform without opening up to the world, while thorough internal reform leads necessarily to comprehensive engagement with foreign countries. China needs advanced management systems and ideas rather than abundant capital and advanced technology from transnational corporations and the West. Domestic reforms require learning advanced ideas, science, technology, culture and institutions, mainly from advanced Western countries. The process of opening up is a process of acquiring advanced ideas and institutional models rather than capital and technology.

Developing countries should participate actively into the process of globalization on the basis of their own particular conditions. At the same time they should always retain their own characteristics and autonomy. It depends on their strategic choice whether nations find more advantages or disadvantages in joining the process of globalization. Developing countries do not necessarily lose out and developed countries are not necessarily winners in globalization. In fact, globalization is a double-edged sword for both developed and developing countries. Developing countries have their own strong points and are likely to become winners if they take proper steps toward globalization. *Vice versa*, developed countries have their weak points and could end up being losers if they respond wrongly. Successful globalization combines a country's strength with merits of globalization.

It is important to deal properly with the relation between reform, development and stability. Since stability is a precondition for development, it is a practical strategy for developing countries like China to balance reform, development and stability. There is a dialectical relationship between these three factors: stability advances development, development strengthens stability, and reform advances development.

Market-oriented reform is supplemented by strong government regulation. The market economy has become global, deriving its power from the logical allocation of resources. Therefore, economic reform in such countries as China should be oriented toward the market economy. The market has never been omnipotent, however, and developing countries are even more susceptible to the failures of the market system than developed countries. Thus, strong government regulation, or rather the public sector, should play as great a role as the private sector in the allocation of resources. The market economy never rejects strong government. The point here is not whether the government should be strong or weak, but rather when and to what extent.

Incremental economic and political reform is characterized by a strategy of combining overall gradual development with partial breakthroughs. It is only prudent that reforms aimed at globalization should avoid fierce social turbulences. Shock therapy is not worthy of recommendation; instead, the goal should be to land softly by incremental reform. This does not mean that all reform should be gradual without any sudden breakthroughs; conversely, even partial or temporary improvements merit a drastic shake-up. It is a basic principle for both political and economic reform that reform adapting to globalization must enhance national interests, and that the majority of the people derive advantages from reform.

The following strategic elements should be greatly emphasized as the—at times painful—lessons of the "China Model." Centered on economic growth, the state must aim for balanced and sustainable development between society and nature. Economic development should be the first task for social development since it is the basis for national power and livelihood. Social development does not simply mean economic growth, however, and certainly not merely growth measured in GDP. Development in the context of globalization is a comprehensive goal, a holistic and sustainable social progress. Economic development must be accompanied by environmental protection, ecological balance, general civilization, social stability, citizenship and education. It must promote harmony between human beings, society and nature.

The state has to place equal emphasis upon efficiency and equality and seek a balanced development between individuals and society, between urban and rural areas. Efficiency and equality should not be set against each other since both are fundamental goals for a government. It seems rational to break China's egalitarian traditions by carrying out the strategy of "prioritizing efficiency over equality" in the early stages of reform. However, this biased policy must be revised, and a balanced strategy of efficiency and equality must be practiced. The balanced strategy must be biased toward disadvantaged groups and underdeveloped areas, aiming at avoidance of sharp polarization between the poor and the rich and of unbalanced social and economic development between the urban and the rural, and between the developed and less developed.

The state must hasten political reform aimed at good governance and good government as social and economic reform goes on. The process of modernization, according to China's experience, is a process of democratization. Democracy is a goal rather than a means of development. Democracy, just as welfare, is a fundamental human value. The government should take responsibility not only for economic development but also for political development based on democratic governance. Good governance is an ideal for politics in the global age while good government is the key toward good governance. The government must reform with the goals of decentralization, greater efficiency, accountability and good service before it can deal with social democratic governance aimed at the rule of law, mass participation, human rights, transparency and stability. The government itself should be a model of democracy and innovative thinking.

The state must take more responsibility for its citizens. Indeed, globalization has been weakening the sovereignty of the state to some extent while it has strengthened its power in other respects. Citizens' appetite for rights has steadily increased. The capacity of government is reflected not only in promoting economic development but also in improving citizens' rights concerning security, human rights, welfare, participation and employment. For developing countries, sovereignty and a strong state remain the most important insurances for civil rights, despite mounting challenges to traditional sovereignty from globalization.

The state must be conducive to cooperation between the government and civil society, and public and private sectors, as a sign of good governance. A civil society is a consequence of a modern market economy, and also of globalization and democratization. The government should welcome such change rather than being on the defensive. It should support civil organizations by way of creating a favorable political and legal framework. The government should encourage CSOs to exert their positive role in managing social affairs and turn CSOs into subjects of governance and self-governance. Public and private sectors should have equal status in law, and equal accountability for social progress. The public sector should put emphasis upon cooperation and communication with the private sector and allow the latter to play a greater role in governance. Furthermore, the government should provide CSOs and the private sector with much better facilities and assist it in global collaboration. Civil organizations and the private sector are as much the subjects of globalization as are the state and the public sector.

CHAPTER THREE

FROM "CHINA AND THE WEST" TO "GLOBALIZATION": CHINESE PERSPECTIVES ON GLOBALIZATION

"Globalization" has become a fashionable term, in itself as globalized as McDonald's, the internet or the film *Titanic*. In West or East, in developing or developed countries, in capitalist or socialist economies, people are talking about "globalization." China is no exception. All popular theories in the West tend to have repercussions in China sooner or later, as the theoretical discourse of modernization, post-modernity and globalization demonstrates. Modernization theory, which prevailed in the West in the 1950s and 1960s, did not become popular in China until the 1980s, while globalization theory, which came to prominence in the West in the early 1990s, has been a hot topic in China since the mid-1990s. This fact itself is a good indicator that globalization has been an inevitable trend shaping the development process of the world, including China. As an active member of the international community, having introduced reforms that open the country's economy to the world markets, China is necessarily facing the effects of globalization. As a result, Chinese politician and scholars are posing questions about how to respond to the challenges and opportunities posed by globalization.

Perceptive Chinese scholars responded as soon as they noted the lively debates in the West about globalization at the beginning of 1990s. They introduced into Chinese intellectual circles Western academic views on globalization and advocated relevant research. In 1993, the Institute of Comparative Politics & Economics invited Professor Arif Dirlik of Duke University to come to Beijing for a series of lectures on globalization and capitalism, which were published in the initial issue of *Strategy And Management* in 1993 as "Capitalism under Globalization." Dirlik's article was the first to introduce Western globalization theories systematically and it had a great impact in Chinese intellectual circles. Professor Li Shenzhi, former Vice President of the Chinese Academy of Social Sciences, contributed with papers advocating studies on globalization in China. In this respect, he came to be recognized as one of earliest Chinese proponents of intellectual engagement with globalization.

Asia experienced a serious financial crisis in 1997. Its epicenter was located in Thailand and Indonesia, but quickly spread to Malaysia, Singapore, South Korea and Japan. Although China escaped its effects, the Asian financial crisis did alert Chinese scholars to the potential dangers of financial crises that might result from economic globalization. Jiang Zeming, President and General Secretary of the Communist Party of China (CPC), said on March 9, 1998, that "we have to recognize and treat properly the issue of economic 'globalization' Economic globalization is an objective trend of world economic development, from which no one can escape and in which everyone has to participate. The key point is to 'globalization' dialectically; i.e., see both its positive aspect and its negative aspect. It is particularly important for developing countries."[1] The interest in globalization by the country's top leader gave a great impetus to scholars and analysts engaged in studies of globalization, making it relevant to intellectuals. A number of essays on globalization have since been published and some important Western works on globalization such as *The Trap of Globalization* have been translated into Chinese. The Institute of Comparative Politics and Economics has gone even further in editing a Globalization Series, comprised of seven books: *Antinomies Of Globalization, Marxism and Globalization, Socialism and Globalization, Capitalism and Globalization, Globalization and China, Globalization and the World,* and *Globalization And Post-Colonial Criticism.*

The debate on globalization among Chinese intellectuals focuses on the following main issues:

1. *Conception of globalization*: What is globalization and what essential features does globalization embody?
2. *Types of globalization*: Besides economic globalization, are a nation-states' politics and culture affected? If so, what are the patterns?
3. *Implications of globalization for China*: Is globalization above all a universalizing process or one which demands a reinforcement of national autonomy? What policies should China follow?
4. *Globalization's advantages and disadvantages*: Is globalization a blessing or a disaster for China's modernization and development?

We examine each of these issues in the following section of the paper.

---

[1] Jiang Zeming, *Renmin Ribao (PEOPLE'S DAILY)*, March 9, 1998.

Debates on Globalization in China—Concepts of Globalization

In order to study globalization, it is necessary to understand its meaning and to define it. In essence, there are three different opinions among Chinese scholars.

A first argument is that globalization is a process of integrating human life, taking place as a global and holistic tendency that reaches beyond regional and national boundaries. In other words, it stands for "an objective historic process and tendency of contemporary human development beyond nation-state boundaries, which is unfolding as global communication, global networks and global interactions develop."[2] Some go further by explaining that the essential meaning of globalization lies in a global consensus beyond spatial, cultural and institutional barriers, in the global interdependence of nations and regions, and in the fact that as communication develops and international connections become tighter, humanity is facing common problems and seeking to cooperate in order to resolve these problems.[3]

A second view regards globalization simply as global capitalism at a new stage and new form of development. In the viewpoint of some authors, globalization is nothing but the logical result of free economic development, a universalization of the capitalist mode of production. So called issues of globalization are essentially issues of contemporary (developed) capitalism. Concretely, both in its basic nature as well as in the mode of its operation, the explanation of globalization requires placing it in the history of the capitalist mode of production.[4] According to this logic, globalization is only a temporary alternative name for capitalism. Thus, it is also referred to as "late capitalism, developed capitalism, disorganized capitalism, transitional capitalism, globalized capitalism, post-Fordism."[5]

---

[2] Cai Tuo, *"Quanqiuhua yu Dangdai GuojiGuanxi (Globalization and Contemporary International Relation),"* Makesi Zhuyi yu Xianshi (*MARXISM AND REALITY*), No. 3, 1998, p. 20.

[3] Tan Junjiu, *"Guanyu Quanqiuhua de Sikao yu Taolun (Thinking and Arguing on Globalization),"* See: Quanqiuhua de Erlv BeiFan (*GLOBALIZATION AND ANTINOMIES*), edited by Yu Keping, Central Compilation and Translation Press (Beijing: Zhongyang Bianyi Chubanshe, 1998), 1998, p. 127.

[4] Yang Caoren and He Zhiwei, *"Quanqiuhua, Zhidu Kaifang yu Minzu Fuxing (Globalization, Institutional Opening and National Rejuvenation),"* ibid., p. 138.

[5] Wang Fengzheng, *"Quanqiuhua, Wenhuarentong yu Minzuzhuyi (Globalization, Cultural Identity and Nationalism),"* See: Quanqiuhua yu Hou zhimin Piping (*GLOBALIZATION AND POST-COLONIAL CRITICISM*), edited by Wang Ning, Central Compilation and Translation Press (Beijing: Zhongyang Bianyi Chubanshe, 1998), 1998, p. 91.

If globalization merely constitutes the latest manifestation of capitalism, developed Western countries, especially the United States, are its natural representatives. It is then plausible to conclude that globalization does mean Westernization. This is a view shared by a small minority of intellectuals in China. Globalization is interpreted as Westernization simply because, contrarily, "Western" values are represented as "universal" human values. Liberal intellectuals in China are thus inclined to define globalization by terms such as universal "trends" and "values," implying that the Western (and specifically the American) set of political, economic and cultural values represent globally normative standards.[6]

Above all, globalization encourages increasing homogeneity in human development on the basis of financial and economic integration. Economic globalization is a necessary consequence of the development of a market economy that extends beyond national and regional boundaries, creating a genuine world market. Undoubtedly, the Western developed countries are the originators and driving force behind globalization, setting the rules of globalization and controlling its functioning. In attempting to spread their own political and cultural values to the rest of the world, economic and cultural globalization becomes as the expression of a homogenizing human experience.

Contradictory Aspects of Globalization

The process of globalization is, by its very nature, highly contradictory, simultaneously embodying tendencies toward homogenization (integration) and fragmentation, unification and pluralization, centralization and separation, internationalization and reinforcement of national autonomy.

Let us first reflect on the unity of universalization and particularization. On the one hand, globalization is a process of homogenization characterized by a convergence of life styles, modes of production and values among various civilizations. For instance, the capitalist market economy is becoming a worldwide phenomenon, abstracted from its European origins. Democracy and human dignity are being sought

---

[6] Zhang Yiwu, *"Quanqiuhua: Cong Yazhou Jingrong Weiji de Jiaodu Chongxin Shenshi (Globalization: Rethinking in view of Asian Financial Crisis),"* ibid., pp. 82, 86.

by all peoples in the world as basic human values while despotism is rapidly losing its supporters. On the other hand, universalization is always accompanied by particularization. Market economies in various countries are subtly different and these differences among market economies in various countries are not diminishing as the market economy expands into every corner of the world. For example, the post-1945 "Social Market Economy" in Germany is clearly different from the liberal market economy in the United States (or the United Kingdom). The market economy in East Asia is currently different from others due to higher levels of governmental intervention. Democracy is similar. The universal longing for popular participation has a host of different expressions in different countries. For instance the representative systems of Japan and South Korea are based on distinctly different democratic models and cultures compared with those of Western models.

Secondly, there is the theory of globalization as a unity of integration and fragmentation. Indeed, the integration and homogenization fostered by international organizations such as the United Nations, World Bank, IMF and WTO is more important than ever before. International integration also leads to at least some degree of weakening national sovereignty. Moreover, cosmopolitan ideals have come closer to realization with intensifying trans-national integration, as the examples of European integration, the global capital markets and the global flows of information illustrate. Conversely, however, particularity is being reinvigorated at national and regional levels. National identities are being redefined with the creation of new national states. The fate of Yugoslavia may serve as an apt, if extreme, example. Communitarianism and local identities are political issues of heated debate in developed countries. Scholars have coined the term "global localism" to specifically reflect these contradictions, because local autonomy is developing rapidly under the conditions of globalization.

A third argument posits that globalization is a unity of centralization and decentralization. One of the major outcomes of globalization is the increasing centralization of capital, information, as well as power and wealth. The merger of big companies has been the fashion since the 1990s, which pushes the centralization of power and wealth further. A good example is the merger of McDonnell-Douglas and Boeing, two of the world's biggest companies in the aerospace industry. On the other hand, the decentralization of capital, information, power and wealth is also a marked trend. Small capital is still very active and developing very well, appearing not to have suffered as a result of capital centralization of capital. It sounds like a contradiction, but the higher the degree of centralization of information, the more difficult it is to monopolize it. The best example in this regard is the internet. To date, the internet has been the largest medium for the exchange of information, drawing in bits of information from all parts of the world, all fields of society and all aspects of human life. Meanwhile, no one is able to monopolize this information which is highly discursive in the sense that everyone whose computer is linked up to the internet is able to share in this information.

Finally there are those who say that globalization enforces a unity of internationalization and nationalization. As we pointed out above, globalization is breaking down traditional national barriers. As a result, more and more international conventions, treaties, agreements and norms are accepted and observed by states across the world. Many international principles thus have an authentic international meaning for the first time. On the other hand, states and their citizens do not forget their own traditions and characteristics while accepting such international conventions, agreements and principles. International agreements, such as the covenants on the protection of human rights and the environment, are adapted to specific national conditions which draw deeply on national characteristics in reasoning and implementation.

In short, globalization is a term full of contradictions. Nevertheless, it is a fact and an objectively verifiable trend. Antinomy within globalization is inescapable, since it is impossible to leave behind national characteristics, even for the most open of countries. However, globalization as an antinomy is advantageous for human progress. The unity of the plurality of societies is the true meaning of human development.

Types of Globalization

Globalization is based upon the integration of capital, production, communication and technology and economic processes, leading to the global harmonization of economies as well as information.[7] However, globalization has not only economic, but also political and

---

[7] Li Ling, *"Quanqiuhua Beijing xia de Zhongguo falv fazhan (Chinese Legal Development under the Background of Globalization),"* Xuexi yu Tansuo *(STUDIES AND INQUIRIES)*, No. 1, 1998, p. 93.

cultural dimensions. It is "a cultural, a political, and an economic phenomenon."[8]

Many Chinese scholars do not recognize this multiple identity. Most relevant articles strictly refer to economic globalization. There are a few scholars who identify globalization with economic integration, but most refuse to read the term in a political and cultural sense. This may be due to a reluctance to abandon Chinese political values and its political fundamentals. As one author mused: "elements of economic growth, especially elements of capital, technology and human labor, circulate globally dictated by the dynamics of the free market, so that national and regional economies become increasingly integrated into a global economic system. The interdependence, reciprocity and interlinkages of human economic development have increased and increasing varieties of commodities produced in different countries are shared by throughout the world."[9]

Some researchers summarize the features of economic globalization as follows:

1) Globalization of production: a new worldwide division of labor replacing traditional arrangements under the nation-state regime;
2) Formation of a new multilateral trade system as a driving force behind the integration of national and regional economies into a single world market.
3) Rapidly expanding processes of financial integration.
4) A global framework of investment, with investment activity stretching into nearly every part of the world;
5) Transnational or supranational cooperation as the center of international economic life, challenging traditional sovereignties.
6) Skilled labor and professional expertise are becoming globalized commodities.[10]

---

[8] Zhu Jinwen, *"Guanyu Quanqiuhua de Ruogan Wenti (Some Issues on Globalization),"* See: *Quanqiuhua yu Zhongguo (GLOBALIZATION AND CHINA)*, edited by Hu Yuanzhi, Central Compilation and Translation Press (Beijing: Zhongyang Bianyi Chubanshe, 1998), 1998, p. 102.

[9] Mu Guangcong, *"Jingji Quanqiuhua yu Zhongguo Renkou (Economic Globalization and Chinese Population),"* Dangdai Shijie yu Shehuizhuyi *(CONTEMPORARY WORLD AND SOCIALISM)* (Quarterly), No. 3, 1998, p. 19.

[10] See Xue Rongjiu, *"Jingji Quanqiuhua de Yingxiang yu Tiaozhan (The Impact and Challenge of Economic Globalization),"* Shijie Jingji *(WORLD ECONOMY)*, No. 4, 1998, p. 46.

For most Chinese scholars, economic globalization is an inevitable tendency from which no country can escape, China not being an exception. China should actively participate in the process of economic globalization, they claim, rather than being forced into this process. Some people say that China's participation in economic globalization is not only an inevitable fact but also a necessary one for realizing its modernization aims. The most advantageous outcome of economic globalization is thus the optimal distribution of world resources. Regardless of the performance of a single economy, it is always shackled by the availability of its own domestic resources and other limiting features. Moreover, the development of the entire world economy can only be optimized by integrating world resources and markets. Furthermore, economic globalization provides developing countries with a good chance to catch up with developed economies.[11]

Globalization is a holistic progress of historic dimensions, coercing nations to observe common rules and to accept institutional arrangements. In turn, it tends to influence political and cultural values. Some Chinese scholars have thus begun to reflect upon non-economic globalization, for instance in the political, legal and cultural realms. In their eyes, political globalization refers to increasingly similar political values and political institutions across nation-states. Prime examples are democratic values based on freedom and equality and the universalization of democratic institutions underpinning such values. Political globalization has thus been equated with global democratization: "In terms of political implications, globalization and democratization are synonyms. The recent wave of political globalization was started by the fall of the Berlin Wall in 1989, the end of the Cold War and the disappearance of the Iron Curtain. The visible force of globalization is economic integration while invisibly it leads to the integration of [...] democratic and global values."[12]

Other political scientists specifically discuss concrete democratic implications, such as good governance. By this political processes are meant which maximize public goods and which characterize cooperation

---

[11] See Liu Lie, "*Jingji Quanqiuhua: Fazhanzhong Guojia Ganshang Fada Guojia de Biyouzhilu (Economic Globalization: An Necessary Way by which Developing Countries Catch Up With Developed Countries)," Guoji Jingji Guancha (INTERNATIONAL ECONOMIC REVIEW)*, No. 11–12, 1997, p. 32.

[12] Liu Junning, "*Quanqiuhua yu Minzhu (Globalization and Democracy)," Dangdai Shijie yu Shehuizhuyi (CONTEMPORARY WORLD AND SOCIALISM)* (Quarterly), No. 3, 1998, p. 26.

and synergy between governments and citizens in public management. Good governance, as a new, optimal relation between state and civil society, consists of six elements:

- Legitimacy, i.e., public order and authority coinciding with citizens' interests
- Transparency, i.e., access by citizens to pertinent political information
- Accountability
- Rule of law
- Responsiveness
- Effectiveness

The resulting political world is defined as "the political model of the global age."[13]

Internationally binding practices and conventions have gained in importance. In other words, the globalization of law has been put on the agenda of lawmakers. As Chinese jurists have noted: "From the legal perspective, the adoption of a concept of globalization raises a number of serious problems, such as conflicts between the world economy and national interests, traditional culture and modernization, globalization and state sovereignty, the problem of legal pluralism, the status of state legislatures, etc."[14] Others refer to the globalization of law as a new stage of legal development, placing their emphasis on a global consensus on law, the possible resolutions to worldwide problems, changing notions of sovereignty and a weakening of nationalism.[15]

The issue of cultural globalization is already well established in China. In fact, in the history of modern China, there have been two views: a "Westernization View" (*xihua lun*) and a "Chinese Cultural Quintessence" (*guocui lun*) view. The Chinese Cultural Quintessence view has gradually lost its defensibility as Western popular music, clothing fashions, books, magazines, and lifestyles entered China one after the

---

[13] Yu Keping, "*Cong Shanzheng dao Shanzhi (From Good Government to Good Governance),*" *Fangfa (Way)*, No. 1, 1998, p. 38.

[14] Li Ling, "*Quanqiuhua Beijing xia de Zhongguo falv fazhan (Chinese Legal Development under the Background of Globalization),*" *Xuexi yu Tansuo (STUDIES AND INQUIRIES)*, No. 1, 1998, p. 94.

[15] See Zhu Jinwen, "*Guanyu Quanqiuhua de Ruogan Wenti (Some Issues on Globalization),*" See: *Quanqiuhua yu Zhongguo (GLOBALIZATION AND CHINA)*, edited by Hu Yuanzhi, Central Compilation and Translation Press (Beijing: Zhongyang Bianyi Chubanshe), 1998, pp. 111–119.

other after the reforms and opening up of the economy (in fact during the entire twentieth century). Cultural globalization has been a reality in a sense that there has emerged a cultural identity or value identity beyond China's native or national cultural identity. For the Chinese advocates of such a "global culture," global identity and values draw their justification from global processes of socialization. Thus, human socialization is completed in particular cultural environments, which now extend beyond the national boundaries. The outcome is a "global person" surrounded by global cultural information and enjoying all aspects of global civilization, both material and spiritual. Such global identity replaces national ones, persons becoming more "global" at the expense of, say, "Chinese," "American," "French" or "Russian" qualities. As it stands, each national culture is actually a fusion of a variety of cultural influences, despite the fact that each national culture retains its independence. Global culture results from the merger of national cultures, implying that universal values have emerged, transcending national borders, social systems and political ideologies.[16]

The Impact of Globalization on China

Chinese scholars are highly interested as to what extent globalization will influence China, since it can comprise of positive and negative consequences alike. Positive characteristics include the enhanced distribution of resources, increased levels of international cooperation and of sharing scientific and technological information, as well as the best possible resolution of global problems such as (air) pollution, illegal (im)migration and drug smuggling. From a negative perspective, it strengthens the hegemony of developed countries in international economic and political life, increases the risks of international financial crises, widens the gap between South and North, and helps international capital to increase its control over under-developed economies.

Chinese society is experiencing both positive and negative aspects. Globalization certainly provides many good opportunities for China's development. It attracts foreign capital, communicates advanced science and technology, theories of management and of organizational struc-

---

[16] Tan Junjiu, *"Guanyu Quanqiuhua de Sikao yu Taolun (Thinking and Arguing on Globaliza-tion)," ibid.*, pp. 131–132.

tures abroad, is conducive to export and to international cooperation. Negative manifestations, on the other hand, also exist, as politicians and scholars have emphasized since the East Asian financial crisis. Generally speaking, negative evaluations of globalization for China focus on economic security and on national sovereignty. To begin with the former, foreign control of capital and advanced technology is perceived as a threat to both the structure and progress of China's industry. As the domestic financial market opens up to the world on a major scale and accumulates foreign debt, it becomes more subject to global financial fluctuations. Secondly, there is a possibility of weakening the sovereignty of the Chinese state. A general condition for participating in the process of globalization is to observe established international practices and conventions, mostly reflecting the standards and values of the developed world. Developing countries have no alternative but to follow the Western example. As a consequence, their sovereignty tends to decline to varying degrees.[17]

Globalization, Modernization and Development

The Chinese government has taken direct steps to globalization by implementing policies that open its economy to the world, such as membership of the WTO, or by signing the International Covenant on Civil and Political Rights. Chinese scholars mostly agree. The problem for China as a developing country is not whether to join in, but how to do so. As an author notes, the Chinese people must:

> recognize fully the dual impact of globalization dominated by developed countries: opportunity coincides with challenge. It is a fortunate opportunity in the sense that globalization provides avenues for developing countries to absorb international capital and modern technology, to increase exports, to improve their market economies and to enter the world market. China provides a good example in its implementation of reform policies, including economic opening, and the construction of a socialist market economy. Meanwhile, it is a source of mental agony and pain for developing countries that the progress of globalization may

---

[17] See Wang Caocai, *"Shijie Jingji Quanqiuhua yu Zhongguo Jingji Anquan (World Economic Globalization and China's Economic Safety),"* and Liu Jianping, *"Jingji Quanqiuhua yu Woguo de Jingji Anquan Zhanlue (Economic Globalization and Our Strategy of Economic Safety),"* in *Quanqiuhua yu Zhongguo (GLOBALIZATION AND CHINA)*, pp. 180–200.

undermine the foundations of state sovereignty and that their economic independence will suffer due to the hegemony of the developed countries. The financial crisis in East Asia is a good example in this respect.[18]

This crisis has greatly influenced Chinese intellectuals, who are more cautious in their advocacy of the modalities governing China's participation in globalization. Firstly one hears the argument that China should not try to imitate the developed countries because China's socio-economic condition lags behind theirs, and because globalization is actually controlled by a few advanced countries. Attempts to copy the advanced world would bring problems due to undue haste, as well as due to manipulation by the advanced world. An economist summarizes the view of "keeping up" with globalization in this way: "China has entered through the gate of globalization and will not be able to improve its economy without keeping up with advanced countries in the progress of globalization." He then goes on to criticize this view as "too simplistic and removed from the Chinese situation, and therefore as one-sided and improper."

Secondly, some think that China should participate more selectively, that priority should be given to economic globalization, although politics, culture and the economy are difficult to separate from each other. As the above-mentioned scholars have pointed out, "globalization" equals economic globalization. Some caution that since China would never be able to catch up with the West even in economic terms, China should open up to global markets at a moderate pace. They warn of dreams of economic globalization concealing the tremendous risks involved and highlight inequalities within the existing global economic order through which (Western) developed countries manipulate developing countries (including China). China must thus insist on an independent strategy of economic development, on its guard against Western economic and political hegemony.

Finally, some intellectuals put their emphasis on national economic autonomy as a basis for economic globalization. As pointed out at the beginning of the article, globalization both preserves national autonomy and internationalizes it. On the one hand, economic globalization is breaking down national barriers by accelerating global economic inte-

---

[18] Wang Weiping, *"Quanqiuhua yu Zhongguo Zhengzhi Gaige (Globalization and China's Political Reform),"* See: *Quanqiuhua de Erlv BeiFan (GLOBALIZATION AND ANTINOMIES),* pp. 50–51.

gration. Calls for the protection of national economic autonomy have become louder. Protectionism, even in developed countries, remains as strong as before as agricultural subsidies illustrate, and trade wars continue to take place.

In such a situation, how should China deal with the relationship between economic globalization and national autonomy? In other words, should joining the global economy or developing the national economy be given priority? Scholars express the need for the latter by arguing that globalization can be justified due to its wholesome effects on China's national economy. The more global the world economy becomes, the more this is in the national interest. They conclude "it is absolutely mistaken to stress opening to the global market rather than protecting the national economy. It is a basic principle to develop our national economy."[19]

Conclusion

The globalization debate has been one of most important discourses in Chinese academic circles in recent years, drawing scholars from political science, economics, philosophy, sociology and other disciplines. We have been able to discern some new features from this discussion although it is still in its infancy. It represents progress in two relevant ways: firstly because the discourse is gradually transcending the traditional "East-West" dichotomy, and secondly because the ideological paradigm of "Socialism vs Capitalism" is being relegated to history.

The "East-West" discourse might constitute the most time-honored intellectual debate in modern China, evaluating the relative merits of "Sinification" or "Westernization" in terms of China's relations with the world. It is a discourse which began with the Westernization Movement during the late Qing period. The dominant doctrine has always been "Chinese values as the core, Western values for usefulness" (*zhong-ti xi-yong*). This doctrine implies that China should only use Western sciences and methods as a tool while insisting on its traditional values. The doctrine has remained essentially unchanged, throughout the Republican period and under the People's Republic. It quintessentially

---

[19] Gao Debu, *"Quanqiuhua Haishi Minzuhua? (Globalization or Nationalization?),"* Zhongguo Dangzheng Ganbu Luntan (CHINESE CADRES' FORUM), No. 5, 1997, p. 44.

stipulates that China and the West are diametrically opposed in their interests and that China can only use Western sciences and techniques as tools while never being able to learn from Western core values.

This doctrine, however, has changed during the globalization debate that began in the 1990s. Globalization is, mostly, no longer simply equated with Westernization, though the dominant role of Western developed countries is recognized. Chinese intellectuals argue that globalization must treat nations on an equal basis, no matter whether the nations are large or small, and even though its main agents are from the advanced West. It follows that China should participate actively and intuitively in globalization processes while never becoming Westernized. This reveals that the old "East-West" dichotomy is being relinquished.

The international community divided into communist and capitalist spheres after the Second World War. Since 1949, China belonged to the former bloc while the developed West belonged to the latter. Since due to this division, Western countries became synonymous with capitalism, the traditional dichotomies were turned into one of "Socialism vs Capitalism." This ideological mantra was repeated also when China was implementing its policies of opening to the Western world. More recently, however, Chinese intellectuals increasingly distinguish globalization and capitalism, although they understand the leading role of the developed capitalistic countries. They do not advocate capitalism publicly in China while they do welcome globalization in China. In this respect, we can say that the discourse of globalization is dissolving the dominance of the ideologizing dichotomy of "Socialism vs. Capitalism."

CHAPTER FOUR

AMERICANIZATION, WESTERNIZATION, SINIFICATION: MODERNIZATION OR GLOBALIZATION IN CHINA?

China has long since embraced the concept of the Golden Mean, yet, since the beginning of the twentieth century, extremism has prevailed. The Cultural Revolution is a typical example of extremism turned catastrophe. The reforms promoted by Deng Xiaoping were not only significant on the socio-economic level, but also for politics and ideology. In essence, they constitute an attempt to strike a balance between "left" and "right." Twenty years of reforms have shown that Deng succeeded in principle, in as much as extremist ideology no longer dominates Chinese politics. Yet, as the old extremisms faded, new forms were taking their place. Currently the two most popular extremes in China's ideological spectrum are Westernization and its opposite, i.e., anti-Westernization, or—in more concrete terms—Americanization and anti-Americanization. In fact, these new extremes have affected China's politics, economy, academia, education, literature, arts, media and also to a great extent people's everyday habits.

I would like to highlight a few examples of this Westernization or Americanization that I personally experienced. In 1999, I was invited to deliver a lecture entitled "Globalization and its Impacts on China" for local executives of the Chuyong regional government, in an ethnic minority region. It was striking in itself to be asked to discuss globalization in an area where the economy is underdeveloped and most people live below the poverty line as defined by the state. What was even more telling was that my lecture on globalization was warmly welcomed by the audience and I was asked to present another. One of the topics this audience focused on in particular was the relationship between China and the USA, and China's attempts to become a member of the World Trade Organization. Chuyong is located in a subtropical region that is ideally suited for agriculture. Flowers are one of the major sources of income for the local peasants. A wide range of colorful flowers is available on the market at extraordinarily low prices. Confounded by the price level I was told by my hosts that it was equally low all year round except for February, when prices rise because of Valentine's

Day. This holiday, for the most part, is not known in China, yet it has become a focal market date in this marginal, underdeveloped area. This only hints at how Western marketing, and in particular the American economy, have influenced poor regions such as Chuyong.

Americanization does not stop with flowers. Something I do not like doing in Beijing is taking my young daughter to McDonald's. This is not primarily because I have not adapted to Western food, since I am used to waiting in line and even to the discomfort of eating on the go. McDonald's is my daughter's favorite reward for bringing home excellent marks; so her enjoyment is the exact counterweight to my unhappiness. Over 70 McDonald's outlets have opened in Beijing alone during the past ten years. McDonald's is perceived as a symbol of American culinary culture, which the Chinese used to sneer at. Today American fast food is firmly established and represents a challenge to traditional Chinese food because it has captured Chinese children's taste buds before their parents have been able to inculcate the enjoyment of traditional foods.

The signs of Westernization or Americanization are apparent to anyone living in China, language being a prime example. Learning English is a major preoccupation for students at school and in higher education, sometimes even in primary schools. An English test is required not only for the equivalent of SSATs but also as a prerequisite for job interviews and promotions. English terms and names used to be transcribed with Chinese characters, while today Western advertisements decorate the main streets in China's metropoles. The operating system used on personal computers is the Chinese version of Windows and for word processing we use Microsoft Word, both marketed by the American Microsoft Corporation. American novels, movies, music, painting, cartoons and other aspects of popular culture are quickly translated into Chinese and become as popular as they are in the USA. Blockbusters such as *Titanic* were screened in China simultaneously with cinemas in the West, receiving the same enthusiastic welcome. American public figures such as Bill and Hillary Clinton, Alan Greenspan, Monica Lewinsky, Madonna and Michael Jordan are discussed among ordinary Chinese people. Publishers vie for American copyrights of books, since publishing these in Chinese translation is more lucrative than marketing local books. The academic bestseller list includes many American scholars, such as Samuel Huntington, Milton Friedman, Alvin Toffler and Paul Samuelson. Any self-respecting Chinese scholar has them on his or her bookshelves. Most textbooks in management and economics currently used at Harvard have been translated into Chinese, as bedrocks of students' required reading lists.

These are but superficial examples. More importantly, American values have become adopted by the Chinese, and in particular by the young, producing an "Americanized mindset." The American lifestyle, its political, economic and managerial systems, as well as American ideas and liberal arts have become pursuits sought after and imitated by many Chinese. The USA is perceived as a paradise, making the American Dream the greatest aspiration of the generation that came of age after the Cultural Revolution. Life in the USA, including its people, institutions, economy and culture, is viewed as so perfect and attractive that "the American moon may just be rounder than in China." Attending an American college or university is the fondest hope cherished by Chinese students and their parents. Study abroad programs have multiplied since the 1980s, above all to the USA. Many young students long to be American citizens or at least permanent residents. Even the powerful and rich worship America and send their children on expensive trips to the USA. It is ironic that some former revolutionary cadres—the self-declared enemies of the USA—have sought opportunities for themselves or their children to go to the USA to gain first-hand knowledge of "capitalist evil and adversity."

One author depicts China's Americanization as follows:

> Since the 1980s, more and more commodities, such as movies, videos, country music, rock-and-roll, Donald Duck, Mickey Mouse and Made-in-USA toys, values and culture have hit the Chinese market. Even products for pure entertainment, with little ideological content, illustrate and advocate something of the Western life style that exerts enormous impact on people, especially young people in developing countries. In particular, the rapid growth of the Internet has resulted in an information explosion. Information is very different from other industrial products because a great deal of data flowing on the information highway by necessity contains implied political and cultural values. The US and other Western countries control most of the software and hardware on which the circulation of information depends. For instance, the US possesses over 70 percent of the world's databanks. Moreover, the US decorates its laws, human rights and technology with an international label and imposes these on developing countries. Thus, "Americanization" via the Internet has begun to threaten some countries' social, political, legal and cultural values. (Qi, 1999)

A few writers have gone further, arguing that leading Chinese intellectuals and officials have been Americanized due to intentional pressure and policies, so that the culture of the Chinese elite has in fact become American. In their view, there is a deep-seated conflict between the "Americanized" elite and the "Chinese" masses. An article written under the pseudonym "Mathematics" recently published in the on-line edition of *The People's Daily* stresses that the US (government):

> has paid off some Chinese to sing the praises of the multi-party system...,
> in order to divide China. The US has been successful to some extent in
> the sense that many Chinese intellectuals and officials have been Ameri-
> canized. The US can harvest a few members of the social elite but is not
> able to buy off all 1.3 billion Chinese people. What emerges is that the
> lower classes are patriotic while the "elite" is exerting its utmost efforts
> to destroy the people's nationalism.

Anxiety over Americanization not only comes from Chinese intellectuals and officials, but from ordinary people as well. I occasionally read articles dealing specifically with the dangers of Americanization and the concomitant eclipse of our national identity in an informally published newsletter issued by a local government, which mainly reports on the activities of its political leaders. This type of article typically puts forward statistics and facts to explain the dangers of Americanization, for instance that the US controls 75% of all TV programs, with the effect that many TV stations in developing countries act as US retransmission stations. Furthermore, that 90% of news is manipulated by the US and Western countries or that US films account for over half of all global screenings. A survey indicates that in the general imagination, American culture reflects the following: romantic Hollywood movies, untamed American cowboys, convenient McDonald's, technologically excellent Windows and Intel. Today's Chinese children eat McDonald's, drink Coca-Cola, play American games, watch American and European movies, listen to Western music and speak English. There is nothing of the traditional Chinese culture in their minds, only cultural symbols such as Donald Duck, action toys, *Jurassic Park* and the *Lion King*. This Americanization is true not only for Chinese intellectuals but also for ordinary Chinese people who do not even know where the USA is. They capitulate to American cultural hegemony because of its predominance in academia, culture and information. (*Newsletter of Zhuji*, published by the Office of Zhuji Government, No. 8 (2000): 38–39.)

Judging by such evidence it seems hard to disprove that China is being Americanized. Yet it would be a mistake to ignore the other side of the ideological coin, namely that of anti-Americanization, anti-Westernization and Sinification. Post-1949 China has seen a permanent national complex against Westernization and Americanization, specifically directed against the USA. This attitude was partially responsible for Mao Zedong's closed-door policies. Anti-US emotions have been greatly mitigated since the end of the Cultural Revolution, but a new wave of anti-US feeling has resurfaced since the 1990s, especially since the US-led NATO bombing of the Chinese embassy in Yugoslavia in 1999. A wave of critical articles and essays were penned against the USA, concerning international relations, national culture and globalization. Some Chinese intellectuals have attempted to "reveal" American intentions to "Westernize and divide China," while others decry the USA as a world policeman. Disdain for "American arrogance" and the subservience of sections of the Chinese elite also figured. To those harboring conspiracy theories, US foreign policy can be reduced to the quest for hegemony—a new manifestation of imperialism. Ideologically, the USA regards not the former Soviet Union but rather China as its strategic enemy since the Cold War ended with the collapse of Communist regimes in central and eastern Europe. As a result, they claim, containing China, curtailing her sovereignty and even removing socialist China from the political world map has become US policy. Fighting between China and the US could begin with thorny issues such as Taiwan, Tibet, Xinjiang or the Korean Peninsula. The US could make tactical use of military force, as a continuation of its carrot and stick strategy. (Qin Jiaxi, 1999: 18)

For some post-Cold War intellectuals in China, this is a debate beyond the theoretical. In their view, the USA has begun to put China under siege, and each strategic step that the USA take in the Western Pacific is aimed against China, directly or indirectly. As one commentator put it in his analysis of regional US military activities in 2000 (Zhang Xin, "Look Out, the US is Besieging China!" 2000): "The US is firmly grasping the Taiwan card to threaten China strategically, and is eagerly developing a quasi-military coalition in the Western Pacific while tightening its strategic siege of China." The author calls on the Chinese never to forget the American "insidious conspiracy":

> In recent years, the US has been working hard not only to develop relationships with its old allies, but to penetrate other Asian countries. In northeast Asia, the US is strengthening military alliances with Japan and South Korea while adjusting its policies to North Korea in an attempt to throw a spanner into China's relationship with North Korea. In southeast Asia, the US has increased its political influence on countries by renewing its military relations with the Philippines while cottoning up to Vietnam.

> In south Asia, the US has begun to implement its new policies of "looking up to India while looking down on Pakistan" seeking to make India one of the powers to counterbalance China in Asia, through the active pursuit of military and other exchanges. In central Asia, the US wants to strengthen its relationships with the five central Asian countries for two reasons. The first is to checkmate China, and the second is to use them as a bridge to penetrate China's western borders. Meanwhile, the US is extending its hand to northern China by improving its relationship with Mongolia. Furthermore, the US supports Taiwan's separation from the Mainland under the table by selling weapons and bringing it into the US regional defense missile system. (Zhang Xin, 2000)

Other scholars believe that the USA has devised new strategies in dividing and hindering China but that its aim remains the same. One new US tactic to "divide and Westernize" China since the 1990s is to heavily increase the pressure of globalization. Globalization is hence seen as the latest tool in establishing a US hegemony, as a ruse toward Westernization or Americanization:

> The US combines "soft" and "hard" tactics through its control over the dissemination of information, so as to place the Western Pacific region firmly in its grip. Globalization in the information age stands for Americanization. This has its roots in the American preconception that US economic and military power is derived from its social system and cultural values, rather than from its advanced technology. Globalization in this sense is neither gospel nor inevitable. The true face of such globalization was fully exposed in the US-led NATO invasion of Yugoslavia. (Zhao Chu et al., 2000: 43–44)

Chinese intellectuals are loudly proclaiming that "globalization is Americanization." Many globalization theorists do not stop at the emotional anti-US level. As a young professor specializing in globalization studies states:

> Many people thought globalization was purely an economic process. However, it is not as simple as that. Clearly there is a powerful political and economic hegemony lurking behind globalization. This is not only true for developing countries but also for developed ones. In essence, globalization is global homogenization towards American values and standards. (Wang Ning, 1999: 32)

One writer provides a detailed illustration of the "globalization trap" laid jointly by the USA and the UK, the principal institutions used to manipulate the trap, its elements and typical tricks, the mass media and scholars advocating globalization, and so on. Readers of such articles must arrive at the conclusion that globalization is a swindle initiated by the USA. "It is vital to see that the essence of globalization lies in its evil concealed purpose, rather than its visible surface, viz. the American brand name" (Lin Fangshi, 1999: 15).

For some theorists, also other aspects of American culture contain the "evil intent" to Americanize China and the world. Films, for instance, are seen by some as vehicles of Americanization and of the CIA. The author begins by quoting from a CIA program stating that "[we] must do everything possible to propagate, by means of movies, the media, TV programs, radio, etc.... [We] will be successful in part only if foreigners are longing for our clothing, foods, houses, entertainment and education." He then points out that:

> the stars of American movies, whether they are playing ordinary people or soldiers, are characterized as individuals coping with disaster and saving all other people from their sufferings. Many American movies propagate "the American spirit" and "Pan-Americanism"...What is the image of China in American movies? The Chinese or residents of American China Towns are usually demonized. Hollywood exerts its "magic power" in that few Chinese are employed as actors, who in fact denigrate their own people. (Anonymous, "The vile purpose behind American Movies," www.netsh.com (14 August 2000)).

Like Americanization, anti-Americanism is universally reflected in Chinese literature and arts. A satire of the Olympic women's football game between China and the USA was aired on Beijing television's evening news on September 19, 2000, with the comment: "Four years ago, the US women's football team defeated China by an obvious foul and the Chinese women's football team lost the gold medal. One year ago, the US women team's goalkeeper broke the rule by blocking our penalty shot while the judge ignored it. Chinese-US women's football teams met again in the Sydney Olympic Games and it was very clear what the referee did. Thanks to the excellent performance of Gao Hong and Sun Wen we achieved this result."

Anti-Americanism is manifest not only through hatred of the USA or by exposing the "Conspiracy of Americanization," but also through forms of slander and attempts to convince the Chinese that the USA itself is in a disastrous state and unworthy of being an example for China. For instance, many articles have been exposing corruption within the American education system, despite the fact that an estimated 200,000 Chinese students study abroad every year. Many intellectuals try systematically to shed light on the shortcomings and evils of the modern-day USA in terms of culture, politics and the economy. Politically, it is claimed that American "democracy" is merely enjoyed by a powerful and rich oligarchy rather than truly by the people. Elections are rigged, it is said, and political scandals and behind-the-scenes quarrels abound. Economically, America is facing imminent disaster and the gulf between the rich and the poor is ever widening. Culturally, consumerism prevails as morals decline. Some Americans are said to be aware of these shortcomings and crises although pessimists believe that the USA is too sick to be saved (Guang Zhikun, 1994).

To many Chinese, the USA does not deserve to be viewed as a role model for China. On the contrary, China has been able to contend with the USA and should take uncompromising diplomatic stances against it. In 1996 three young journalists published a book entitled *China Can Say "No"* (Song Qiang et al., 1996), which became one of the bestsellers of that year. Several other publishing houses quickly realized that this type of literature was a money-maker, publishing similar books such as *Holding China Back* (Sun Keqing et al., 1996), *Behind the Denigration of China* (Li Xiguang et al., 1996), and *Why China Can Say "No"* (Qian Peng et al., 1996). All shared a common purpose, namely to allow Chinese intellectuals to let off steam against the USA. In fact there would have been more titles in this vein if the authorities had not stepped in. These books cater to the tide of anti-US feeling among young nationalists, whose reasoning is that China's power derives from its huge population, its nuclear capacity and its rapid economic growth, outstripping the USA. Conversely, the USA is a paper tiger, strong outside but inwardly weak, as Chairman Mao had once pointed out, doomed to imminent collapse. The USA lost to the Chinese Communist Party (CCP) during China's civil war and the Korean War. This prompted a few young intellectuals to make an appeal to the Chinese people to "stop buying American commodities, watching American movies and eating American food, and reject the US most-favored-nation clause." People should "burn down Hollywood and prepare to fight against the US."

At first glance, anti-Americanism and Americanization appear to be two extremes of the spectrum. A closer look, however, shows that they are in some ways bound together. Anti-Americanism is a reaction against the ongoing process of Americanization, manifesting the all-pervasive signs of Sinification. Deng Xiaoping postulated all-embracing reforms, including opening up to the world by means of introducing advanced Western, above all American, science, technology, products, management techniques, market systems, culture and knowledge. The politics, economy and culture of the West have subsequently exerted such a profound impact on Chinese society that Westernization, Americanization and anti-Americanism have taken root. On the other hand, in order to integrate advanced Western methods, China experienced a renaissance of its traditional culture. Mao Zedong launched the twofold policy of locking China's door to the West, while rooting out traditional Chinese culture. His "Destroying the Four Olds" campaign aimed at replacing old ideas, culture, customs and habits. Taking a diametrically opposed stance, Deng Xiaoping advocated opening up to the West and reviving traditional Chinese culture, by both accepting Western civilization and systematically reviving Chinese traditional culture. This can be termed Sinification of Western civilization.

Deng Xiaoping's "Socialism with Chinese characteristics" differs from socialism in the Mao era by welcoming "Chinese traits" in politics, economy, culture, academia, education, literature. The "Chinese culture fever," which reached its peak in the 1990s, canonizes traditional Chinese civilization. It is striking that Confucianism, which used to be viewed as opposed to a market economy, is now interpreted as the basis of economic success in East Asia and China. In the eyes of the partisans of traditional Chinese culture, all good things originate from traditional Chinese civilization, which can overcome the shortcomings of its Western counterpart. The twenty-first century is thus said to be the century of Chinese civilization.

Chinese traditions are also experiencing a renaissance. Chinese traditions in literature, opera, folk arts and crafts, martial arts, rituals, customs and habits which were opposed after 1949 have resurfaced to broad popularity. Traditional celebrations such as the Spring, First Lunar Month, Dragon Boat, Double Nine, Mid-Autumn, Wine, Foods and Tea festivals have been reinstated. Since the 1980s, Chinese people have been so eager to revive the traditions that disappeared during the Cultural Revolution that they made little distinction between positive and negative. Thus many negative customs have also returned. For example, the deeply rooted concept of "getting a promotion and striking it rich" can doubtless account for the terrible rise in corruption, while old superstitions challenge modern science. It is an ironic misunderstanding to attribute the pervasive phenomenon of entertaining mistresses to "corrupt Western capitalist notions," (Lijun, "Don't Neglect the Fact that some Party Members are being "Westernized" and "Separated," www.netsh.com) when it is merely the revival of the custom of concubinage.

What best accounts for the fact that Americanization, anti-American-ism and Sinification coexist in contemporary China? What does this say about Chinese society? What attitudes should Chinese intellectuals and politicians take? The answers can be found in modern Chinese history and the impact of globalization on China today. China is an ancient civilization, for centuries one of the most highly developed ones. Traditional Chinese society existed for thousands of years on the basis of political absolutism, a feudal peasant economy and cultural Confucianism, which snuffed out Chinese creativity and the ability to innovate. China has very slowly made social progress and has scarcely contributed to the world since the South Song Dynasty (1127–1279). Meanwhile, Western countries experienced the Industrial Revolution and its resulting progress. Consequently, China has lagged behind West-ern countries since the start of modern times. Some Chinese intellectuals identified the gulf between China and Western countries as early as the middle of the nineteenth century when the Western powers forced ancient China's door open with superior weapons and commodities. They came to the conclusion that if China were to regain its former splendor, the only way was to learn from Western industrial countries and introduce Western civilization into China. The Qing Dynasty had no other choice than to accept the intellectuals' demands to initiate the "Westernization Movement."

Already the "Self-Strengthening Movement" of the 1870s saw a quest to put an end to relative underdevelopment and to catch up with the West and with Meiji Japan. This and subsequent movements also vied to reduce the dominance of the Western powers in China. In other words, modernization and national independence were two interlinked imperatives in modern China (Liu Danian, 1996). In essence, the con-tradiction between Westernization and Sinification can be explained in this context.

If we define modern civilization as one dominated by modern industry, from steam power to electricity and scientific medicine and chemistry, then modernity arose in the West. Modernization is thus a process of learning from and approximating the West. Some intellectuals simply equate modernization with Westernization in this narrow sense, reasoning that an underdeveloped country must follow the well developed West in order to become modernized. Axiomatically, the greater a country's preservation of tradition, the greater its relative backwardness. The debate between radicals and conservatives, which typified the clash between Westernization and Sinification, hinged on the question of whether Western civilization could be regarded as synonymous with progress, while traditional Chinese culture could be equated with underdevelopment. As a well-known CCP thinker has pointed out, conservatives refrained from advanced Western civilization by overemphasizing the values of Chinese traditional culture and the corruption of Western civilization (Ai Shiqi, 1990).

However, China's other aim, the one of national independence, runs somewhat counter to this. One of the dilemmas facing modern Chinese intellectuals and politicians is how to learn effectively from Western countries while simultaneously preserving China's independence. If Western powers were the cause of China's semi-colonization, China's sovereignty is defined as being free from Western control and influence. Yet China's modernization depends on learning from the West. Chinese intellectuals and politicians have therefore had to deal with both facets of Westernization, with the aim of avoiding colonial dependence. This is why a balance has emerged between Sinifying all things Western while simultaneously Westernizing Chinese society. Strikingly enough, an identical relation between Sinification and Westernization has held under three different regimes: the Qing Dynasty, the Republic of China (Guomindang) and the People's Republic of China (CCP). The modus operandi has been to Sinify Western industrial civilization to ensure China's modernization. This goal has been known respectively as the "Chinese ways as the body, Western methods for use" under the Qing Dynasty, as "Chinese indigenization" under the Kuomintang and as "Chinese characteristics" under the CCP.

There is a general consensus that China accomplished one of these two tasks while failing to achieve the other. The CCP established the People's Republic of China after it came to power in 1949. In so doing, China obtained complete independence yet without modernization. Mao Zedong and his comrades took on this unaccomplished task, expecting that China could catch up economically with the West before long. It would be a mistake to believe that Mao Zedong did not want a wealthy and powerful China. Mao actively sought a way for China to modernize by advocating the "Great Leap Forward," which in retrospect proved disastrous. Mao refused to follow in the footsteps of Western modernization, resisting both capitalism and contacts with the West. Among the many reasons why Mao refused the Western road to modernization was his concern that China would lose its independence once opened up to the West. Therefore, there was no Westernization or Americanization during the Maoist period, since Mao was too afraid of dependence on the West.

Mao's development strategy succeeded in securing China's independence while it failed in attaining modernization. As a matter of fact, by the end of Mao's reign, the economic gap between China and the West widened. Many intellectuals and the Party elite realized that China lagged far behind the developed world in terms of economy and culture after Mao had been in power for thirty years. That China had to learn from the developed world in order to achieve modernization became the basis for Deng Xiaoping's reform of Maoism. This once again brought the debate on Westernization and Sinification center-stage, reproducing the well-known dilemma of how to balance Western innovation with China's independence.

Chinese intellectuals concerned about China's modernization need to address this issue. Two juxtaposed, at times antagonistic positions have arisen. Some emphasize development by all means for the sake of national independence, placing traditional values into the back seat. Others focus on national independence for the sake of national development, even at the risk of eliminating elements of foreign civilizations. We are presented with the dichotomy that for the former the traditionalists are too conservative, while for the latter the modernizers are too Westernized.

Deng Xiaoping launched his reforms at a time when Western countries generally were the most developed in the world. The process of modernization of developing countries, including China, remains to a large extent to "catch up" with the development levels attained by the West, chiefly with those of the USA. Indubitably, the USA has exerted a greater impact on developing countries than other nations. In this sense, not only developing countries but also other Western nations have felt the lure of Americanization. It follows that the "Sino-West" debate has now become the "Sino-US" debate, turning "Westernization" and "anti-Westernization" into "Americanization" and "anti-Americanization."

Globalization is sometimes viewed as a process of homogenization, as a process of world capitalism leading to Westernization or Americanization. Yet, globalization is rather a plurality of contradictions, of unity and antinomy, containing elements of both homogenization and fragmentation, centralization and division, internationalization and nationalization.

1) Globalization as a unity of universalization and particularization. On the one hand, globalization is a process of homogenization characterized by a convergence of lifestyles, modes of production and civilizational values. For instance, the capitalist market economy is becoming a worldwide feature [beyond its European origins], while people worldwide are seeking democracy and human dignity. On the other hand, universalization is always accompanied by particularization. Although the market economy has become international, market systems in various countries are consistently different. The same is true of democracy. People all over the world are longing for democracy, which, however, has many diverse versions in different countries. For instance, Japan and South Korea have adopted representative democracy, which is quite different from the forms of democracy found in the USA or the UK.

2) Globalization as combining integration and fragmentation. Integration and homogenization are highlighted by the rapid growth of international organizations such as the United Nations, the World Bank, the IMF and the WTO, whose roles are much more important than before. A greater degree of integration among nations leads to a breakdown of traditional national sovereignty and barriers. A cosmopolitan ideal has begun to materialize in the sense that there is a growing movement toward the integration of nations (such as in the European Union), global floating of capital and global sharing of increasingly common information. At the same time, however, there has been a growing trend toward particularity and independence for both nations and regions. Movements of national independence or regional autonomy provide a good example. The trend toward individuation has developed steadily as global integration increases. More and more small ethnic groups are demanding independence. The yearning for regional, local and communal autonomy is not disappearing, but rising along with globalization. Community movements and communitarianism are key political issues in developed countries. The term "global localism" was coined to reflect the fact that local autonomy is developing rapidly against the backdrop of globalization.

3) Globalization as combining centralization and decentralization. A major feature of globalization is the significant centralization of capital, information, power and wealth, especially in transnational corporations. Big companies have increasingly merged since the 1990s, accelerating the centralization of power and wealth. A good example is the merger of McDonnell-Douglas and Boeing, two firms dominating the aviation

industry. On the other hand, there have been major trends to decentralize capital, information, power and wealth. Small capital is still very active and developing, apparently unaffected by the centralization of capital. This shows that the higher the degree of centralization of information, the more difficult it is to monopolize. The best example is the Internet, which has become the prime distribution vehicle for information. No one has the monopoly over this information, since anyone whose computer has been connected to the Internet can share information.

4) Globalization as unity of internationalization and nationalization. As mentioned above, globalization has broken down traditional national barriers. Consequently, ever more international conventions, covenants, agreements and standards have been signed and implemented. "Bringing into line with international practice" is becoming a typical phrase and many international principles have an authentic international meaning for the first time. On the other hand, no nation will ever forget its own traditions and characteristics while accepting international conventions, agreements and principles. Instead it will attempt to deal with international principles in the light of its own specific national conditions, so as to "nationalize" these international principles and norms. For instance, most countries in the world accept international agreements on the protection of human rights and the environment, while imbuing them with their own national characteristics when interpreting or applying them.

Thus globalization has become an objective reality, an inescapable trend in human development. When a country opens up to the outside world, it will enter into the process of globalization, and China is no exception in this global age. Globalization is initiated and dominated by the US-led Western world. However, no country, including the USA, can completely control the process of globalization. Developing countries, including China, also influence the process. Globalization is thus a double-edged sword for both developed and developing countries. Both can either benefit or lose out from globalization. Globalization changes modern civilizations into cosmopolitan units, regardless of whether their civilization originated in the East or the West. Therefore, learning from Western civilization never simply results in Westernization, just as learning from Eastern civilizations will never mean Easternization. China's membership of the WTO and the introduction of a market economy will never result in China's "Westernization" or "Americanization." Internationalization, nationalization and localization complement each another. China must participate actively in globalization if it wants to preserve its own unique civilization, just as China must enhance its national resources if it wants to participate in globalization effectively. Globalization in its true sense is by no means Westernization or Americanization. Those who express their anxiety about China's participation in globalization lack foresight.

References

Zhao Chu, (2000), "Quanqiuhua shi Fu shi Huo? (Is Globalization a Good Fortune or Misfortune?)," *Guide To Opening Up 9*: 43–44.

Liu Danian, (1996), "Zhongguo Jindai Lishi de Zhuti (The Subjects of China's Modern History)," Jindaishi Yanjiu (*Studies in Modern Chinese History*) 6, pp. 4–11.

Lin Fangshi, (1999), "Quanqiuhua de Beihou: dui Yingmei Zhanlue Xianjing de Fenxi (Behind Globalization—An Analysis on the US and the UK's Strategic Trap)," *Zhongliu* 2: 13–17.

Chen Jiaxi, (1999), "Meiguo Baquanzhuyi Lishi Guiji Zhuizong (History of American Hegemony)," *Huazhong Ligong Daxue Xuebao (Journal of Technology University in Central China)* 3: 17–32.

Sun Keqin, et al. (eds) (1996), Ezhi Zhongguo (*Holding China Back*). China Yanshi Publishing House (Beijing: Zhongguo Yanshi Chubanshe).

Wang Nin, (1999), "Quanqiuhua Shidai de Wenhua Zhenglun yu Huayu (The Cultural Debates and Discourses in the Age of Globalization)," *Dongfang Wenhua (Eastern Culture)* 3: 31–36.

Qian Peng, et al. (eds) (1996), Weishenme Zhongguo Keyi shuo bu (*Why China Can Say "No"*). New World Press (Beijing: Xin Shijie Chubanshe).

Bian Qi, (1999), "Dui Wenhua de Tongzhihua Xianxiang de Sikao (Reflection on the Cultural Homogenization)," *SheKe Zongheng (Aspects of Social Sciences)* 5: 56–57.

Song Qiang, et al. (eds) (1996), Zhongguo Keyi shuo bu (*China Can Say "No"*). China Industrial and Commercial Press (Beijing: Zhonghua Gongshang Lianhe Chubanshe).

Ai Shiqi, (1990), "Lun Zhongguo de Teshuxing (On Chinese Characteristics)," in Luo Rongqu (ed.), Cong "Xihua" dao Xiandaihua (*From Westernization to Modernization*). Beijing University Press (Beijing: Beijing Daxue Chubanshe): 592–93.

Li Xiguang and others (eds) (1996), Yaomohua Zhongguo de Beihou (*Behind the Denigration of China*). Chinese Social Sciences Press (Beijing: Zhongguo Shehui Kexue Chubanshe).

Zhang Xin, (2000), "JingTi Meiguo zai Baowei Zhongguo! (Look Out, the US is Besieging China!)," *http://jczs.sina.com.cn/2000–07–09/2286.html*.

Guang Zhikun, (1994), "Quanpan Xihua zhi Miu (A Mistake of Complete Westernization)," Qingdao Daxue Shifan Xueyuan Xuebao (*Journal of Teacher's College of Qingdao University*) 2: 23–27.

CHAPTER FIVE

CIVIC ORGANIZATIONS AND GOVERNANCE IN RURAL CHINA: A CASE STUDY OF DONGSHENG VILLAGE, CHANGQIAO MUNICIPALITY, ZHANGPU COUNTY, FUJIAN PROVINCE

Foreword

Since China implemented its policy of reform and opening to the outside world, rural areas have undergone great changes. As far as economic restructuring is concerned, the current contract responsibility system replaces the "people's communes." As to the political system, civic organizations are beginning to emerge and a self-governing system based on civic organizations in villages is gradually being implemented. Economic and political restructuring is taking place in rural areas. This reflects Deng Xiaoping's strategy for reform: "Since 80% of our people live in the country, China's social stability and its economic development depend above all on the development of the countryside and the improvement of rural living standards" and: "Devolving authority to the local level and to the people, which in the countryside means the peasants, is the height of democracy" to cite but two pronouncements.[1] Actually, China's problem can be equated with the rural problem, because there are over 800 million peasants among an overall population of 1.2 billion Chinese people. The same is true of civic organizations. At present, there are 2,135 counties, 44,689 townships and towns and about 740,000 administrative villages in China.[2] Since the 1990s, civic organizations have mushroomed in townships, towns and villages. According to conservative estimates, more than 3 million civic organizations at sub-district level have been registered or are awaiting registration, accounting for over two-thirds of all civic organizations. Without a thorough analysis of rural civic organizations

---

[1] Deng Xiaoping, *Selected Works of Deng Xiaoping (Volume III)*, [Beijing:] Renmin chubanshe, 1993, pp. 77–78 and p. 252.
[2] *China's Statistical Yearbook for 1998*, China Statistics Publishing House, 1999.

and governance, we can hardly expect to gain an understanding of China's political state.

In the present study, the author takes the village of Dongsheng in Changqiao municipality, Zhangpu county, Fujian as a case in point. The development of rural civic organizations and the changing mode of rural governance are of particular importance because the village is advanced in terms of economic and cultural development as well as in its social and political structures. Zhangpu County, in which Dongsheng village is located, lies under the jurisdiction of Zhangzhou in Fujian, one of China's coastal "open counties," approved by the State Council. Zhangpu is located between the two special economic zones of Xiamen and Shantou. It is close to the Taiwan Straits in the east, to Shantou in the south and to Zhangzhou and Xiamen in the north. The county has twenty townships and towns and eleven farms, as well as forestry stations, saltworks and tea plantations, with a total population of 790,000. Its area encompasses 1,981 square kilometers, its cultivated land 35,351 hectares (530,000 *mu*), while mountains cover 109,388 ha (1.64 million *mu*) and shoal 62,164 ha (932,000 *mu*). In 1997, the gross national product of the whole county was RMB 4.06 billion. Its total output value of industrial and agricultural production was RMB 9.95 billion, of which industrial production accounted for RMB 7.772 and agriculture for RMB 2.182 billion. Local revenue was RMB 216 million. The yearly per capita income of urban residents was RMB 5,096, compared with an income for peasants of RMB 2,920. This contrasts with an approximated RMB 2,160 in 1998.[3]

Before 1949 Dongsheng was called Xiyan village. Its exact history cannot be ascertained. But "Yiyuan Hamlet"—the core of its architectural heritage—has a history of over 300 years. For most of their history, villagers lived mainly in the "Yiyuan Hamlet," comprising more than 30 houses.[4] Generally speaking, there was one household per house. After 1949, the population increased and the village gradually expanded. At present, the village counts 1,156 people, in 265 families. Just over 100 residents migrated from other places, mostly hired laborers from neighboring counties or further north. Most villagers share

---

[3] People's Government of Zhangpu County (eds), *Zhangpu*, Zhangpu County Newspaper, 1998.

[4] *Tulou* is a traditional local-style compound, built as a round multi-storied edifice, which can accommodate dozens of households. People of the same clan usually live in the same compound.

the surname Huang, and only a couple of families are not Huangs. The Huang clan consists of seven branches, of which the third has left the village. Presently, the first and fourth branches form the majority. The fourth branch alone counts more than 400 people. The village covers an area of 1,534 ha (23,000 *mu*) of hills and 97 ha (1,450 *mu*) of cultivated land. Dongsheng is one of the most advanced villages in Zhangpu county, in terms of living standards and social development. In 1998, the production value of the village exceeded RMB 80 million. Only recently the per capita income of the whole village was RMB 3,500, rising to RMB 4,290 in 1998, 1.45 times as much as the equivalent peasant income throughout the county and about twice as high as the average per capita income. Each villager enjoyed a statistical living area of over 80 square meters, up from 50. The main source of income is fruit farming. The whole village has over 300 orchards, on average one per household.[5]

In addition to the high levels of economic development, Dongsheng is more advanced than neighboring villages in other aspects. For example, the rate of participation in birth control is 100%, its serious crime rate is zero, while every single child attends school. 98% of households are connected to the telephone network, and all receive television. Therefore, Dongsheng has been awarded honorable titles, such as:

1) "Community commended for ideological and cultural progress," conferred by the Fujian CCP committee and the provincial government (April 1987 and December 1995);
2) "Advanced collective commended for family planning in Fujian," conferred by the provincial government;
3) "Telephone model village" conferred by the general office of the government of Zhangpu county and the Posts and Telecommunications Bureau (November 1997);
4) The title of the "1,000 advanced villages in China commended for afforestation" conferred by the National Greenification Committee (1998);

---

[5] CCP (Dongsheng), "Achieving Common Prosperity and Making Concerted Efforts to Build a New Village—the Party of Dongsheng (Changqiao) Leads the People in Efforts to prosper and to Build a New Village" (Report).

5) "Star village," conferred by the Fujian CCP committee and the provincial government (1991);
6) "Advanced primary Party organization," by the Zhangzhou CCP committee (July 1997);
7) "Advanced primary Party organization," conferred by the Fujian CCP committee (July 1997);
8) The title of "Modern village commended for improvement at the village level," conferred by the Zhangpu CCP and the county government;
9) "Village of ideological and cultural progress," by the Fujian CCP committee and the provincial government (February 1998).[6]

Development of Civic Organizations in China's Rural Areas

Civic organizations in China's countryside have a long history. The reach of the central government never extended beneath district level, dynasties instead relying on the cooption of the rural gentry (*shenshi*). After 1927, the Guomindang government led by Jiang Jieshi established village offices for the first time, to serve as grassroots administrative organs. But civic organizations in rural areas did not disappear. Buddhist and clan associations, as well as mutual aid foundations of all descriptions existed in most rural areas and continued to exert an important influence there.

After the CCP took the helm in 1949, it gradually implemented collective ownership and command economics. Politically, a centralized administrative system under the Party's leadership became the norm. Party offices (*zhi*, "branches") were established in almost all rural areas, serving as the nuclei of administrative power. The Party branches and production brigades micro-managed the political and economic affairs of the countryside. Before 1980s, traditional rural civic organizations as temple fairs or clan associations were decried as "feudal" or "reactionary" and were eliminated. They were replaced by new rural organizations, such as peasant associations, the Women's Federation, the Youth League, agricultural cooperatives, mutual aid groups and production teams. In fact, they were little more than executive organs of the Party branches and the rural organizations imposed by the Central

---

[6] *Ibid.*

Government. Regardless of whether or not peasants were willing to join, membership became compulsory. Voluntary organizations were not allowed and banned as soon as they were discovered. Therefore, for about 40 years from 1949 to 1980, strictly speaking, there were no voluntary, self-governing civic organizations in China's rural areas.

In 1978, China implemented major economic and political restructuring under the leadership of Deng Xiaoping. Reforms were spearheaded in rural districts. The household contract responsibility system, with remuneration linked to output, rivaled the people's communes, and a private household economy began to develop. Thanks to the new economic structure, peasants enjoyed the freedom to use (though not to own) their land and labor force and engage in business activity. This greatly stimulated rural initiative and productive forces, significantly raising living standards. From 1978 to 1998, the per capita income of rural households increased from RMB 133.6 to 2,160, a net increase of 350% after allowing for price rises, the yearly average growth rate exceeding 8%.[7] Because of the disintegration of the people's communes and the implementation of the household contract responsibility system, the rural economic activities and, in fact, the social and political life in the countryside, underwent earth-shaking changes. One of these changes was that rural civic organizations slowly began to recover and even grow.

After China introduced market reforms in 1978, the development of rural civic organizations underwent two stages. The first stage extended from 1978 to 1992. Important rural civil organizations began to recover or emerge, for example Villagers' Committees, temple fairs, Family Planning Associations, Public Security Committees, and unlicensed private banks (as private cooperatives). In Dongsheng, rural civic organizations were characterized by three features. Firstly, civic organizations developed rapidly, nearly reaching today's state of development. Secondly, management was rather chaotic. There were neither regulations on the internal management of such organizations, nor on their external management. Thirdly, the Party branch exercised absolute leadership over the various civic organizations. In fact, the Villagers' Committee, which served as an autonomous agrarian organization, was created as an executive organ of the Party. The second stage began in 1992. Its

---

⁷ State Statistical Bureau, *China's Statistical Yearbook for 1999*, China Statistics Publishing House, 1999.

main features are that rural civic organizations are becoming increasingly autonomous and that organizations such as the Villagers' Committee or the Senior Citizens' Association begin to play an important role in the management of village affairs. Governments at all levels have promulgated new laws and regulations, such as the Organic Law on Villagers' Committees in the People's Republic of China, or the Regulations on the Registration and Management of Social Associations (Revised) and the Regulations on the Management of Civilian-Run Charities, drafted by the Central Government. The above as well as other laws and regulations, such as the Detailed Rules on the Elections of Villagers' Committees or the Rules of Family Planning Associations (drafted by Fujian Province) and the Village Regulations (drafted by the Villagers' Representative Assembly, Dongsheng), underline that the internal and external management of civic organizations is becoming more standardized.

At present, Dongsheng Village has eighteen civic organizations: the Villagers' Committee, the Youth League, the Women's Federation, the Senior Citizens' Association, the Association for the Study of Fruit Trees, the Public Security Committee, the Family Planning Association, the Mediation Association, the Economic Cooperative, the Population School, the Senior Citizens' School, the Village Militia, the Villagers' Association, the Villagers' Representative Assembly, the temple fair, the Talented Persons' Association, the Working Group for Publicizing Village Affairs and for Exercising Democratic Management, and the Villagers' Group for Financial Affairs. Almost all adults join one or more civic organizations. These can be categorized according to different standards for classification. In typological terms, they can be subdivided into power and service organizations. The Villagers' Committee, the Family Planning Association, the Senior Citizens' Association and the Villagers' Representative Assembly belong to organizations vested with actual powers, playing an authoritative role in looking after villagers' everyday lives. The Public Security Committee, the Association for the Study of Fruit Trees, the Mediation Association and the Economic Cooperative can be counted as service organizations. The Youth League, Women's Federation, Population School and the Village Militia are subsidiaries of the Party. In terms of relative activity, they can be divided into permanent and provisional organizations. The temple fair, the Population and Senior Citizens Schools, the Villagers' Representative Assembly, the Villagers' Group for Financial Affairs and the Working

Group for Publicizing Village Affairs and for Exercising Democratic Management are provisional civic organizations. Most other organizations are permanent in nature.

In comparison with urban civic organizations, the civic organizations in Dongsheng have the two distinctive features. Firstly, almost all of these do not go through the legal registration formalities of the department for the management of civic organizations. They are nevertheless legal organizations, since their legitimacy is based on the following aspects:

1) State laws, for example the Organic Law on Villagers' Committees and the Law on the Elections of Deputies to People's Conferences, also apply beneath county level;
2) The regulations of local Party and government departments apply, such as the Regulations on Family Planning formulated by the provincial government;
3) They have the consent of local Party and government departments. All civic organizations in Dongsheng are approved by the municipal government of Changqiao, and most of these are established according to the general requirements of the municipal Party committee and government.

Secondly, the influence and status of certain revolutionary organizations are weakening. The Youth League, the Women's Federation and the Village Militia are mere shadows of their former selves, now seldom engaged in political activities. On the contrary, some reinstated or newly-emerged organizations have become powerful, such as the Senior Citizens' Association or the Economic Cooperative.

Profile of Rural Civic Organizations

Civic organizations in Dongsheng greatly reflect the current conditions of rural organizations in southern China. A non-analytical depiction of the former presents the following situation:

1) The Villagers' Committee—at present the most important civic organization in China' rural areas. In fact, it has replaced or is replacing the local Party, becoming the most authoritative administrative organ in many localities. According to the provisions of the Organic Law on Villagers' Committees (for Trial Implementation), the Villagers'

Committee is the villagers' grassroots organization for self-management, self-education and self-service. It handles all village affairs and matters of public interest, mediates in civil disputes, helps safeguard public security, reports villagers' opinions and requests and makes suggestions to higher authorities. The Villagers' Committee does not report to the local government but directly to the villagers.[8]

The Villagers' Committee of Dongsheng was established in 1988. It consists of five members: one director (also called village head), two deputy directors (deputy village heads), a women's representative and a militia member. All members of the villagers' committee are Party members. As in most other rural parts, village heads serve as deputy secretaries to the local Party office. Members of the Villagers' Committee of Dongsheng are directly elected by villagers, but "sea elections" as in other economically better developed areas are not implemented in Dongsheng.[9] After candidates have been recommended by the local Party and are approved at the Villagers' Representative Assembly, they are elected universally and by secret ballot. From our investigation, we can conclude that candidates for the Villagers' Committee reflect the will of the Party office, enhancing its ability to implement policies.

The main responsibilities of Dongsheng's Villagers' Committee are to organize and lead villagers in developing the economy. Village cadres, for example, take the lead in cultivating hillside fields and in planting fruit trees. Other examples include taking the initiative to provide services and coordinate the production of village cooperatives and producers' associations (e.g., for an increased yield of fruit production), protecting the legitimate rights and interests of collectively-owned economic organizations, of villagers, contractors, jointly operated households and businessmen from other areas. Further to manage land and property collectively owned by the villagers, to instruct villagers to make rational use of natural resources and preserve and improve the ecological environment. Finally, to publicize the Constitution, laws, regulations and state policies, inform and urge villagers to perform their due obligations according to the law, be entrusted with public property

---

[8] See *Organic Law on Villagers' Committees in the People's Republic of China*, revised and adopted at the Second Plenary Session of the Standing Committee of the Ninth People's Congress.

[9] "Sea election" refers to local Party bosses and government departments failing to designate or recommend specific candidates as village heads or members of the villagers' committee in the direct, free and public elections.

and help villagers conduct activities designed to promote ideological and cultural progress.

Like other localities, members of the Villagers' committee of Dongsheng are not divorced from production. But they often attend meetings and handle village affairs in light of actual need. Every member thus has to spend a considerable amount of time on the public village affairs every year. The government does not provide funds to the Villagers' Committee, but funds for the operation of the Villagers' committee and economic compensation for its members are reimbursed from the public village budget. Dongsheng has a vibrant economy, and peasants are not unduly taxed. The public finances of the village are mainly derived from land contracting, management fees and rent from land used by businesses from other areas. According to current regulations, the village head and secretary of the Party branch get a remuneration of RMB 150 per month, the deputy village head RMB 120, and ordinary members RMB 100.[10]

2) The Senior Citizens' Association (also called the Elderly People Association). This is a civic organization developing rapidly, both in urban and in rural areas. At first, it was a mass organization, mainly consisting of retired urban cadres and workers, but it gradually established a foothold in the countryside. The rural Senior Citizens' Association in parts of Fujian and Jiangxi is of special significance, since they often become transformed into traditional clan organizations. Even when this is less the case, they have a special status. This is also true of the Senior Citizens' Association in Dongsheng.

There is only one requirement for membership, namely to be an elderly villager. Pursuant to national standards on senior citizenship, the senior citizens' association of Dongsheng consists of citizens above 60 (men) and 55 (women). It has some 130 members. The leading body of the Senior Citizens' Association is the executive council, responsible for preparing its activities. The president of the executive council is the leader of the Senior Citizens' Association. The Association has a president and a vice-president. The current president is nearly seventy, a veteran village head and Party member, enjoying a high reputation in Dongsheng. His opinion is consulted in every discussion of any importance arising in the village. It also has a secretary-general and

---

[10] See Record of Interview 990722.

seven members. They constitute a rural elite, enjoying high prestige and commanding universal respect.

Senior Citizens' Associations comprise groups for management, finance, recreation, coordination and for funerals. Every group has a head, a deputy head and three to four members. In addition, the local Association operates a Senior Citizens' School. The village head concurrently serves as its principal, while the secretary of the local Party concurrently serves as honorary principal. The president and the vice-president of the Association also serve as deputy principals. The Senior Citizens' School dean is responsible for the teaching carried out by its two teachers. The members of the Senior Citizens' Association are naturally its students. The school gives lessons in the afternoons of the first and fifteenth days of every lunar month. Courses cover the general political situation (the secretary of the village Party branch usually teaches the first lesson) as well as village planning, construction, health care for the elderly, culture and science, and technical knowledge. Students enroll free of any tuition fees, on a voluntarily basis, and usually unassisted. The activities of the Senior Citizens' Association are varied and colorful, routinely including

a. Recreational activities: There is a room for activities, where senior citizens can play chess, mahjong and poker, read books and chat;
b. Health care: Doctors of the village clinic give regular physical examinations to senior citizens and teach them how to exercise and practice *qigong* and *taijiquan*;
c. Discussions on politics and policies: local Party decisions concerning economic development or any major changes in the village are usually preceded by sessions soliciting the opinions of veteran Party members within the Senior Citizens' Association. These concurrently hold the leading posts of other important organizations. The president of the Association, for instance, also serves as the vice-president of the Family Planning Association, another important civil organization;
d. Public activities: The Association presides over weddings and funerals in the village, organizes public memorial ceremonies and theatrical performances as well as banquets;
e. Services to the elderly: Concrete assistance in the daily difficulties faced by the elderly, as well as with their endeavors at studying.

The engagement of all Party veterans and members of the Association is voluntary and unpaid. But the senior citizens' association requires a considerable income to be used as a financial cushion for its activities. For example, in the first quarter of 1999, the total income of the Senior Citizens' Association was RMB 7,810, its total expenditures being RMB 6,015. Its income is mainly derived from the following five sources: membership fees (RMB 10 p.a.), voluntary donations (donations are mainly made to support individual activities), fixed financial assistance from the village (RMB 10,000 from the villagers' committee p.a.), donations from the local Party, the Villagers' Committee and other bodies (donations for specific needs of the association and the village, culminating around the Double Nine Festival), as well as proceeds from the business operations of the Association, its most important source of income (annual profits from its 0.667 ha (10 *mu*) fruit tree station and other enterprises, such as the leasing of tools and paid services amount to circa RMB 30,000).

The outgoings of the Senior Citizens' Association can be broken down into operating costs (investment into fruit tree operations and tools, costs for weddings and funerals), expenses for social activities (such as tourism, health care, recreation or stationery), invoices (office equipment, telephone rates and reception fees), expenditure on festivals (Chinese New Year, Double Nine and Mid-Autumn Festivals, birthdays) as well as miscellaneous other costs, such as for offering sacrifices to the ancestors, looking after the elderly poor or organizing theatrical performances. The Senior Citizens' Association of Dongsheng implements a transparent and regulated system of financial management. Its finance department is responsible for all financial activities, keeping and publishing detailed accounts of all income and expenditures. The finance department is subject to the scrutiny of its members.[11]

3) The Family Planning Association. It holds a central role in China's vast countryside, because the strict implementation of family planning is one of the basic state policies of the Chinese government. The Family Planning Association is responsible for organizing the implementation of this policy. The relative success of the "one child policy" is the touchstone issue in assessing village cadres. For years village cadres in many localities used crude means to punish villagers violating this policy, giving rise to antagonism between cadres and peasants. Since the 1990s, local authorities have revised the rural policy on family planning, amending the "one child policy," which has been strictly implemented in the cities: If the first child is a boy, a couple can have

---

¹¹ See Record of Interview 990726.

only one child. If it is a girl, the couple is allowed to give birth to a second child three to five years later. The peasants in Dongsheng call this the "one and a half child policy," greatly easing the antagonism between peasants and cadres. But family planning poses major difficulties, hence the importance of the association.

The Family Planning Association of Dongsheng operates in an office housed in its own building. It is run by a six member council, the deputy secretary of the Party branch concurrently serving as its president, while the president of the Senior Citizens' Association concurrently serves as vice-president. It also has a secretary-general. All women of childbearing age are members. It has a total of over 140 members divided into six groups. Funds for the Family Planning Association come from the village budget. Every year circa RMB 1,000 are made available for various activities. The members, president and vice-presidents of the association do not receive any remuneration and provide their services on a voluntary basis.

The main responsibilities of the Association are to publicize the government's policy toward family planning, supervise villagers' implementation of the policy, punish villagers who violate the policy, reward couples who set a good example, provide medical and health services to young couples and console and help the women who suffer from complications. The family planning association runs the village "population school," the secretary of the Party branch serving as its principal. Both men and women aged between eighteen and 45 are counted as students. Attendance is compulsory, with fines imposed on those who refuse to go. Classes are held twice per year. The Party secretary, the association's president and specific town leaders offer honorary lessons on family planning, medical provisions and information on prenatal and postnatal care.

The family planning association relies on a series of compulsory arrangements and regulations to perform its responsibilities. The Dongsheng Family Planning Association formulates and implements fifteen different state policies, laws and regulations. These include the Regulations on the Work of Family Planning Associations at Village Level in Fujian Province, the Responsibility System of Making Cadres of Two Village Committees Take Charge of Family Planning, and Work of Family Planning Associations at Village Level. Furthermore regulations governing the Association presidents, working standards, the issuing of family planning certificates, the reporting of individual cases, statistical accounts, and migration. Other specific regulations are entitled Provision of Family Planning Services, Birth Control Targets during the Period of the Ninth Five-Year Plan, "Six Goods and Three Nos" and "Four Haves and Three Implements" for Qualified Villages, Regular Meetings on Family Planning Work at Village Level, Family Planning Publicity and Education at Village Level, as well as the Responsibility System of "Two Checks and Two Supplements" at Village Level.[12]

All villagers must observe the above-mentioned regulations or face punishment. This is usually meted out through the imposition of fines. According to the regulations of Fujian Province, if the first birth is a girl, a second attempt at birth is permitted four years later. In the case of boys being born this is not permitted. Heavy fines, reaching tens of thousands of RMB, are imposed on couples who give birth to more children than permitted by family planning. So far such cases have not occurred in Dongsheng. If the second birth is still a girl, "households with two girls" are not given the option of having additional births but they do enjoy a series of privileges:

a. RMB 200 of arrangement fees are reduced or waived;
b. RMB 86 is taken off the children's tuition fees;
c. RMB 50 is rewarded for voluntary labor;
d. RMB 46 of miscellaneous tuition fees are waived;
e. Free attendance of the agricultural correspondence school (RMB 65); and
f. RMB 500 worth toward the old-age pension.[13]

"Households with two girls" enjoy such preferential treatment for two reasons. Firstly, male villagers still account for the main labor force in rural areas. Secondly, the traditional bias in favor of men in society still strongly persists.

4) The Youth League. The village's Youth League is the rural manifestation of the Chinese Communist Youth League. Both the local Youth League and the local Party played a major political role prior to the onset of the reform period. Within the village, it assisted the Party in managing the local young. But its role has been greatly weakened since, firstly, the power of the Party is reduced and, secondly, because the

---

¹² See General Office of the Government of Zhangpu County (eds), *A Collection of Standard Documents of Zhangpu County (1990–1997)*.
¹³ See Record of Interview 990729.

Youth League lacks authority and is facing certain image problems. The Youth League in Dongsheng has five officers, including one secretary and one deputy secretary, and some 150 members. Its secretary obtains a monthly remuneration of RMB 150, while the others work in honorary function. The Dongsheng Youth League receives circa RMB 1,000 in annual aid, paid out of the village budget. Rather than organizing events for the village youth, the Youth League aims to fulfill the tasks assigned by the Youth League committees at higher levels, such as celebrating Youth Day (May 4), doing voluntary labor, celebrating parties and attending functions for League members elsewhere.

5) The Women's Federation. Like the Youth League, the Women's Federation is an official mass organization which has existed since the dawn of the People's Republic. Its main vocation has experienced a gradual shift away from political organization to the protection of women and their children, marriage guidance as well as to the resolution of conflicts between women and their mothers-in-law. Any active involvement into the lives of women has been effectively transferred to the Family Planning Associations. Its remaining functions include organizing International Women's Day (March 8), village clean-ups and other voluntary labor, as well as publicizing and safe-guarding women's rights and interests. The Dongsheng Women's Federation counts three officers and one director, who also sits on the council of the village family planning association. A small amount of its operating funds comes from the village budget.

6) The Public Security Committee—a subsidiary of the Villagers' Committee, consisting of four members. The Village Head concurrently serves as its director. Its basic responsibility is to guarantee public security as well as law and order, for example by organizing nighttime patrols. It also features a five-person Joint Defense Group, three of whom are members of the Public Security Committee, with the remaining two recruited from the general public. Commissars, as well as members of the Joint Defense Group, are remunerated for joining patrols. All funds are derived from the village budget.

7) The Mediation Association. Its permanent office consists of three persons, namely the director (a Party member) and two other members, one of whom is the director of the women's federation, the remaining one being a villager. Its main task is to mediate in disputes among family members and between neighbors. It does not seek active engagement, but once disputes arise, the association requests the persons engaged to attend the office. Mediation office members may also take the initia-

tive to visit homes. Its role in settling small disputes through mediation should not be underestimated, greatly assisting the local public security police, who can concentrate on more serious conflicts. The funds of the Mediation Association also come from the village budget.

8) The Economic Cooperative. Consisting of three permanent members, its office is managed by the director, who is also the deputy village head. The other two members are villagers chosen for their ability to engage in business. Its main role is to assist enterprises, by providing services such as business consultancy and advice to villagers selling farm products. The most important annual event is to provide the logistics of the fruit harvest season sales, when merchants flock to Dongsheng in order to purchase fruit. Being an anchor of commercial activity both within the village and for outside entrepreneurs visiting Dongsheng, the Economic Cooperative collects a commission appropriate to the size of each transaction, forming its financial foundation.

9) The Association for the Study of Grain and Sugarcane and the Association for the Study of Fruit Trees. It is a permanent, yet unregistered organization, in effect being one organization under two names. The deputy village head concurrently serves as its president. Its five members are villagers experienced in grain, sugarcane and fruit cultivation and with scientific and technical knowledge. They provide scientific and technical services, including the dissemination of scientific and technical know-how and concerning plant diseases and pest control. Its members provide services free of charge. Funds for some crucial activities come from the village budget. Its yearly funding of RMB 1,000 is mainly used for its library and experimental equipment.

10) The Village Militia. The Militia consists of a primary and reserve militia. Recruits to the primary militia are young male villagers—physically, mentally and morally strong—who receive systematic military training. There are eighteen primary militia troops in Dongsheng. The reserve militia counts all men between 18 and 45 years, currently several hundred in number. During the annual one-month training, some reserve troops are prepared for dealing with public emergencies, such as floods, to provide emergency rescue services and be on duty for war. Others never undergo training. An annual, publicized, meeting is held. Funds for militia training can be collected from villagers according to the government's regulations, while the upkeep of the local militia itself is guaranteed through the village's public budget.

11) A common phenomenon referred to as "unlicensed private banks" or "vermin control associations" encountered in rural Fujian

also exists in other agrarian areas of southern China. In fact these are nothing but unlicensed private banks. Such enterprises attract deposits by offering high interest. Although they often violate PRC financial laws and regulations, they usually operate with the support of local governments. Financial fraud by such unlicensed private banks, mismanagement of money entrusted to them by common farmers and the associated squandering of monies by cadres have become a frequent occurrence. Villagers often appeal to the authorities for help or protest more violently, seriously affecting rural stability. Fortunately for Dongsheng there are no such illegal banks, merely a foundation for the welfare of senior citizens in the village. The latter is organized and managed by the Senior Citizens' Association and confined to voluntary contributions intended for mutual help. The Welfare Foundation also makes small investments, the profit of which is used to fund activities of the Senior Citizens' Association.

Organizations such as the Villagers' Representative Assembly, the Working Group for Publicizing Village Affairs and for Democratic Management, the Villagers' Group for Financial Affairs, the Talented Persons' Association and temple fairs are ad hoc organizations, conducting activities at irregular intervals. They lack fixed assets and fixed organizational structures and have no guaranteed funds. The Villagers' Committee summons the Villagers' Representative Assembly and the Talented Persons' Association. The main function of the former is to elect a new Villagers' Committee and discuss important village affairs. Following its election, semi-annual meetings are held, presenting reports by the villagers' committee and opinions about village affairs. The Talented Persons' Association mainly consists of the professionally active villagers. When the Villagers' Committee discusses problems affecting the entire village, it often summons this group of professional persons in order to solicit their opinions. The main tasks of the Working Group for Publicizing Village Affairs and for Democratic Management and the Villagers' Group for Financial Affairs are to make village and financial affairs known to the public. There is no Buddhist temple in Dongsheng, the nearest temple being the "Xizai Buddhist shrine" in a neighboring village. It is a regional attraction, with a big temple fair being held every four years. Every family in Dongsheng attends the fair. Villagers voluntarily raise funds and donate these to the temple. There are no organized religious activities, but families go to the temple in light of their own needs. The Buddha statue is available on loan for private worship, which is called "visiting." When the statue passes by, villagers hail it, since they have faith in it. There is little other religious activity, for instance, there are only two Christian households in the whole village.[14]

Environment for Growth of Rural Civic Organizations

The development of rural civic organizations is determined by political, legal, economic and cultural parameters. Prior to the reform period, rural China's economic structure and political system were highly centralized, thus providing no political, legal or economic basis for the development of voluntary organizations. Consequently, no independent civic organizations emerged. The prevalent political conditions dictated that all civic organizations were to be regarded, and eliminated, as remnants of feudalism or of the bourgeois system. Even the time-honored clan organizations disappeared.

The reason for the rapid development of civic organizations in Dongsheng as of the 1990s was the disintegration of the people's commune system, coupled with the serious economic pressure caused by the new household contract responsibility system, linking pay to productivity. Within the people's communes, villagers did not own land or any other property. Nor did they have private interests which they controlled. Villagers did not even have the power to make decisions about what to grow in the fields. This mandatory and entirely collectively-owned system of the people's communes greatly dampened the peasants' initiative for production and seriously impaired the development of rural productive forces. The peasants' income was generally low and many lived in dire poverty. Neither time nor money could be made available to participate in voluntary organizations. Following the implementation of the household contract responsibility system, farmland was distributed to villagers for private and individual use. As a result, the rural command system lost the basis for its existence, and farmers were given wide-ranging powers to take economic decisions. For instance, they were entitled to control land, time and labor, greatly raising living standards. In 1998, the rural per capita income in Dongsheng reached RMB 4,290, almost eleven times as much as the national per capita income in the countryside in 1978 (RMB 378). Under such economic

---

[14] See Record of Interview 990722.

conditions, senior citizens dispense with farming, allowing for various recreational activities to be organized. The village enjoys sufficient levels of public finance to provide financial support for the running of civic organizations such as the Villagers' Committee, the Family Planning Association or the Senior Citizens' Association. From the experience of economic change and the development of civic organizations in Dongsheng, we can conclude that the free disposition of property and labor as well as high living standards are two necessary economic pre-conditions for the growth of rural civic organizations.

The standard thesis arrived at when discussing China's reforms is that China should primarily pursue economic restructuring, only then followed by political transformation. It is precisely because the PRC has failed to introduce important changes to its political system that reforms are succeeding. Conversely, the former Soviet Union pursued a line of reform under the primate of political restructuring, which is perceived as the reason for the failure of its reforms.[15] This view has its limitations. It defines China's political development in Western political terms and regards multi-party systems, separation between executive, legislative and judicial powers as well as Western representative democracy as the sole criteria for political restructuring. Accordingly, we can state that China's political system has yet to undergo any substantial reform. There remain, however, other criteria for judging political development, such as relations between central and local authorities, between Party and state, government and citizens, as well as between the government and business. Other criteria include cadre selection, leadership of Party and state, political management, culture, tolerance, and respect for human rights. Seen from this angle, the only possible conclusion can be that the entire political system has undergone tremendous changes since the reform policy was implemented. Political change is hence the prime determinant for the growth of rural civic organizations.

As elsewhere in China's countryside prior to the reforms, Dongsheng exercised a highly centralized political system. During the Cultural Revolution, the village leadership was in the hands of the local Revolutionary Committee, with the Party firmly in control. Although neither the Party nor the Revolutionary Committee acted according to any legal provisions, they were actually vested with full executive authority. Combining political, economic and cultural leadership, both bodies

---

[15] See Susan Shirk, "The Political Logic of Chinese Economic Reforms."

were in command of six production teams. The village population, on the other hand, was devoid of any democratic and autonomous powers and was tightly controlled. Farming, as well as the distribution and time allocation of labor, was imposed on every villager by assignment to production teams. Villagers had no choice but to accept the political or economic arrangements made by their production team leaders. Disobedience triggered economic penalties, for instance by reducing the cash value of their remuneration vouchers. Political punishment included compulsory participation in study classes, public self-criticism and even struggle sessions where perceived enemies were denounced. The Party and the state incorporated every peasant into a highly centralized political process, a tight hierarchical system which consisted of the local Party, the Revolutionary Committee, as well as production brigades and teams, resulting in a high degree of civil dependence.

During the early 1980s, the Chinese government began to implement a policy of separating government from commune management, Party from government and economic management from the rural administration. In particular, it was stipulated that the Party was no longer to serve as an administrative organ for the direct management of village affairs. Furthermore, the Revolutionary Committees were banned, the administrative functions of the production brigades were removed, an autonomous local body, namely the Villagers' Committee, was established and democratic participation increased. Because of these rural reforms, the vestiges of former centralism began to disintegrate, being replaced by a political model of relative pluralism. By the late 1980s, this process was basically complete in Dongsheng. The hierarchical production teams had disappeared, replaced by loosely organized village associations. The Party no longer interferes in the lives of villagers, having been replaced by the Villagers' Committee. For the first time, villagers enjoy the right to freely elect village cadres. Compulsory political study sessions, night schools, mobilization meetings and mass movements are gone forever. Villagers can air disagreement without facing criticism. Rural political pluralism based on rural economic pluralism is the basic political environment for the rapid development of civic organizations in Dongsheng.

The legal environment for rural civic organizations differs from the urban model. Civic organizations in Dongsheng, as opposed to their urban counterparts, which must be first registered with the Department of Civil Affairs to become legal, are essentially unregistered. Only the Villagers' Committee, established in strict accordance with the Organic

Law on Villagers' Committees in the People's Republic of China, is registered. The Committee is governed pursuant to the Regulations on the Registration and Management of Social Associations and the Regulations on the Management of Charities. The Village's Association for the Study of Fruit Trees and the Senior Citizens' Association are civil social organizations and ought to, according to the regulations, be registered with the department of civil affairs. However, no formalities for any formal registration have been processed to date. The Economic Cooperative is a charity. According to government stipulations, it is meant to be registered with the County Bureau of Civil Affairs, but again no formal steps have been taken. To ordinary villagers, these unregistered civic organizations are legal, their legitimacy based on documents issued by Party and government at provincial and central level. In the eyes of villagers and village cadres, informal regulations and promulgated laws have the same value. In conclusion, the legitimacy of China's rural civic organizations is mainly based on the approval by Party and government at higher levels, rather than on PRC laws.

Rural civic organizations are also governed by traditional cultural parameters. Prior to the reform period, both Party and government took all conceivable steps to eliminate China's political and cultural traditions, by initiating mass movements such as the Eliminate the 'Four Olds' (i.e., old ideas, culture, customs and habits) campaign and the Cultural Revolution. In a powerful political offensive, the influence of traditional culture was meant to be minimized. But traditional cultural notions remained intact in the hearts of villagers and could not be destroyed. During the decades of political calm that followed, traditional culture gradually restored its influence over rural life. In Dongsheng we cannot fail but to notice the tremendous influence of country worthies, clans and autonomous associations. Organizations such as the Villagers' Committee, Talented Persons' Association, Senior Citizens' Association, Public Security Committee and the temple fair have deep historical roots. The temple fair reflects the influence of the traditional Buddhist culture, the Talented Persons' Association that of the country worthies, the Senior Citizens' Association is the inheritors of the clan organizations, while the Villagers' Committee can be regarded as a continuation of traditional village autonomy.

*Funding Sources of Rural Civic Organizations and
Their Internal Mechanisms*

The financial sources of rural civic organizations are very different from those of their urban counterparts. Urban civic organizations possess three main sources. Firstly, full government funding for mass organizations such as the trade unions, the Communist Youth League, Women's Federation as well as professional organizations such as the Chinese Association for International Understanding, China National Light Industry Council, China Law Society and the China Association for Science and Technology. Secondly, partial funding from official sources, supplemented by privately raised moneys, for instance from the chamber of commerce or certain academic associations. Thirdly, fully privately raised funds, for example from charities. Rural civic organizations get no government funds, with all money raised or donated by villagers.

Civic organizations in Dongsheng have three main sources of funding. Firstly, there are membership fees. Most organizations do not charge members, but significantly the temple fair, the Senior Citizens' Association and the Communist Youth League thus derive their income. By rule or convention, members pay fees in order to fund the activities of these organizations. Middlemen collect the dues for the temple fair from villagers, and the latter also voluntarily contribute money. Members of the Senior Citizens' Association pay annual fees, currently RMB 10, which are entirely controlled by the Association. Members of the Communist Youth League pay on a monthly basis according to their income, but most of the proceeds are passed on to the local Youth League committee. A second type of source is obtained from services paid for by civic organizations, such as the Economic Cooperative or the Senior Citizens' Association. Fees are collected for the provision of services to villagers and used to fund their activities. Finally, there are official village funds, the main source of funding for civic organizations in Dongsheng. Except for the Senior Citizens' Association, the Economic Cooperative, the temple fair and the Communist Youth League, the other organizations have village funding as their only source of income. Except for the Economic Cooperative, organizations with alternative sources also enjoy subsidies from the village. It is a common occurrence in China's rural areas that villages provide subsidies to local organizations. But in the case of Dongsheng this is more remarkable, because its financial situation is rather exceptional. The village has a village-run enterprise, namely the fruit tree station with about 2.67 ha (40 *mu*) of land. The station can be leased at an annual cost of **RMB** 100,000. The village counts two Taiwanese investments, the Jingu Preserved Fruits Factory and Dongsheng Mineral Water. The village collects land rent for the 1,534 ha (23,000 *mu*) of the collectively-owned hill land,. Villagers can lease land for up to 30 years. Villagers pay **RMB** 8 per year for every *mu* (0.0667 ha) of fruit trees to the village. In 1998, the village's net income approximated **RMB** 600,000.[16]

Membership qualifications in villages are less strict than those of urban organizations. In Dongsheng, all adult women are automatically members of the Village Women's Federation, without the need to apply and pay for membership. This is also true for the Senior Citizens' Association. All men over 60 and women over 55 years of age automatically qualify, though continued membership is subject to the payment of membership fees. The requirements set by the local Communist Youth League are relatively strict. Applicants can become League members provided they are young, and able to handle a series of administrative and financial procedures on behalf of the League. Once members, they are subject to membership fees. About one quarter of potential candidates qualify to become League members. Equally stringent are the criteria for membership applications for the Talented Persons' Association and the Association for the Study of Fruit Trees. Candidates must possess professional skills and have relevant work experience, but application procedures and membership fees are absent. As to the Mediation and the Family Planning Associations, members should have a strong sense of responsibility, have experience in handling public matters and be reputable. Public Security Committee members should be physically strong, know about technology and show experience in matters of security. Usually, they are selected from demobilized soldiers. The Mediation Association, the Family Planning Association and the Public Security Committee have no procedures for application and registration. Instead, candidates are suggested by the Villagers' Committee and the Party.

In order to qualify for leadership positions, however, restrictive conditions apply. Personal qualities required are enthusiasm for public welfare, strong organizational and managerial skills, financial prowess, willingness to participate in the administration of village affairs and a good

---

[16] See Record of Interview 990719.

team spirit. Because the Villagers' Committee is a local autonomous body and the most important civic organization in the countryside, its leader is elected by general vote according to the legal provisions. The electoral procedures for the Dongsheng Villagers' Committee are simple: the local Party presents a list of candidates for the posts of director and deputy directors as well as for ordinary membership after soliciting the opinions of representative villagers. One candidate in excess of the available posts for director and deputy directors respectively, and two names in excess of posts available for members are required. Once the candidates have been determined, the list of candidates is presented to all voters for a direct ballot. If any one candidate attains at least half of the votes, he or she is formally elected. If all candidates reach or surpass a minimum of 50%, those who obtain the most votes will be elected. After the village head, the deputy village heads and the members have been elected, their list must be submitted to the next higher Party committee and government body for approval. According to the provisions of the Organic Law on Villagers' Committees, candidates for the positions of village head, deputy village head and ordinary membership can be nominated by the local Party, by more than ten individual villagers or by groups of villagers. However, all previous candidates for this position in Dongsheng were selected by the Party. The vetoing of candidates nominated by the Party, reported in other localities, is unheard of in Dongsheng.[17]

Just as the Villagers' Committee, the Youth League elects its leaders by general membership ballot, pursuant to the Constitution of the Communist Youth League. In contrast, the leading cadres of the other civic organizations in Dongsheng are not elected. The secretary of the Senior Citizens' Association and the chief organizer of the temple fair are recommended by their members, the choice of the Senior Citizens' Association pending the approval of the local Party and the Villagers' Committee. Directly appointed by both bodies are the leading officers and members of the Family Planning Association, the Public Security Committee, the Mediation Association, the Village Militia, the Association for the Study of Fruit Trees, the Talented Persons' Association, the Senior Citizens' School, the Population School, the Women's Federation, the Villagers' Group for Financial Affairs and

---

[17] See Record of Interview 990723.

the Working Group for Publicizing Village Affairs and for Exercising Democratic Management.

Most of Dongsheng's eighteen civic organizations lack strict internal organizational structures and do not even have subsidiaries. The Villagers' Committee, Senior Citizens' Association and the Family Planning Association, all crucial contributors to the development of the village, are more strictly organized and managed. The formal subsidiaries of the Villagers' Committee are the Villagers' Associations, the Villagers' Representative Assembly, the Public Security Committee and the Village Militia. The Villagers' Committee also controls most of the other organizations. The subsidiaries of the Senior Citizens' Association are six sub-groups and the Senior Citizens' School. Those of the Family Planning Association are six local groups and the Population School. Although most organizations have their own regulations, the Villagers' Committee, the Senior Citizens' Association and the Family Planning Association have the authority to influence other associations. Except for the Organic Law on Villagers' Committees in the People's Republic of China, the most authoritative regulation governing the Villagers' Committee in Dongsheng are the Regulations for Dongsheng Village. The current Regulations, in fifteen articles, were promulgated in 1994.[18] It becomes apparent that almost all articles list obligations, beginning with "it is not allowed" or "it is prohibited." The Family Planning Association also has fifteen rules and regulations, mostly members' obligations, with only a few emphasizing their rights. In its rules, the Senior Citizens' Association formulates detailed provisions on the rights and obligations of its members. Mandatory provisions on punishment are nigh absent, but its members are held to abide by the above rules as conscientiously as those of the Villagers' Committee and the Family Planning Association. We can thus conclude that the Villagers' Committee and the Family Planning Association rely on mandatory rules to manage members, while other organizations emphasize common understanding and harmony among theirs.

Rules and regulations aside, rural civic organizations rely on the personal ability and prestige of their leading cadres. The more influential and active villagers' organizations in Dongsheng have cadres endowed with high leadership qualities and public prestige. For example, the deputy Party secretary concurrently serves as director of the Villagers'

---

[18] Villagers' Committee of Dongsheng Village, Changqiao Town, "Regulations of Dongsheng Village," October 1994.

Committee and originates from the village's influential Huang clans (first branch). At 36 years of age, the deputy secretary is a strong and talented manager, hence enjoying high prestige among the villagers. Another deputy Party secretary also serves as president of the Family Planning Association. He is deeply respected for being fair and even-handed in public affairs, while bold and resolute in action. The president of the Senior Citizens' Association is simultaneously its full-time vice-president. A former village head of over ten years, he stems from the most powerful Huang clan (fourth branch). He enjoys public trust for being honest and upright while entertaining good relations with ordinary people. The personal charisma of these leading cadres greatly increases the cohesion of their organizations and among their membership base. Furthermore, these three villagers' organizations are also the most active ones in Dongsheng, in particular the Senior Citizens' Association.

Rural Civic Organizations, Party and Government

For civic organizations to exert any influence in China, they must maintain good relations with both Party and government. Rural civic organizations are no exception. To be specific, there are three reasons for this need. Firstly, the countryside was directly subject to Party organizations prior to the 1980s. Self-governance was gradually implemented among villagers from the late 1980s, but it lacks maturity. Party branches operate in most rural parts. Even in places where Villagers' Committees are influential, the local Party offices retain considerable power. Secondly, the Chinese Communist Party is the only governing party setting the tone for all political, economic, military and cultural affairs throughout China, including the countryside. According to the recently adopted Organic Law on Villagers' Committees, Villagers' Committees, as rural autonomous organizations, must subject themselves to the political leadership of primary Party organizations. Thirdly, the Chinese Communist Party has over 60 million members, accounting for almost 5% of the total population. It accounts for most of the elite from all walks of life, including that of rural villagers' organizations.

Except for the liaison persons for the temple fair, most other leading cadres of the eighteen, formal or informal, civic organizations in Dongsheng are Party members, while five delegates of the Villagers' Committee are members. Though there are merely 42 Party members in Dongsheng, they hold the leadership positions in the village's most important organizations. The five cadres of the local Party (one secretary, two deputy secretaries and two other officers) all hold leading positions in other village organizations. Because the Party secretary is in the most senior position, he combines a number of responsibilities, also serving as principal of the Population School and honorary principal of the Senior Citizens' School. One deputy secretary is concurrently the village head and the director of the local Public Security Committee. The other deputy secretary acts as president of the Family Planning Association. One of the two remaining officers plays a key role in the Mediation Association, while the other acts as commander of the Village Militia. The president of the Senior Citizens' Association is an old Party member and a former secretary of the local Party. Its vice-presidents and secretary-general are also old Party members.[19]

Pursuant to the relevant provisions of the current Constitution of the People's Republic of China and the Constitution of the Chinese Communist Party, Party committees at all levels exercise unified leadership over all aspects of public life, but this "leadership" cannot compete with the remit of the government. The Party does not intervene directly in the administration and management of social affairs, but it exercises political influence. This is done by three means: firstly by recommending cadres to the government and other relevant authorities, secondly by formulating guidelines, principles and policies, and finally by implementing the political programs of Party organizations with the help of civil servants at all levels who are also Party members. The Dongsheng Party office thus exercises political leadership over all village organizations. It does so by recommending to the relevant organizations the right type of leadership material. The village head and deputy heads, the candidates for Villagers' Committee as well as leadership candidates for the village's committees and associations, the Youth League and the Women's Federation are thus selected. Any major village affairs, for example plans relating to infrastructure, capital construction, the village budget and its public investments, are discussed both within and in between the Party and the Villagers' Committee. As the highest organ of self-governance in Dongsheng, the Villagers' Committee reports to the local Party at regular intervals and requests

---

[19] See Record of Interview 990719.

instructions on all major matters. It must accept the supervision of villagers and the leading role of the Party. The Party office holds regular bi-weekly meetings, to deliberate matters of concern to the village, to assign tasks and to set out guidelines to the Party members in the village. The CCP Central Committee's principles and policies on rural work and the peasantry are implemented by the Villagers' Committee and other local organizations by Party committees at all levels and through the local Party office.

China's administration constitutes a matrix system, integrating departments and regions at different levels. Laterally, all authorities have to accept the leadership of the Party committees and of the corresponding government level. Vertically, authorities need to accept the prevalence of higher Party and government departments. This management system also applies to rural civic organizations. In Dongsheng, only a few civic organizations, such as the temple fair and the Talented Persons' Association, do not follow this example. Most other organizations, such as the Family Planning Association, the Senior Citizens' Association, the Village Militia, the Association for the Study of Fruit Trees, the Youth League, the Economic Cooperative are subject to decisions taken at higher levels within said organizations. All must accept the guidance and leadership of the Villagers' Committee and of the local Party, as well as of the authorities at higher levels. Especially the Family Planning Association, the Youth League, the Women's Federation, the Village Militia and other civic organizations of official nature maintain close ties with their parent organizations. District town authorities habitually issue instructions and orders to village organizations. The Villagers' Committee is nominally independent, being the highest administrative organ, but it is implicitly to respect the authority Party committees and government bodies at town and township levels. The town exercises its leadership over the Villagers' Committee through the assignment of "cadres residing in the village." The latter are also called "cadres responsible for the village." Both terms refer to town and township cadres now residing in the village, since they were dispatched to the village for assigned work (generally one to three years, in rotation). The number of "cadres residing in the village" is determined according to the size of the village and to the nature of their task. Team numbers range between a maximum of four to five cadres and a minimum of one or two. Their main responsibilities include the implementation of Party and government principles, policies and instructions, taken at town and township levels and to report on the local situation, problems and requirements to the higher authorities. They are also expected to guide and assist the local Party and the Villagers' Committee in their work, to examine family planning, and to collect taxes to the state and fees toward town and township funds. In fact, the collection of taxes and fees has become the main task of most "resident cadres."

This is at least true in Dongsheng. Paying its dues is generally not a problem for Dongsheng because of its enviable economic position. Nevertheless, there are three "resident cadres" in the village. Since Dongsheng easily outperforms other localities in aspects such as economic development, family planning and villagers' self-governance, the "resident cadres" can concentrate on other matters, mainly on raising funds for the township. Central government policies permit that villages can retain some of the general funds collected by the township in order to stimulate local initiative. The value of the fiscal discount varies in proportion to local income. Officially referred to as "retention of funds," the total of general funds collected by the townships but retained by the village cannot exceed 5% of the net per capita income, based on 1995 figures. In townships where such fiscal retention does not exist, the local population will be compelled to pay. This, however, many are unable—or unwilling—to do. The ensuing conflicts are affecting the stability of rural China. Dongsheng is a case in point. Because the village is economically developed, peasants are exempt from certain fees and taxes. In 1998 and 1999 the per capita "general funds collected by the township" in Changqiao, the municipality where Dongsheng is located, was RMB 48, with an educational surcharge of RMB 50. But some 10% of the local population refused to pay. About half of the rural population in Zhangpu, the County in which the village is located, has not paid their taxes. Imposing fiscal discipline on China's rural parts is evidently a problem.[20]

Fundamentally speaking, the relationship between rural civic organizations, the Party and government departments at lower administrative levels provides leeway for cooperation and conflicts. In most cases, harmony and compromise prevail, since the public authorities at the lower end of the administrative ladder hold concrete power. Civil organizations, however, must represent the interests of their members. They thus frequently generate conflict with administrative bodies at higher levels and with the local Party organizations. In some cases,

---

[20] See Record of Interview 990722.

Party members serving as leading cadres of civic organizations back the views of their members, thus running into conflict with their Party or government superiors. As to Dongsheng, Villagers' Committee and other local organizations have managed to maintain a harmonious relationship with Party and government. Frictions certainly exist, as in any situation where there is conflict of interests. But such frictions have never developed into large-scale conflicts, as opposed to the situation in a neighboring village.

In 1995, with local Party approval, the Villagers' Committee of Youche, a village next to Dongsheng, signed a contract with the County Bureau of Civil Affairs on leasing land to be used as a cemetery. Traditional belief, however, prohibits the building of cemeteries adjacent to villages. Resolute local opposition led the village elders and the Senior Citizens' Association to organize villagers to protest against the planned lease. Instead of negotiating with the local Party, they amassed over one hundred villagers to directly petition to the county government for two days in succession, requesting to abandon the plan. Government and Party organizations implored the villagers, but in vain. When the government ordered an on-site survey of the leased land, the Senior Citizens' Association organized more than two hundred villagers for a violent protest, resulting in destroyed surveying equipment. The police detained three key perpetrators, charging them with the offence of obstructing the performance of official duties. After violent clashes, the Senior Citizens' Association gathered several hundred villagers to hold a demonstration in front of the county government, forcing the latter to negotiate with the villagers. After the government conceded defeat, the demonstration came to an end. This event shows that rural civic organizations can be more powerful than the local Party office, forcing the Party into a contest of strength—with a fair chance of victory.

Functions of Rural Civic Organizations

Different rural civic organizations perform different functions. In the case of Dongsheng, these can be subdivided into management and service provision: promoting village autonomy, providing concrete services to villagers, mediating in personal disputes, assisting the old, weak, sick and disabled, maintaining rural stability, improving relations between the rural population, Party and government, furthering the development of the rural economy, to name but a few.

The primary function of rural civic organizations is to enhance village autonomy. In the late 1980s, the Chinese government decided to gradually abandon the political system in place since the 1950s, which allowed the local Party or the Revolutionary Committee to exercise direct management over the village population. One precondition for greater autonomy was that there had to be at least one autonomous element differing markedly from both Party and Revolutionary Committee. Pursuant to central government regulations, the authority for rural self-governance rests with the Villagers' Committees. Their main responsibility is to manage village affairs, as evident from the above-mentioned functions of the Villagers' Committee in Dongsheng. The Committee's functions are clearly marked: its five members divide tasks according to administrative need, the village head manages the affairs of the whole village, and while one deputy village head is responsible for economic management, the other is in charge of public security. One of the additional members covers work concerning women and family planning, while the other member is responsible for the Village Militia. Because economic affairs and public security are arduous, there are two subordinate organs: the Economic Cooperative led by a deputy village head and the Public Security Association led by the village head and one deputy village head. A village of several thousand people has a variety of public affairs, and villagers quite naturally subject themselves to traditional forms of administration. Merely the Villagers' Committee which consists of five part-time officers finds it hard to engage in active governance. The local Party and other civic organizations jointly manage village affairs. As the policy-making nucleus of the village, it exercises direct influence over the important Family Planning Association and the Mediation Association and also monitors the Villagers' Committee.

Rural civic organizations are self-governing and self-managing and the second basic function of these organizations is to provide concrete services to villagers. To the government, villagers' organizations exist primarily to allow the rural population to administer itself autonomously. To ordinary villagers, however, the organizations are welcomed because they provide practical services. Organizations which do not provide such services and consultation find it hard to exist. There are, however, some which lay particular emphasis on management rather than services. In Dongsheng, the latter include the Villagers' Committee, the Family Planning Association, the Villagers' Associations, the Youth League and the Women's Federation. These organizations manage the village's development, capital construction, public property and its collectively-owned economy as well as villagers' taxation, military service, marriage, family planning, and public security. To the government, they constitute indispensable organs of self-governance and self-management. Villagers regard them as managing consultants. For example, if villagers want to build a house, they first need to present applications to the Villagers' Committee. After securing its approval, the project needs to be registered with the town government and land and house taxes paid. Applications for marriage should first go to the Villagers' Committee, before registering their marriage with the municipal department of civil affairs. If a couple wants to give birth to a child, the approval of the Family Planning Association must be sought. Once agreed, the couple can obtain a birth license from the municipal Family Planning Association. Only then a woman is allowed to become pregnant. Other village organizations, such as the Senior Citizens' Association, the Association for the Study of Fruit Trees, the Economic Cooperative, the Mediation Association, the temple fair and Village Militia mainly provide services. These include health care for villagers, recreational activities, mediation in family disputes, as well as between parents and their children, between married women and their mothers-in-law as well as between families. Streets are being patrolled for public security.

An important function of rural civic organizations is to help the old, weak, sick and disabled. Respecting old age, cherishing the young and helping the poor are treasured Chinese traditions and are particularly deep-rooted in the vast rural hinterland. For rural organizations, official or civil, not to provide such assistance would be to their own detriment. Prior to the reform period, the system of the "five guarantees" was generally implemented for China's rural households. These "five guarantees" referred to the guaranteed supply of food, clothing, medical care, housing and burial expenses for the childless and infirm old. Production brigades covered the expenses for the "five guarantees" system. With the disintegration of the production brigades, the system was duly abolished. Although rural living standards have risen considerably since then, problems affecting disadvantaged villagers are unavoidable. How to provide a social safety net has thus become a pressing problem. In Dongsheng, this problem is being tackled by the Villagers' Committee and other village organizations through the following methods. Firstly, the Senior Citizens' Association was established, providing a sufficiently large sum of money to assist senior citizens in matters of health and recreation. The annual financial assistance thus provided, directly or indirectly, amounts to circa **RMB** 40,000. Secondly, some organizations offer to help through voluntary work. For instance, the Senior Citizens' Association established a Senior Citizens' Welfare Foundation, subsidizing poor senior citizens. The Family Planning Association provides aid and tax relief or exemption to "households with two girls." Thirdly, the Villagers' Committee prioritizes households in dire poverty, granting relief funds, exempting such households from communal taxation, tuition and other school fees. Finally, a medical insurance system was established to encourage villagers to take out insurances. This coincided with the opening of a village clinic, instantly improving access to medical treatment and health services.

Another important function is to provide economic services, mainly through public economic management, general economic guidance in matters affecting the whole village, as well as demonstrating and endorsing methods of agrarian production and management. This has helped villagers transform barren hills into agricultural land, where they can now grow fruit trees to supplement their income. Ten years ago, this would have been unheard of. But in the view of the Villagers' Committee this is the best way of guiding Dongsheng villagers toward prosperity. The Committee thus decided that its own cadres take the lead in working the barren hill land, setting a positive example. All but a small minority of farmers now cultivate the formerly barren hills. The recalcitrant few can be persuaded through economic coercion. Such measures are referred to as "compelling villagers to become rich." In fact, this is a way of compelling villagers to accept good advice, which has caused some uproar in academic circles. This is because similar measures have wrought disastrous consequences. Others, however, are proving successful, and Dongsheng is a case in point. The barren hills of the past have now become a major source of income. In addition, the Villagers' Committee and organizations such as the Association for the Study of Fruit Trees and the Economic Cooperative assist in marketing, scientific and technical guidance, and by introducing improved varieties.

Village organizations also assume public management responsibilities. One of the overriding concerns in Dongsheng is to plan for building activities, in the form of capital construction and housing for villagers. From 1998, all newly built accommodation had to conform to the plan. The Villagers' Committee also coordinates road construction, fresh water supply and sewage canalization, as well as other construction and engineering projects. Public funds are used toward the costs for public facilities, for the upkeep of the primary school buildings and teachers' wages in non-state schools, with the remainder being paid by township and town authorities. The Villagers' Committee, the Senior Citizens' Association, the temple fair and other village organizations organize the celebration of traditional festivals, as well as weddings and funerals. These celebrations are much valued in rural China, also being occasions when rewards can be apportioned to villagers performing meritorious deeds and for addressing the whole village community.

Concluding Remarks: Rural Civic Organizations
and Good Governance

The emergence of civic organizations in China's rural areas is the inevitable result of the country's market-oriented economic restructuring. This process thoroughly changes the structure and reality of rural politics, promoting democracy and good governance.

Since the introduction of autonomous Villagers' Committees, consultation in financial and other village affairs has greatly increased, significantly enhancing rural political transparency. Increased consultation is a consequence of systematic changes introduced by the Central Government. Its influence is clearly stipulated in the Organic Law on Villagers' Committees and other relevant documentation issued by the CCP Central Committee. Party and state authorities at all levels formulate detailed rules for implementation pursuant to the above-mentioned law and regulations. County and township councils have established special offices for the rural consultation policy and are responsible for its guidance, surveillance and examination.

Local consultation policies are subject to those endorsed by the county government. In the case of Dongsheng, this is Zhangpu County. For its implementation, Dongsheng established two provisional bodies, namely the Working Group for Publicizing Village Affairs and for Exercising Democratic Management and the Villagers' Group for Financial Affairs. The former consists of the principal cadres of Party and Villagers' Committee with the secretary of the local Party serving as its leader and the village head being responsible for the management of democratic processes. The latter consists of the leading cadres of the Villagers' Committee and of the Senior Citizens' Association, with one deputy secretary of the Association serving as leader. Furthermore, the

Party and Villagers' Committee appoint four supervising consultants, chosen from among the Party, the Villagers' Committee and ordinary villagers. The contents, times and methods of specific consultation work must be logged in an official file deposited with the Zhangpu County government, while the working group is to present a report to the township government.[21]

Aspects to be addressed include the level of wages, bonuses and subsidies given to village cadres, the income and expenses of the cooperatives, family planning, land cultivation, as well as the use of ponds, orchards, mountain forests and other enterprises. Other consultation tasks refer to the bidding for construction projects, distribution of land for accommodation, requisitioned land and compensation claims, the apportioning of voluntary labor, and the financial planning and application behind planning procedures. Finally, the allocation of grain taxes, distribution of public aid and machinery, the use of anti-poverty funds, as well as practical advice. Most of the desired consultation work is advertised twice a year, namely during the first ten days of January and of July, respectively. Important aspects touching upon land cultivation and business activities, project bidding, and land requisitioning can be made public at any time. Relevant yet more routine-natured aspects, such as family planning reviews, income and expenses of the cooperatives, are publicized at monthly and quarterly intervals. Two methods of publicizing village affairs exist, namely by posting an official announcement on the outer walls of the villagers' committee and through blackboard bulletins or by radio broadcasting within the village, reproduced at least in part. In addition, "comments boxes" are installed at the main village intersections to solicit public opinion about village affairs.

The emergence of rural civic organizations greatly promotes the rule of law in China's countryside—a basic aim of the Chinese government. For the longest time China implemented not the rule of law, but of personified power. Rural citizens lack awareness of the importance of law, and the rule of law is thus hard to implement. Ignorance of the law is a great obstacle to implementing its rule. Rural civic organizations play a tremendous role in promoting the rule of law in two respects. Firstly, they assist the government in legal education. The Villagers' Committee,

---

[21] Zhangpu County CCP (Organizational Committee), "Public consultation in Zhangpu County."

the Family Planning Association, the Senior Citizens' Association, the Public Security Committee and other Dongsheng organizations publicize state laws by holding meetings, running voluntary schools, through broadcasting, slogans and informative billboards. Villagers attest that some knowledge of the law comes across. The Population School in Dongsheng, for instance, spends more than 50% of its teaching on the national population policies, laws and regulations. Secondly, and more importantly, the Village Regulations exist as rural adaptations of state laws. Because rule by law has no place in China's history, general awareness concerning its importance is lacking. Villagers are not used to resorting to the law, but are rather accustomed to following village regulations. The incorporation of laws into village regulations is thus an effective means of implementing the rule of law in rural areas. The Regulations of Dongsheng Village amount to fifteen articles, basically legal norms affecting villagers. Article 1 stipulates that villagers must pay taxes and village development fees on time. Articles 2 and 3 stipulate that disruption and sabotage of public places such as schools and markets are prohibited. Articles 4, 5, 6 and 7 stipulate that gambling, theft, damage to crops and sabotage of public facilities are prohibited. Almost all articles apply or localize state laws and government policies in light of the actual conditions in Dongsheng, facilitating their application by villagers.

Strong village organizations are also an effective counterweight against corruption among township and village cadres. Because the Villagers' Committee promotes public political and financial consultation within the village as well as decision-making transparency, villagers can exercise effective supervision over their cadres. In Dongsheng, important economic activities, such as the salaries and other income of cadres, the village budget, political decision-making, the allocation of business contracts and of land as well as the use and distribution of land for housing, are made known to the public and supervised by specially designated officers. Embezzlement and corruption are thus made less likely. In the past, municipal cadres came to the village during the fruit harvest season regardless of whether they were needed, but always in return for donated fruit. This is no longer possible, since the orchards are now cultivated by individuals. The Villagers' Group for Financial Affairs is mainly responsible for examining the public budget of the village and for publicizing its findings at regular intervals. The Villagers' Representative Assembly, the local Party and the Working Group for

Publicizing Village Affairs and Exercising Democratic Management also have the right to examine the village's finances. Villagers can question the above organizations and even submit anonymous reports.

There are a number of mechanisms for public consultation and supervision in rural civic organizations, aimed at ensuring that their leading cadres work honestly. This matters to the Senior Citizens' Association in Dongsheng because it handles large sums of money. It publicizes members' contributions, membership fees and other income, as well as expenses through publicly displayed posters and clearly records every financial item to the last digit. The Association's finance team consists of four members, whose main responsibility it is to manage and supervise all financial activities, also those of its leading cadres. All expenses are subject to strict examination and formal approval. Major expenses must be approved by collective vote.

The rise and very existence of rural civic organizations are based on the need to maximize public interests. Good governance thus equals the promotion of society's interests. In this sense, civic organizations in China's rural areas play a most important role in promoting good governance. All organizations, including the Villagers' Committee, represent the interests of village society to varying degrees and promote its interests at higher levels. When the interests of local society are threatened, they act to protect their fellow villagers. This can take the following forms:

1) By soliciting the attention of governments at higher levels. For instance, in the promotion of local products, village organizations lobby the town government to apply preferential policies, in order to attract loans from the rural credit cooperative as well as agricultural experts from all over the county to offer their scientific and technical guidance. A recent example is the planned construction of a primary school in Dongsheng, requiring an investment totaling circa RMB 200,000. According to the regulations, investment should be drawn from the village budget, but the county government can offer proportional financial assistance to poorer villages. In order to lobby for such funds from the county government, the secretary of the village Party and director of the Villagers' Committee presented an application to the town and county governments of their own accord to persuade the relevant officials. In the end, the higher authorities conceded, agreeing to provide the unrepayable sum of RMB 30,000. Although this amount only accounts for a small percentage of the whole investment, it does

contribute toward the building costs. Dongsheng Village will not get the additional investment.[22]

2) In case of conflicts of interests between the village and higher authorities or neighboring villages, village organizations protect those of the village. With regard to taxation, fees and quotas, land demarcations, road building and water conservancy, conflicts between village and town as well as between neighboring villages are unavoidable. During such conflicts, the Villagers' Committee and other local organizations in Dongsheng defend the villagers and protect their interests. For instance, the fixed contribution for the development budget and educational surcharge payable by every resident of Changqiao municipality totals RMB 98 per annum, 20% of which can be retained at village level. In Dongsheng, however, the village uses the proportion retained strictly to protect the interests of its residents and agrees to pay upfront for those villagers who are unable to pay on schedule. Relations between Dongsheng and its rural neighbors are harmonious, although serious conflicts do occur in other rural areas in Zhangpu County. In case of such discord, the Villagers' Committee, the Senior Citizens' Association and other local organizations strive to protect the interests of their village. In exceptional circumstances, they take recourse to extreme measures, organizing armed resistance while appealing to the higher authorities for help.

3) An important task of rural civic organizations, and especially of the Villagers' Committee, is to maximize the economic interests of villagers. The recent development plan ("striving to build a prosperous new village") is spearheaded by the Villagers' Committee. In essence, the Committee takes the lead in cultivating barren hill land with fruit trees, imparting scientific and technical knowledge and in establishing experimental fruit plantations. Any financial returns are distributed evenly throughout the whole village. Committee members demonstrate to villagers how to cultivate the barren hills, introducing scientific fruit growing methods to all villagers. At harvest time, the Villagers' Committee promotes the sale of local fruit on the wider market. There are also three fruit processing enterprises operated by the Committee, while villagers are given marketing advice. As a result, the formerly barren hills, measuring an area of over 840 ha (12,600 *mu*) have been

---

[22] See Record of Interview 990721.

miraculously turned into high-quality fruit groves. The per capita income of villagers increased from circa RMB 2,000 five years ago to over 4,200 in 1998.[23]

4) Village organizations develop the collective economy and increase public welfare. After the household responsibility system featuring the redistribution of land to rural households had been implemented, private initiative concerning agrarian production, productivity and living conditions was significantly strengthened. But this policy also produced some negative consequences. Following the disintegration of the rural collectives, villages' public finances collapsed and public welfare was seriously impaired. Disrupted irrigation facilities, damaged roads and collapsed bridges became a common sight. For the government no longer to interfere in rural economic affairs, the responsibility for public welfare has had to shift to the villagers themselves, organized into village associations. The Villagers' Committee and other village organizations in Dongsheng have greatly contributed toward the development of the local economy and raised levels of public welfare. Following the creation of three village-run enterprises and of a fruit cultivation cooperative, its groves covering an area of 1,534 ha (23,000 *mu*), the net income of the village's economy attained RMB 600,000 in 1998. The Villagers' Committee, the Villagers' Representative Assembly and other civic organizations are using this income to improve public facilities throughout the village, for example through public construction programs, road building, the provision of facilities for irrigation and drinking water, cable TV, telephony, FM broadcasting, as well as education and healthcare. Public welfare thus shows signs of significant progress. The village's construction program alone cost RMB 1.8 million, while the cable TV project required RMB 170,000, and school buildings accounted for RMB 180,000. Without the effort of Dongsheng's village organizations, these sums would have been hard to raise.

5) Village organizations comprehensively improve the quality of life, and not merely in financial terms. Other contributions include the pursuit of a safe and clean living environment and a rich cultural life. In most rural areas, quality of life is not guaranteed by governments or individuals, but by village organizations. The Public Security Committee and Mediation Association in Dongsheng provide for a safer, more harmonious village. The Youth League, Women's Federation, Senior

---

[23] See Record of Interview 990719.

Citizens' Association, the temple fair and other organizations provide villagers with public services concerning culture, recreation, health and religion. The Public Security Committee, for instance, organizes training for collective self-defense and safety. At night, it patrols the village streets, ensuring public security. Its funds are entirely derived from the village budget. In addition to providing services to the elderly, the Senior Citizens' Association organizes performances for Chinese New Year and other festivals, enriching the cultural life of the village. In 1998, the Villagers' Committee organized a five-fold competition namely in terms of fruit production, fruit sales, variety of cultural life, talented children, and of personal contribution to the village. Its purpose was to increase social cohesion and local pride.

Rural civic organizations in China have only been developing for a short period of time. In terms of the political and economic environment as well as of their structure and functions, there are many problems. In Zhangpu County, and particularly in Dongsheng, these manifest themselves as follows:

The roles ascribed by civic organizations to themselves fall far short of their actual abilities. At times they can even assume negative roles. For instance, the county-wide public consultation initiative (Working Group for Publicizing Village Affairs and for Exercising Democratic Management) rests on two provisional groups and a number of supervisors. Many tasks are taken lightly, as mere formalities with only a few items actually being recorded in Dongsheng's official public consultation logbook. Only some five lines of text were made known to the public in the first quarter of 1999. Furthermore it is difficult to gauge the public income and outgoings, as well as the official expenses of village cadres. The Dongsheng Population School only offers half-a-day courses twice a year. Nevertheless, it has a principal as well as school regulations. But the Senior Citizens' Association operates quite well, going well beyond its declared remit. Its finances are made known to the public in greater detail than those of the Villagers' Committee, on a monthly basis. And its own school is more active than the Population School.

Rural civic organizations play a predominantly positive role within rural society, though there are some exceptions. Some civic organizations, for instance, encourage the public to withhold state taxes, encourage outdated and superstitious practices, provoke clan disputes and organize armed conflicts between villages. Although nothing of the like has recently occurred in Dongsheng, neighboring villages are frequently affected. One of the most infamous examples must be the

Youche Senior Citizens' Association, inciting villagers to violently resist the county government. Such phenomena are indicative of two problems. First, they point to the pervasive influence of village clans, more influential in rural life than the Villagers' Committee or other organizations. Second, some village organizations go to dangerous lengths to protect the interests of their groups, in violation of state laws. Civic organizations in Dongsheng set a good example in handling relations between the authorities' government and the villagers, yet the clans do exert palpable influence. For example, the populous fourth and first branches of the Huang clan control almost all the village organizations. The clan's fourth branch accounts for some two-thirds of members within village organizations.

Most of the village organizations excessively rely on the leadership of the Party and rural authorities and display a rather official image. Few civic organizations are entirely divorced from the Party and government departments and, even if they are antagonistic to the latter, they tend to lack legitimacy. The Villagers' Committee, the Youth League, Women's Federation, Village Militia, Family Planning Association, Public Security Committee, the Mediation Association and other organizations in Dongsheng rely on the local and municipal Party and government departments to varying extent. Both directly control these organizations and their internal activities, requesting reports and issuing instructions. Almost all leading cadres and principal members are Party members and are thus subject to the guidance of the local Party. However, while displaying a certain air of officialdom few civic organizations go to extremes. They are legally and organizationally autonomous, and are often not even properly registered. The Dongsheng temple fair and Senior Citizens' Association are particularly independent of either local or municipal Party and government departments.

A number of organizations manage their members with excessive compulsion. In contrast to official organizations, members are meant to join and become active on a voluntary basis. Many rural organizations still lag behind in this regard. In Dongsheng, all activities organized by the Villagers' Committee are compulsory, with fines imposed in case of non-participation. For example, villagers within a stipulated age bracket have to attend classes at the Population School and join the local Family Planning Association. All adult villagers must participate in the elections for the Villagers' Committee or face fines. The "Village Regulations" issued by Villagers' Committees and the rules of the Family Planning Associations are intended as voluntary agreements, also offering corresponding rights. But we cannot find any articles for the protection of members' rights. Village Regulations for Dongsheng and the rules of the local Family Planning Association emphasize prohibitions and limitations.

Many rural civic organizations are plagued by chaotic internal management and lack of any standards. Although the Villagers' Committee, the Villagers' Representative Assembly, the village associations, the Family Planning Association and other organizations have well-defined standards, their activities are still conducted at random. The Village Regulations are meant to be the basic guideline for public behavior, but most villagers are either ignorant of these or reject them. In comparison with other villages, Dongsheng's organizations are sound, but the same problems nevertheless apply to varying degrees. With the notable exceptions of the Villagers' Committee and the Senior Citizens' Association, chaotic internal management is rife. Even the Youth League and the Village Militia, which were once tightly managed, now appear loosely organized and are no longer widely respected.

The development of rural civic organizations is uneven, and the social, political and economic influence and status between these organizations differ widely. In Dongsheng, the most influsential and respected village organizations are the Villagers' Committee and the Senior Citizens' Association, but the formerly influential Youth League, Women's Federation and Village Militia are now of very limited appeal. The main reasons for the great differences between local organizations are as follows:

1) Legal status. For example, the status and prestige of the Villagers' Committee are mainly based on the national Constitution, the Organic Law on Villagers' Committees and the relevant regulations of the CCP Central Committee;
2) Traditional culture. China has a long tradition of respect for the old and for one's ancestors. The prestige of the Senior Citizens' Association is based on such traditions;
3) Economic strength. It is hard to attract members, pursue practical matters and win support without great economic strength;
4) Influential leadership. Even if the above-mentioned conditions are met, no organization can thrive without a powerful leadership. From our survey of Dongsheng, we find that the three residents who enjoy the greatest reputation in the village are the leading cadres of the three most influential organizations: the secretary of the local Party, the village head and the president of the Senior Citizens' Association.

Central Government officials, local officials, scholars and the rural public fail to reach a consensus on the nature, functions and significance of rural civic organizations. Most opinions converge on their positive contribution toward greater democracy and rule of law in rural areas and toward the development of the rural economy, improvement of living standards, conflict mediation between peasants and the government and in maintaining rural stability. Some scholars, however, argue that civic organizations in China's countryside cannot operate independently as long as they are controlled by Party and government, becoming nothing more than their local puppets. Many grassroots cadres, however, think that village organizations are indomitable and out of control. In their eyes, these organizations, which are meant to manage villagers, act largely beyond the control of Party and government and are frequently controlled by self-serving individuals or clans, causing great harm to the collective good. In fact, such examples are not unheard of.[24]

From our case study of the village of Dongsheng, we can conclude that as a market economy is gradually being established and the political and legal environment undergoes changes, civic organizations of all descriptions inevitably emerge in China's vast rural areas. Their emergence will play a positive role in improving democracy and governance. The emergence of civic organizations symbolizes the political progress China has been experiencing following the implementation of the reform policy. However, there are problems relating to the relative lack of independence and to coercion toward members. If effective measures to tackle these problems can be taken, China's rural civic organizations will develop on a sound basis, in turn propelling good governance in China's rural areas. The suggestions presented in this chapter were put forward with this vision in mind.

We propose that the management of rural civic organizations be standardized, both by the government and internally within the organizations. National laws and regulations on their management should be revised and the Regulations on the Management of Civic organizations currently in force reformulated with great attention to detail. Training ought to be systematically provided to the principal members of rural civic organizations to safeguard members' interests, increase their authority and cohesion, publicize state laws and policies and enhance management expertise and skills. Party and state should

---

[24] See Record of Interview 990716.

create a sound environment for rural civic organizations and promote the freedom and initiative of their members. Party and state influence over rural affairs should be diminished as quickly as possible, as should the powers of village cadres and of the village Party office, while village organizations ought to be made more autonomous.

CHAPTER SIX

THE EMERGENCE OF CHINA'S CIVIL SOCIETY AND ITS SIGNIFICANCE TO GOVERNANCE[1]

Introduction: Civil Society and Good Governance

"Civil society" is a term open to interpretation. By and large, definitions fall into two categories, namely those championed by political science, and others used in sociology. Both categories define civil society as a public sphere, mainly consisting of civic organizations. The emphasis, however, is different. Political scientists emphasize society's "civil" nature, i.e., of the influence of civic organizations protecting citizens' rights and enhancing political participation and civic engagement. Sociology emphasizes the "intermediate" nature of civil society, as an intermediary between state and commerce. Civil society is thus interpreted as all civic organizations and other civil relations not determined by state or political authority. It is comprised of various non-state or other civic organizations not linked to a governing political force, including NGOs, voluntary civil and civic organizations, residential community organizations, as well as spontaneously organized interest groups and civic movements. Such organizations are also referred to as "the third sector" between government and commerce.[2]

---

[1] This article is based on the report for the research project "The Emergence of China's Civil Society and its Impact on Governance." The research was funded by the Ford Foundation and carried out by Yu Keping, Liu Junning, Wang Ying, Wang Yizhou, Sun Liping, Sun Bingyao and Deng Zhenglai.

[2] The English term "civil society" can be translated as "shimin shehui," "minjian shehui" and "gongmin shehui" in Chinese. In fact, the three Chinese terms differ in meaning, however fine the nuances. "Shimin shehui" is the most commonly used term and the classical translation of "civil society," derived from Chinese translations of the Marxist classics. Within the latter, however, the term actually has predominantly negative connotations, referring to bourgeois society. "Minjian shehui" is the translation used in Taiwan, and preferred by Chinese historians. This term is also widely used in research on China's contemporary civic organizations. Neutral in tone, some scholars and a majority of government officials treat the term with caution. "Gongmin shehui" is a recent translation, dating back to the beginning of the reform period. Used in a commendatory sense, the term emphasises the political dimension, namely citizens' political participation and checks on state power. En vogue with younger academics, most terms are actually used interchangeably.

The civil society organizations (CSOs) mentioned in this article have the following four features. First, they are non-official, i.e., "civil," and they do not represent the position of any government or state. Secondly, they are charities, not founded for the sake of making profit, but for the provision of public welfare and services. Thirdly, they are relatively independent, meaning that they have their own organizational and management mechanisms as well as independent sources of funding, and that they are thus independent from the government to some extent in terms of politics, administration and finance. Finally, they are voluntary in nature, implying that members are not compelled to join CSOs, but rather do so out of their own free will. Therefore, these organizations are also called civil voluntary organizations. As CSOs develop, they play an increasingly important role in social management. The process of social management exercised by CSOs independently or in cooperation with the government no longer belongs under the term "government," but "governance."

The basic meaning of governance refers to a governing authority's efforts to maintain order and to enhance public welfare. The objective of governance is to utilize power in order to guide, control and institutionalize citizens' activities and to maximize the public good in its various institutional expressions. From the perspective of political science, governance relates to the process of public administration. Governance provides the basis for the institutionalization of political authority, for the handling of public affairs and the management of public resources. It highlights the role of political authority and the exercising of administrative power needed to maintain social order. At a first glance, "governance" and "government" appear to be very similar, but the deeper implications are quite different. In order to distinguish between the two terms, we need to examine similarities and divergencies. Both terms express the need for authority and power, for the purpose of maintaining social order. However, there are two basic differences between the concepts.

One key difference is that governance requires authority. This authority not only rests with government departments but also to NGOs. Government always determines society through public institutions, whereas governance can act through public or private institutions, as well as through private-public partnerships. Governance requires cooperation between state and civil society, between government and extra-governmental bodies, public and private institutions and between compulsory and voluntary service. Therefore, governance is a more extensive concept than government. Modern companies, universities and even grassroots community initiatives can operate efficiently without government, but they cannot do so without governance.

Secondly, the direction of the flow of power in administration is different. Government power always emanates from above. It uses its own political authority and exercises a one-way management of public affairs by issuing orders and by formulating and implementing policies. Governance, however, chiefly exercises management of public affairs through cooperation, consultation, partnership and common interest. Its essence is defined by cooperation based on market principles, as well as the interests of the public. Management mechanisms do not rely on government authority, but on cooperation and networking. Power in relation to governance is not exclusive and imposed, but pluralistic and mutual.

The reason why political and management sciences experts advocate governance and the replacement of government by governance is due to a perceived better used in the allocation of social resources. Governance can remedy some defects of the state and the market by influencing their regulation, control and coordination, but governance is not a panacea. It cannot take the place of the state and enjoy compulsory political power. Governance cannot replace the market, allocating most of the resources spontaneously and effectively. Governance failure is not unheard of, and scholars are looking at ways of preventing or mitigating this, for the sake of more effective governance. Solutions offered by academics and international organizations include "meta-governance," "effective governance," "good governance." The "good governance" theory is most influential.

In a nutshell, good governance refers to social management aimed at maximizing the public good. The essence of good governance is the management of public life through cooperation between government and citizens, a new relationship between political power and civil society and the best possible relationship between the two. Key elements include 1) legitimacy; 2) transparency; 3) accountability; 4) the rule of law; 5) responsiveness; 6) effectiveness; 7) uprightness; 8) civic engagement/participation; 9) social justice and 10) stability.[3]

---

[3] Yu Keping, "The Model of Political Management in the Era of Globalization," *Methodology*, 1999, no. 1.

Good governance equals the return of state power to society, indicative of a high level of cooperation between state and society and between government and citizens. As far as society is concerned, there can be no good governance without the involvement of government and—especially—citizens. Smaller social groups are managed not by government, but through public scrutiny. Good governance relies on the voluntary participation by citizens and on the conscientious acceptance of authority by the latter. There can be no governance, at most good government without their active cooperation. Therefore, the basis for good governance is the citizens, i.e., civil society, rather than any government or state. Good governance in its true sense cannot prosper without a sound, developed civil society. Therefore, one of the reasons for the emergence of good governance since the 1990s, in theory and practice, is the growth of civil society, with a clear impact on the structure and status of governance. This has become explicit in China following the implementation of the reform policies.

The Reform Period and the Emergence of Civil Society

Traditionally, civil society was contained within the political state, while the emergence of a relatively independent civil society is a historically recent phenomenon. Although self-governing professional organizations existed in commerce and transportation, they were not modern civic organizations, but traditional formations, such as guilds or village associations. With the onset of a new industrialized social order in the early twentieth century, independent civic organizations began to operate. Research into quantitative aspects of such early civic organizations and into the nature of their activities has been limited. Estimates on their number hence differ greatly. Some researchers suggest that there were about one thousand civic organizations in the first half of the century, while others put the figure at over eighty thousand.[4]

After the Chinese Communist Party (CCP) came to power in 1949, it implemented an economic policy of socialist public ownership and of a planned (mandatory/command) economy. At a political level, a highly

---

[4] Wang Ying and Sun Bingyao, "Introduction to the development of Civic organiCivic organizations in China," in *The Emergence of China's Civil Society and Its Significance to Governance*, Edited by Yu Keping, Social Sciences and Academic Press of China (Zhongguo Shehui Kexue Wenxian Chubanshe), 2002, pp. 1–28.

centralized administrative system was put in place, with the Party in a pivotal position. Almost all civic organizations which emerged prior to 1949 disappeared. Long-established rural organizations, such as temple fairs, clan associations, ancestral halls, country worthy associations and civil corps evaporated.[5] Only a select few organizations continued to exist—for instance "Democratic Parties" (Minzhu Dangpai) comprising of the China Democratic League, the "September 3rd" Society and other organizations which had helped the CCP. The trade unions, the Youth League organizations and the women's federations established by the CCP developed into centralized mass organizations, though the number and diversity of these organizations was very limited. There were only 44 national "centralized mass organizations" in the early 1950s, fewer than one hundred in 1965 and only about 6,000 local ones in 1965. These could be classified into nine types of mass organization, mainly trade unions, youth leagues, women's federations, associations for science and technology, and federations of industry and commerce (Wang Ying and Sun Bingyao, 2000). Almost all centralized mass organizations were subordinate to Party and government and funded entirely by the state. The trade unions, Youth Leagues and women's federations were led by Party committees at all levels, while associations for science and technology were under the aegis of local, provincial or central government commissions for science and technology. Substantial change only occurred with the implementation of reform policies in the late 1970s.

In 1978, China began to implement reform measures under the leadership of Deng Xiaoping, bringing fundamental and far-reaching changes to China's society in their wake. Significantly, the economic, political, legal and cultural environment for the creation and development of civil society underwent fundamental changes, engendering a growth of civic organizations unparalleled in Chinese history. The market-oriented restructuring of the economy led to a gradual abandoning of the post-1949 planned economy, in favor of a socialist market economy. Concomitantly, a shift toward more diverse forms of ownership occurred, allowing for economic control by the state, collectives, individuals, joint ventures and through foreign investment. These momentous changes greatly increased productivity and raised

---

[5] Yu Keping, "The Emerging of China's Civil Society and Changes in Governance," *Chinese Social Sciences Quarterly* (Hong Kong), 1999, fall.

people's living standards. They were also to become the main impetus for the vigorous development of civic organizations.

A first basic requirement for any market economy is that enterprises must be independent from the government, autonomous in management and with full financial responsibilities. In this type of economy, with far-reaching powers for private enterprises, some professional and trade organizations can become civic organizations, largely independent from government. However, and in contrast to planned economies, a market economy also entails increased risks. Instead of relying on the government, they must bear responsibility for their profits and losses. Enterprises thus become more aware of the need to protect their own interests, while a variety of professional interest groups are given the opportunity to proliferate.

Following the implementation of market reforms, China's ownership structure began to undergo tremendous changes, witnessing the coexistence of diverse forms of ownership. Because China remains socialist in its political and economic systems, public ownership is still the basis for the national economy, with great differences in the status and roles of enterprises. Individual and private enterprises face much higher risks than their state-owned counterparts. To create an environment for fair competition, state and non-state enterprises alike require trade organizations which represent their interests. For the sake of increased competitiveness, private entrepreneurs and individual landlords in particular seek cooperation and mutual assistance through voluntary organizations, such as entrepreneurs' clubs.

Thirdly, the tremendous economic returns brought by the market reforms created the necessary conditions for the establishment and functioning of civic organizations. Most civic organizations need to raise funds on their own. In an economy where penury and a lack of power to make economic decisions prevail, it is hard for civic organizations to raise funds without official financial support. Economic development brings enormous excess profits to enterprises and increases personal disposable income. Such funds become the main source of funding for civic organizations.

Finally, the living standards of Chinese citizens have risen rapidly over the last twenty years. From 1978 to 1998, the per capita income of rural residents increased from circa RMB 133 to RMB 2,160, an actual increase of 350% after allowing for price rises, with average annual growth exceeding 8%. The per capita income of urban residents increased from some RMB 343 to RMB 5,425, an actual increase of 200% factoring in price rises, with yearly growth averaging more than 6.2%.[6] The rise in productivity has also reduced citizens' working time. A two-day weekend was introduced to urban employees as recently as in the early 1990s. As a result, more citizens have more time and financial resources to pursue their personal interests, especially through literature, arts, sports and tourism. Many civic organizations which have emerged in the last decade exemplify this trend, such as recreational clubs, sports associations, private amicable organizations and travel organizations.

In addition to the economic prerequisites, civic organizations also require a conducive and tolerant political environment. Some Western scholars have argued that China after 1978 has experienced thorough economic restructuring, but that its political system has basically remained unchanged.[7] This is a one-sided view. If these voices refer to political reform as a process of introducing a multi-party system, with separate executive, legislative and judicial powers, on the basis of Western representative democracies, we can indeed say that China's current political system has survived in its original state without substantial changes. However, "political systems" are multi-faceted. In addition to the above-mentioned features, they include legal and administrative systems, the rule of law, leadership models, electoral systems, checks and balances, the relationship between ruling party and government, between central and local authorities, etc. Accordingly, there can be little doubt that since the 1980s, China's political system has undergone tremendous changes, directly or indirectly promoting the development of civil society.

Firstly, the government has paid increasing attention to the legal system and the rule of law. According to the constitution of the People's Republic of China, citizens have freedom of association. This right forms the legal basis for civil society. Prior to the reform period, however, this constitutional guarantee was a mere scrap of paper. Without authorization from the authorities, ordinary citizens could not organize themselves into associations. Worse still, they might suffer political con-

---

[6] Information Office of the State Council, "Progress in China's Human Rights for 1998," *People's Daily*, April 14, 1999.

[7] See Barrett L. McCormick, "Democracy or Dictatorship?: A Response to Gordon White," *The Australian Journal of Chinese Affairs*, No. 31 (Jan., 1994), pp. 95–110; or Bruce J. Dickson, "China's Democratization and the Taiwan Experience," *Asian Survey*, Vol. 38, No. 4 (Apr., 1998), pp. 349–364.

sequences. As a result, applications were rare and all civic organizations highly integrated into Party and government departments. Subsequent reforms have emphasized the legal system and the rule of law, as the basis for state policy and public administration. The right to freely form associations has thus been fulfilled to some extent. If citizens apply to establish non-political civic organizations, they have every chance to escape political pressure and to see their applications approved.

Secondly, the government has delegated many powers to lower levels. In a political sense, we can say that the process of political and economic reform over the past twenty years has seen a shift from high integration between state and society to gradual disintegration, leading the government to delegate powers to society. First, the functions of government were separated from those of enterprises. The government delegated business management and decision-making powers (also over personnel matters) to enterprises, and most economic powers to society. Then, the central government began to delegate powers to local governments at all levels, which attained more powers ranging from cadre management, administration, social management and political and economic policy-making to taxation, finance and banking. The last stage saw the gradual lifting of controls over the management of citizens, with an unprecedented increase in associational freedom. Following the gradual delegation of powers to society, the state needed to retain an effective grip on society and citizens alike to maintain social order. Where government had receded from management, civic organizations filled the void. For example, the Central Committee of the CCP decided from the mid-1980s that village leaders should no longer be appointed by the Party and by government departments at higher levels, and that rural autonomy was to be implemented. Quite obviously, autonomy could not be imposed, but had to grow from self-governing organizations. Hence the villagers' committees emerged, becoming the principal civic organization in China's rural areas.

Thirdly, the government began to change its role. China's society prior to the 1980s resembled a patriarchal family. Government at all levels played the parental role, and citizens the part of children, the parent being responsible for the future development of the children and their livelihood. A panoply of departments and overstaffing caused problems. Since the 1980s, China's leaders have tried to streamline government departments and to restructure their roles. These reforms have generated useful lessons, and one point has become clear: the roles of government have undergone great changes. Its economic and social functions have been weakened, while its administrative profile has increased. The government no longer manages production, business operation, civil affairs, culture, art and academic research, but rather entrusts relevant civic organizations, for instance non-governmental professional associations, as well as commercial and voluntary organizations, with this purpose.

Because of the above-mentioned economic and political changes brought about by the reform measures, China's civil society began to grow rapidly and reached a peak during the 1980s. In 1989, China-wide civil organizations increased sharply to 1,600, while local ones numbered over 200,000. After the political disturbances in Beijing of 1989, the Chinese government forced civic organizations to re-register and the number of CSOs decreased slightly for a short while. In 1992 there were 1,200 national and about 180,000 local associations. But soon the number of civic organizations increased once again. In 1997, civil organizations at and above county level came to over 180,000 throughout the country, including 21,404 provincial and 1,848 national ones.[8] There is no formal statistical data about the various civic organizations below county level, but these are reputed to be in excess of three million according to conservative estimates.[9] Other than civic organizations, another type of special CSO developed in China following the implementation of reforms: the so-called civilian-run non-enterprise units—in other words, civil service institutions. They do not receive financial support from the state, and maintain their operations by providing paid services to the public. However, according to regulations, these organizations cannot seek to make profits. According to preliminary estimates, in 1998 such organizations numbered more than 700,000.[10]

There are no set standards for the classification of civil service organizations. The government departments, responsible for their management, classify them into four categories. Firstly, academic organizations engaged in research in the natural and social sciences and interdisciplinary studies; secondly, professional business organizations; thirdly, specialized social organizations staffed by professionals, established

---

[8] *The Yearbook of China's Civil Affairs for 1999*, Ministry of Civil Affairs, China Social Publishing House (Zhongguo Shehui Chubanshe).

[9] Yu Keping, "Civic organiCivic organizations and Changes of Governance in Rural China: A Case Study of Dongsheng Village, Changqiao Town, Zhangpu County, Fujian Province," Chinese Social Sciences Quarterly (Hong Kong), 2000, summer.

[10] *The Yearbook of China's Civil Affairs for 1999*, Ministry of Civil Affairs, China Social Publishing House (Zhongguo Shehui Chubanshe).

for specific purposes and relying on specialized skills and technology as well as special funds; finally, common interest associations, such as trade unions. In 1996, these four categories embraced 680 (38%), 410 (23%), 520 (29%) and 180 (10%) national civic organizations, respectively.[11]

Some scholars classify according to area plus function. Accordingly, there are eighteen national civic organizations at present, including industrial associations (Wang Ying and Sun Bingyao, 1999). For example associations for:

- specialized professions and management
- social services and welfare, e.g., foundations and charities
- public affairs, such as mayors' and exchange associations
- information and technical services, e.g., consultation and consumers' associations
- public health associations, for instance for medical services
- physical culture and sports
- education, such as educational service organizations
- culture and art, e.g., film and music associations
- press and publication, such as radio and television associations
- science and technology, e.g., popular science organizations
- the study of natural sciences
- humanities and social sciences
- environment and energy
- specialized professions
- vocational groups, e.g., trade associations
- regional groupings
- individual initiatives, such as interest groups and neighborhood associations
- miscellaneous others

Civic organizations can be classified according to varying standards, for example, status of the subject, functions or regional origin. However, the most important features of the organizations which have emerged can be categorized as thus:

---

[11] Wu Zhongze, "Management of Civic organiCivic organizations," China Social Publishing House (Zhongguo Shehui Chubanshe), 1996, p. 6.

1. Trade organizations, that is, professional associations representing a shared trade. These do not provide legal management but provide guidance in matter pertaining to their trade. These include chambers of commerce and associations for manufacturing, the supply of materials and goods and marketing.
2. Professional management organizations. Organizations of this category are a special product of social transition. Their predecessors are mostly administrative government departments or professional bodies. These organizations are well versed in management and resemble quasi-administrative departments. Examples include the Chinese Light Industry Association, the Chinese Textile General Association, the Chinese Trade Association for the Promotion of Import and Export.
3. Charity organizations, whose main role is social relief. Examples are the Red Cross Society of China, the All-China Charitable Society, the China Welfare Fund for the Handicapped, etc.
4. Academic organizations, i.e., organizations for scholars, such as the China Physics Society, the China Chemical Society, the Chinese Society for Political Science, the China Atheism Society, etc.
5. Residential community organizations. Their main feature is to engage in community management and services. These can include autonomous village organizations, independent resident organizations and community security committees.
6. Professional interest groups, such as associations working for the professional interests of business people, teachers or lawyers.
7. Citizens' self-help groups, mutual aid organizations organized voluntarily to safeguard citizens' interests. They exist in cities and in villages, providing concrete help or insight into agrarian production.
8. Interest organizations representing citizens' hobbies. Often clubs, such as poets' or dramatists' clubs.
9. Non-profit organizations for consulting services. Many are charities belonging to civic organizations.[12]

Thus, we have established that political reform and the introduction of market principles resulted directly in a sharp increase in the number and types of civic organizations. More importantly, the nature of

---

[12] Yu Keping, "The Emerging of China's Civil Society and Changes in Governance," Chinese Social Sciences Quarterly (Hong Kong), 1999, fall.

these new civic organizations is quite different from that of the "civic organizations" which existed prior to reform. The self-governance and legitimacy of such civic organizations have been greatly augmented since the 1980s. Let us now take a closer look at the relationship between civil society and the state, and at the far-reaching changes which have taken place.

China's Civil Society and the Party-State

The CCP gains its understanding of civil society through a process of negation and affirmation. Prior to the implementation of the reform policies, civic organizations were denied by the CCP, as well as by the Chinese government under its guidance, under the premise that independent civil society could not emerge in a socialist China. A mandatory economic structure and a centralized political system do not allow for the existence of a relatively independent civil society. As China's leaders often like to remind us, many things occur independently of man's will. This is also true of the emergence of civil society in China. As mentioned above, in the changing economic and political environment following the reforms, a relatively independent civil society has been inexorably forming, exerting an increasingly important influence on China's politics, economy and culture. This phenomenon ought to convince China's leaders to face up to reality, by changing their negative attitude toward civil society, and by recognizing its legitimacy and its increasingly important role in society, politics and economic life. Effective measures encouraging the sound development of China's civil society would thus seem natural.

Prior to the reforms, civil society was nigh illegal, and "civic organization," "civil society," "civilian society" and "citizens' society" had become politically sensitive phrases. China implemented a highly centralized political system of administration and leadership. Public and private interest, state and society, government and citizen almost merged into a single whole. Against this political background, "civil society" became "bourgeois society," and "civil society" or "civilian society" was seen as antagonistic to socialist government.

Since then, however, a large number of relatively independent civic organizations have emerged, and people are taking note. Civil society has become a public buzzword. On the other hand, as the economic structure and political system are undergoing changes, profound transformations are taking place in China's political culture. People are gradually abandoning traditional views of political ideology and values and replacing them with a new political ideology. At the same time, attitudes toward civil society or citizens' society are also undergoing fundamental changes—from complete rejection of civil society to open acceptance. The reason why "Project Hope," a major initiative by the China Youth Development Foundation providing poor children with access to education, could win the extensive support of the whole society is that it benefits to a large extent from the increased legitimacy of civic organizations.[13] An academic discourse on civil society has existed since the 1990s, rendering the concept legitimate at a scholarly level. In June 1998 the "Department for the Management of Civic organizations" was officially renamed to the "Bureau for the Management of Civic organizations," implying that civic organizations are now officially legitimized by the government.

Accordingly, Party and government have lifted all prohibitive policies vis-à-vis CSOs. In September 1950 the Government Administration Council (the predecessor of the State Council) promulgated the "Interim Regulations on Registration of Civic organizations," followed in 1951 by the "Detailed Rules for Implementation of the Regulations" (Ministry of Internal Affairs). The two regulations were designed to appraise civic organizations which had originated prior to 1949, ban those which did not meet the revolutionary requirements, while transforming "progressive" associations. After the task was fulfilled, the two regulations were gradually abandoned. Government departments were put in charge of the examination, approval and management processes, and the system of centralized registration was no longer implemented. This policy was to stifle the development of civic organizations (Liu Junning, 2000).[14]

After reform measures had been implemented, the State Council promulgated in 1989 the "Regulations on the Administration and Registration of Civic organizations" in order to react to the sharp increase in civic organizations. In October 1998 the State Council made extensive revisions to the above regulations and issued the "Regulations on the Administration and Registration of Civic organizations." At the same time, it promulgated the first ever "Regulations on Management of Civic

---

[13] Sun Liping, "Public Welfare NGOs and Governance: The Case of 'Project Hope,'" in *The Emergence of China's Civil Society and Its Significance to Governance*, Edited by Yu Keping, Social Sciences and Academic Press of China (Zhongguo Shehui Kexue Wenxian Chubanshe), 2002, pp. 67–94.

[14] Liu, Junning, "Civil Society and Limited Government—A Case Study of China's Chambers of Commerce" (Research Report).

charities." Because there had not been any official legislation regarding civic organizations in China, the above-mentioned regulations are extremely important, determining the current framework for the official management of civic organizations. A change of the system regarding civic organizations was implemented after 1949 in favor of a system of dual leadership by the government departments responsible for civil affairs and affiliated Party units. The government departments are in charge of registration, while the routine management rests with both Party and government units. This system is referred to as "registration at different levels and dual management."

The model stipulates that the relevant departments and units:

- approve the appointment of leading cadres, including presidents, vice-presidents, executive directors and secretary-generals
- assess and approve key activities
- supervise routine work and provide professional guidance
- audit finances

The major functions of the government departments for civil affairs are to

- formulate the principles, policies and regulations for the management of civic organizations and civic charities, and supervise their implementation
- be responsible for the registration and yearly assessment of domestic civic organizations (including those established in mainland China by compatriots from Hong Kong, Macao and Taiwan), including civic charities, foreign civic organizations and offices of international NGOs
- provide guidance to the activities of civic organizations, as well as engage in research and planning concerning the development of civic organizations, membership policies and methods of financial management
- supervise the activities of civic organizations and investigate and deal with illegal acts by civic organizations as well as unregistered illegal organizations conducting activities in the name of civic organizations[15]

---

[15] Regulations on the Administration and Registration of Civic organiCivic organizations, State Council, October 1998.

In addition to the above-mentioned, Party and government have adopted two other measures to manage civic organizations. Firstly, by establishing Party organizations within the latter. Permeating China's society with Party cells has been CCP policy since the early 1950s. China's Red Cross Society, for instance, has permanent representatives of Party, trade unions and Youth League (Wang Ying and Sun Bingyao, 2002). A second measure has been to control operating funds. Presently, funds of civic organizations are derived from three possible sources: either through full government funding, through government-private co-financing or by raising all funds by private means. The state furnishes most funds of influential civic organizations such as the Chinese Disabled Persons' Federation, the Chinese Enterprise Management Association, the Chinese Association for Science and Technology, the Chinese Society of Administrative Management, trade unions, the Youth League organizations and the women's federations. However, the number of civic organizations which still fully rely on the state financially is small, the majority raising funds through membership dues, donations, income from non-profit services and other sources. Civic charities receive no funds from the government, and fund their activities by providing services to society. However, they do receive tax breaks. For example, they are allowed to engage in paid consultancy and non-commercial service activities, in exchange for partial or total exemption of taxes.

The above management system is epitomized by a general acceptance of Party and government leadership, while asserting the internal autonomy of the civic organizations. The former is both a mandatory provision and motivated, to a certain extent, out of the organizations' self-interest, namely in order to obtain funds and administrative leverage. There are therefore few civic organizations that decline to cooperate with state and Party. Civic organizations usually take the initiative by requesting advice from the relevant departments on major problems, by reporting back to them, often cementing the leadership of the authorities in their statutes. The rules of the All-China Chamber of Commerce, for instance stipulate that it is a civic organization under the leadership of the CCP, that the establishment of chambers of commerce at all levels has to be scrutinized by the leading bodies of the Party and the government at all levels and that any major activities must conform to Party and governmental provisions (Liu Junning, 2000).

However, it must be stressed that since the 1980s, organizations have been moving away from central control, with the notable exceptions of the traditional trade unions, Youth League organizations and the women's federations, plus a few special associations committed to organizational subordination. A growing body of grassroots organizations enjoy extensive autonomy. These include professional associations, chambers of commerce and community organizations, not to mention spontaneously established civil organizations. Organizations not registered with the authorities have no legitimacy. Moreover, new legal regulations actually require civic organizations to be independent of Party and government in terms of their leadership. According to opinions formulated by the Central Committee of the CCP,[16] Party and government officials cannot serve as leaders of civic organizations, including civic charities. However, as we will see later, these regulations tend not to be adhered to, in the case of many trade unions, Youth League organizations and women's federations.

Civic organizations proactively engaged toward greater independence include the China Youth Development Foundation, established by the Central Committee of the Communist Youth League of China (CYLC) and led by the League's Central Committee in terms of organization, leadership and professional work. However, as soon as the Foundation was established, its leaders did everything possible to increase its independence. It eventually obtained the right to directly control its operations at the local level and has a relatively independent management structure (Sun Liping, 2000). To summarize, civic organizations' obedience to Party and state contravenes their independence. This contradiction determines the relationship between China's civic organizations and the authority of Party and state.

Other than funding arrangements, and the relative degree of control and independence, a third area of interaction between civic organizations and Party and state is over policy. Firstly, civic organizations attempt to influence the Party and the state to revise current policies or formulate new ones, in order to maximize their own interests. Local and professional organizations, both in cities and in the villages, often take direct action in order to make their concerns heard, for instance by

---

[16] "The General Office of the Central Committee of the Chinese Communist Party and the General Office of the State Council issued notices to require leading cadres of Party and government departments not to concurrently serve as leaders of civic organicivic organizations," *China's Policies for 1999* (Volume II), China Policy Research Group, China Building Material Industry Publishing House (Zhongguo Jiancai Gongye Chubanshe), 1999, p. 2089.

presenting petitions, canvassing, organizing sit-ins, marches and demonstrations around Party and government buildings. In doing so, they put pressure on the relevant authorities to solve policy-related issues touching upon the immediate interests of local residents, in matters of eviction, security concerns, pollution, unemployment and poor public services. This has been analyzed for the Market for Farm and Sideline Products at Quxi Road in Wuliqiao Street, Shanghai (Wang Ying, 2000),[17] as well as for the chambers of commerce (Liu Junning, 2000). Secondly, more and more civic organizations and especially those dominated by intellectuals, try to influence national policy-making. For example, in recent years, the Tianze Research Institute of Economics, the Friends of Nature and the "Three-Flavours" Study (an intellectual organization which held discussions or lectures periodically among scholars) offer concrete suggestions on issues concerning China's economy, politics, diplomacy and environment (Wang Yizhou, 2000).[18]

The Emergence of Civil Society and of Good Governance

China's economic and political restructuring has created a conducive political, economic and legal environment for the creation of a civil society. At the same token, its emergence has been influencing social politics and economic activities, effectively promoting good governance. Good governance has been of particular benefit to general political participation and self-governance, while the government has become more honest, efficient and democratic.

In China's traditional political culture, superiors set an important example for their subjects. In tandem with government organs, civic organizations engage with the issue of governance. Their success or failure thus has a direct bearing on the governance of society as a whole. The reason for this lies in the many distinctive features and practical advantages setting civic organizations apart from government

---

[17] Wang Ying, "Self-Governance for City Residents and Changes in Community Management Styles," in *The Emergence of China's Civil Society and Its Significance to Governance*, Edited by Yu Keping, Social Sciences and Academic Press of China (Zhongguo Shehui Kexue Wenxian Chubanshe), 2002, pp. 95–123.

[18] Wang Yizhou, "Domestic Progress and Foreign Policy in China," in *The Emergence of China's Civil Society and Its Significance to Governance*, Edited by Yu Keping, Social Sciences and Academic Press of China (Zhongguo Shehui Kexue Wenxian Chubanshe), 2002, pp. 150–188.

organizations. The high degree of change China's society is undergoing has also affected China's civil society, albeit to differing degrees. Civic organizations resembling government organs tend to exercise weak governance, while others are exceptionally strong.

More independent-minded bodies, such as the senior citizens' associations or community organizations, tend to enjoy a higher degree of pride and membership participation than organizations of a more official nature, such as the Youth League or women's federations. The Youth League, for instance, acted as the Party's "assistant" in various political functions prior to reforms. Its degree of internal identity and participation was originally very high, but its role declined during the reorientation of society toward economic development. The state's financial support increased at such a slow rate that the Youth League is often short of funds. At the same time, members became more inert and the organizational drive greatly reduced, at times to the point of paralysis. The China Youth Development Foundation, a product of Youth League reform efforts, enjoys on the contrary a high degree of internal self-identification and participation. Participants often take the initiative regarding auditing the budget and offer their views on various aspects. Some participate actively, becoming involved even in its management, organization and policy-making. Their involvement in Project Hope, sponsored by the China Youth Development Foundation greatly motivated its development (Sun Liping, 2000).

Many civic organizations do better with regards to internal transparency. This is particularly true of those civic organizations active at grassroots level, such as the villagers' committees and senior citizens' associations. Villagers' committees and urban neighborhood committees are greatly conducive to making information known to the public, while their political transparency is much higher than that of grassroots organizations with political power. The election process for villagers' and neighborhood committees, as well as their activities, income and expenses are also made public knowledge. In Shanghai, cadres of neighborhood committees must display employee cards while at work. Every neighborhood committee must publicize the affairs, documents, procedures, deadlines, responsible persons and other relevant items on wall posters, ensuring that residents are clear about all these at a glance (Wang Ying, 2000).

In Dongsheng Village, Fujian Province, information revealed to the public includes the wages, bonuses and subsidies of village cadres, the income and expenses of the collectives, but also measures of family planning, the contracting of arable land, ponds, orchards, mountain forests and enterprises. Also included are the bids for construction projects, distribution of land for housing, land requisitioning and compensatory payments and voluntary labor. Finally, the finances for planning, grain tax revenues, the distribution of relief materials and machinery, the use of anti-poverty funds and items of practical concern. Most is made known to the public twice a year, namely during the first ten days of January and July, respectively. Major items, such as the contracting of land and enterprises, bidding for projects and requisitioning of land can be publicized at any time, while other important issues such as family planning or the income and expenses of the collective are advertised on a monthly or quarterly basis.

There are two methods of communicating village affairs to the public. Firstly, by posters affixed to the walls of the villagers' committee, or through blackboard bulletins. Secondly, through local radio broadcasts. In addition, "suggestion boxes" are installed at cardinal points to solicit opinions about village affairs.

An important consequence of the high internal transparency of such local organizations is, at least compared to the rather grave situation of high-level corruption, that the leadership is perceived as "clean." The ascent of villagers' organizations effectively checks corruption at township and village levels. The finances and politics of the village being relatively transparent, villagers can exercise effective supervision over cadres. In Dongsheng Village, important economic activities such as enterprise contracting, land requisitioning and the use and distribution of land for housing are supervised by specially designated people. Hence, even if someone wanted to engage in corruption, this would be far from an easy undertaking. In the past, urban cadres came to the village at the time of the fruit harvest regardless of whether there were any matters to attend to, and were paid off with fruit by village cadres. This cannot occur nowadays because all orchards have been contracted out to individuals. Specific villagers' groups responsible for financial affairs are now responsible for examining public finances and for communicating results and accounts to the public. Bodies such as the villagers' representative assembly, the local Party branch and the working group for public information and democratic management also have this right. Villagers can consult the above organizations and even offer anonymous reports (Yu Keping, 2000).

Another distinctive feature of civic organizations is their pronounced democratic governance. Most community organizations in urban areas choose their leaders by election, at least pro forma. Such organizations include the neighborhood committees, volunteers' associations, landlords' committees, the communal environment-protection team, societies for working people in culture and sport, community education committees, senior citizens' study associations, family education guidance teams, villagers' committees, associations for the talented, those for science and technology and senior citizens' associations. Civic organizations both in urban and in rural areas consider free election as increasingly important. Second, civic organizations are in the habit of regularly sampling the opinions of their members to underpin policy decisions and secure membership approval. Civic organizations generally have clear provisions on member consultation, in particular for matters of major importance. State laws further stipulate that major affairs concerning residents and villagers must be discussed and put to through plebiscite or at village meetings. Thirdly, civic organizations usually have well-established systems for rigorous internal supervision. In Shanghai, for instance, such regulatory devices include a local residents' conference designed to consult, examine and advise the work of the neighborhood committee. Furthermore, a public consultation process exists for all community affairs. Community supervisors, the systematic supervision of the metropolitan government and a public telephone, mail and visiting system complete these two control methods (Wang Ying, 2000). Some rural organizations also have supervision mechanisms, ensuring that their leaders work honestly. For example, the senior citizens' association in Dongsheng Village publicizes membership contributions, fees and other financial matters through wall posters and the provision of clear original records accounting for every single coin. Its finance group consists of four members, whose main responsibility it is to manage financial affairs and to supervise the financial activities of their leading cadres. All expenses of the association are subject to strict examination and approval. Major expenses must be decided on by means of collective discussion (Yu Keping, 2000).

The internal management of civic organizations is of great significance to good governance. More importantly, it benefits political life on a whole, promoting political participation, democratic policy-making, civic autonomy and efforts to publicize government affairs and to produce clean and honest government.

China's civic organizations are increasing in number and are becoming an important bridge between government and citizens. The essence of good governance is good cooperation between the government and citizens, but this cooperation is not always direct. On the contrary, it often requires coordination by intermediate organizations. Civic organizations have precisely this function, by conveying their members' suggestions and criticisms to the government and by communicating government's policies to their members. Thus, civic organizations promote cooperation between the government and citizens and, ultimately, good governance.

Civic organizations not only call on their members to take an active part in internal matters, but also to actively engage in the political activities of the state. Our case study shows that members of civic organizations participate more actively in social politics than ordinary citizens do. This is not only true of grassroots organizations in urban areas, but for instance of the villagers' committees, mobilizing their members to participate in the election of people's deputies for sub-county assemblies and for villagers' committees. Some localities even resort to mild coercion, for example by offering material encouragement and by issuing subsidies to those villagers who participate in the voting, while imposing fines or forced labor on those who do not take part. Civic organizations also go out of their way to make elections convenient, for instance by setting up mobile polling stations or ballot boxes, to the effect that voter participation can surpass 95%. Civic organizations also have a place in state power and in political administration. This is typically the case with organizations maintaining particularly close ties with the government. In particular, the federations of industry and commerce, the Youth League, women's federations, trade unions, family planning associations, senior citizens' associations and some professional associations have their representatives participate in the People's Congress and at all levels of the legislative process. In addition, the presidents of the federations of industry and commerce usually serve as vice-chairmen of CPPCC organizations (Chinese People's Political Consultative Conference) at all levels.

Some civic organizations have since the 1980s succeeded in shaping government policies, becoming a motivating force for promoting administrative reforms. Academic associations in particular can contribute with a wealth of professional knowledge. An increasing number of professional associations are serving as government think tanks, exerting an important influence on policy-making and promoting democratic processes. Inducing the government to introduce reforms requires both internal and external motivating forces—the former rests on the Party and government themselves, while the latter originates from individual citizens and civic organizations.

In a sense, a civic organization is a kind of pressure group, aiming to promote the interests of its members. As a means to this end the organization participates in policy-making, trying to influence the policies of Party and government for their own benefit. At present, civic organizations employ the following methods of influencing government policy-making:

1. They report problems and make requests to decision-making units on behalf of their organizations or professional bodies and urge the organs of state power to formulate corresponding policies and to take concrete measures. Recent organizations for environmental protection, the so-called "four big green parties" (Friends of Nature, Global Village, Green Home and the Shannuo Society), are engaged in the protection of the natural environment, propagating environmental protection, criticizing eco-crimes and offering advice on environmental protection. Because of their influence, environmental protection has become a major issue at the NPC (National People's Congress) and the CPPCC, held once a year (Wang Yizhou, 2000).

2. At the request of the legislative authorities, the CSOs put forward their views on the formulation and implementation of specific policies. Before formulating or implementing such policies, Party and government seek extensive advice. For example, before the Constitution was revised at the First Session of the Ninth National People's Congress, expert opinion on the revision of certain articles was urgently required. Because the articles to be revised related to non-public sectors of the economy, the NPC, the Party and government organs paid particular attention to the views of the chambers of commerce, which studied and discussed the articles with great scrutiny. They eventually succeeded in communicating their heartfelt desire that the status of non-public enterprises be raised in the revised constitution and in related economic directives. The Nanjing chamber of commerce thus eloquently summarized commercial aspirations in its Seven Hopes (Liu Junning, 2000).

3. When government policies impair the interests of their members, they negotiate with the relevant authorities. The landlords' committees in some parts of Shanghai have, on a few occasions, demanded

compensation for losses caused to their members through demolitions. Through reports and appeals, the residents' group of Zhayin Road No. 1 Neighborhood Committee finally solved three outstanding problems, namely the repair of the road at 60th Lane, Zhayin Road, the removal of the LPG station, and the location of bus route no. 90. These achievements generated widespread admiration (Wang Ying, 2000).

A major step for China's political development since the 1980s has been the promotion of grassroots autonomy. This policy is at present implemented on a trial basis in mainly three areas: autonomy in villages, urban communities and in the professions. Their implementation rests with the villagers' committees, neighborhood committees and various professional associations, respectively. Civic organizations thus provide an organizational basis for grassroots democracy and, in particular, social autonomy.

According to the provisions laid down by the Constitution, the Organic Law on Neighborhood Committees in the People's Republic of China and the Organic Law on Villagers' Committees in the People's Republic of China, urban neighborhood committees and villagers' committees are not first-level organs of political power or the extension of government, but civil and self-governing organizations. A neighborhood committee is an autonomous grassroots mass organization for the autonomous management, education and the provision of services among community residents in the city. According to the law, the major tasks of the neighborhood committee are to:

- publicize the Constitution, laws, regulations and state policies
- safeguard the legitimate rights and interests of residents, and teach them to perform their duties in accordance with the law
- protect public property
- actively promote socialist ideological and ethical progress
- handle public affairs and public welfare for residents
- mediate in civil disputes
- help maintain public security
- assist the government and its offices in public health, family planning, special care and relief and education among young residents
- report the opinions, requests and suggestions of residents back to the government and its offices (Wang Ying, 2000)

Villagers' committees are the most important civic organizations in China's countryside. In fact, it is gradually replacing the Party as the most authoritative administrative unit. Again, according to the law, the Villagers' committee is the villagers' grassroots organization for the autonomous management, education and provision of services. Villagers' committees are not answerable to local governments, but very much so to the villagers' conference. Their main responsibilities are to:

- manage all village affairs for the public good
- mediate in civil disputes
- help safeguard public security
- organize and lead villagers in developing the economy
- take the initiative in providing services and coordinating village production
- protect the legitimate rights and interests of collectively-owned enterprises, villagers, contractors, joint households and businessmen from other areas
- manage the land and other property collectively owned by villagers, providing advice with regard to the responsible use of natural resources and the protection of the environment
- publicize the Constitution, laws, regulations and state policies, urging villagers to perform their obligations according to the law and to protect public property
- help villagers in their active pursuit of ideological and cultural progress
- report villagers' opinions, requests and suggestions to the local government

Urban neighborhood committees and rural villagers' committees invariably do not play a great role in grassroots democracy and self-governance, pursuant to the above-mentioned laws. However, our research has found that both urban and rural grassroots communities are increasingly relying on such civic organizations in order to improve democratic self-governance (Yu Keping, 2000).

Civic organizations also serve as an important medium for raising political transparency, and their proliferation has exerted a positive influence with regard to this in recent years, primarily by encouraging political openness. This requires perseverance and the willingness to put pressure on the government. In China's vast countryside, the only possible channel for villagers' opinions to cadres in the village, township or town is the villagers' groups. Secondly, some civic organizations act as media for diffusing political information. A variety of research societies, federations and associations organize conferences and training courses to discuss political information, often the most important means of obtaining political information. Thirdly, some civic organizations establish their own mass media, in print or through the internet. Finally, independent bookstores which emerged after the reforms greatly increased the availability of information and the mechanisms for its diffusion.[19]

Civic organizations also take an active part in social welfare, improving the government's image and enhancing citizens' political self-awareness. It is the government's responsibility to develop public welfare, but state-organized welfare may not produce the best results. Civic organizations play an indispensable role in this respect. For example, they outperform the government in providing relief and counseling services, and in providing assistance to women, children, the old, weak, poor and disabled. The All-China Society of Charity and the Soong Ching Ling Foundation are cases in point, while the China Youth Development Foundation sponsors Project Hope and the Anti-Poverty Project, providing education to poor children and relief to victims of disasters and poverty. In doing so the organizations improve their own social image, ease relations between the government and citizens, thus increasing the latter's identification with the state. Project Hope is an excellent example in this respect. It is a large-scale public welfare undertaking sponsored by the China Youth Development Foundation, enabling poverty-stricken children to attend school. The project provides assistance to millions of poor children and enjoys a tremendous social reputation. The initiators, the China Youth Development Foundation were formed by the Central Committee of the Communist Youth League of China (CYLC). Otherwise badly affected by the transformations toward a market economy, the Youth League's image was greatly improved by the China Youth Development Foundation and Project Hope (Sun Liping, 2000).

Civic organizations effectively check government behavior and power. Prior to the reforms, internal checks existed, but as more and more civic organizations emerged, the government began to introduce external supervision. Some civic organizations have found that some government policies surreptitiously or openly violate state laws, thus resisting

---

[19] Deng Zhenglai, "Civil Society and Reconstruction of National Knowledge Governance System," 2000, (Research Report).

such policies through organized protest. In many cases, the government has succumbed to such pressure, in particular if emanating from more powerful organizations. Fewer violations of the law and reduced indiscipline by local officials in villages with effective villagers' committees prove this point (Yu Keping, 2000). Non-governmental organizations also exert influence over international affairs.

Conclusion

Summary of Features of China's Civil Society

As noted at the beginning of this chapter, civic organizations have in common that they are non-governmental, charitable, autonomous and voluntary. These features are shared by organizations in China and in other countries. Such civic organizations are an important feature of contemporary Chinese society, following the political experiments between 1949 and 1976. However, obvious differences between China's civic organizations and those in Western countries exist, outlined in the following:

1. China's civil society is typically government-led, characterized by public-private duality

According to government regulations, any civic organization to be registered must be affiliated to a relevant Party or government unit. Although smaller, often unregistered CSOs enjoy a great deal of independence, a distinctive feature of China's civil society is that most major civic organizations above country level are well established and influenced by the government. This is particularly true of legally registered organizations representing the professions, commerce, academia and special interests. Although they are separating gradually, in organizational terms, from their official mentors, there are still close ties between the two. Many professional associations, for instance, are supervised by government departments, in terms of organization, personnel, operating funds and activities. In addition, their membership sections are managed by affiliated government departments rather than by the associations themselves.[20]

---

[20] Sun Bingyao, "Professional Associations and Civil Self-Governance in the Economic Field," in *The Emergence of China's Civil Society and Its Significance to Governance,*

As the ultimate organ of political power, the Party is responsible for the political leadership of the civic organizations. The China Youth Development Foundation, for instance, was established and is led by the Central Committee of the Communist Youth League of China (CYLC). Its leading cadres must be appointed or transferred by its Central Committee, and all major activities must be approved by the latter (Sun Liping, 2000). The Chinese chambers of commerce are also masterminded by the government, their personnel having the status of public servants. Just like government departments, they accommodate Party units, and their officials are appointed by Party organizations. Ranks, wages and benefits are determined on the pay scale of civil servants, and their personnel is transferrable between the chambers of commerce, the Party and government ministries (Liu Junning, 2000).

On the issue of leadership, the CCP and the Chinese government try to increase the autonomy of civic organizations, repeatedly issuing stipulations that the cadres of Party and government on duty cannot concurrently hold leading positions within civic organizations and charities. Civic organizations moreover require their presidents and vice-presidents to be elected by their councils. In reality, however, non-officials seldom serve as presidents, with former Party and government officials, retired or removed from government departments after institutional restructuring, serving as major management figures in almost all major civic organizations. An example at hand is the former Minister of the State Economic Commission, who served as President of the Second National Council of the China Industrial Economics Association, formerly director of the Municipal Economic Committee and president of the Shanghai Municipal Industrial Economics Association (Sun Bingyao, 2000). In parallel fashion, retired secretaries of rural Party branches or village heads often serve as presidents of powerful villagers' organizations such as the senior citizens' association (Yu Keping, 2000).

According to government regulations, civic organizations should in principle raise their own funds, but, as we have demonstrated, in prominent cases still receive operating funds from the government. Generally speaking, civic organizations authorized by the government are also financially supported by the government. This rule of thumb goes for

---

Edited by Yu Keping, Social Sciences and Academic Press of China (Zhongguo Shehui Kexue Wenxian Chubanshe), 2002, pp. 124–149.

almost all professional associations established by the government, such as the Chinese Association of Popular Science Writers, the China Law Society, Chinese Society of Administrative Management, China Federation of Literary and Art Circles, the Chinese Dramatists Association, as well as for professional associations (China Industrial Economics Association, China National Light Industry Council, etc.) and the chambers of commerce. Other important organizations, including academic associations, also receive at least some government funds.

As can be seen from the above, civil society in China is currently vastly influenced by the government, in particular the large and influential civic organizations. Chinese civic organizations are more dependent on governments than their Western counterparts.

2. *China's CSOs are incipient and in transition*

In comparison with civic organizations in Western countries, China's are still immature, and far from being autonomous, voluntary and non-governmental. Most of the civic organizations exist since the mid-1980s, and have hence had a relatively short history. They are still undergoing change and development, and are not fixed in terms of structure and functions. In theory all civic organizations are supposed to sever official ties with Party and government, but on the other hand, the government controls their important activities. In contrast to these heavily state-influenced organizations, independent, civic organizations are organized spontaneously by citizens, without registering with the government or accepting its leadership and guidance. The latter enjoy a high degree of autonomy and independence. The development of civic organizations reflects the process of social transition on a whole, in particular concerning China's civil society.

3. *In conformity with the above features, China's CSOs are not institutionalized*

Although the Ministry of Civil Affairs revised existing and promulgated new regulations on the management of civic organizations in 1998, the process of institutionalization has barely begun. At present, there are several categories of civic organizations:

i) Highly hierarchical civic organizations, such as trade unions, the Youth League organizations and women's federations. Actually, there are no essential differences between these civic organizations and administrative departments. They are not bound by the Regulations on the Administration and Registration of Civic organizations, but are directly led by the Party and government departments. They mirror all administrative levels and the appointment or dismissal of their leading officers is decided on by Party committees at corresponding levels.

ii) Relatively hierarchical civic organizations, such as the federations of industry and commerce, consumers' associations and those for professional management. They have authorized staff numbers, administrative hierarchy and perform some administration management. The leading officers are appointed and dismissed by Party and government at all levels, enjoying the privileges of CCP or state cadres.

iii) Civil, academic and civic organizations, for example research societies. Most do without sizeable full-time personnel, administrative hierarchies and do not enjoy the benefits of having official links. Leading officers are chosen and accountable to the members.

iv) Civic charities. A special category of civic organizations, with almost no hierarchical structures. Charities such as the Chinese Academy of Management, the Chinese Institute of Development and the Chinese Academy of Culture engage in research and exchange projects, but also provide specialized services.

As regards funding, China's civic organizations fall into three categories: entirely government funded; both government and independently funded; and entirely independently funded. The latter two enjoy preferential taxation, and include most professional and research societies, commercial and service organizations and all civic charities. In fact, the government's preference toward civic organizations is directly responsible for the recent rise in applications to establish charities.

4. *The development of the civic organizations in China is rather uneven, and there are significant disparities in social, political and economic influence and status amongst civic organizations*
The civic organizations exerting the greatest influence and enjoying the highest prestige in rural and urban areas are the villagers' and neighborhood committees as well as some community organizations such as senior citizens' associations. The Youth League, women's federations and militia's battalion, however, which used to be very influential, suffer from weak influence and now play but a minor role. Comparatively speaking, the professional and management associations, charitable organizations and civic charities at all levels exert increasingly greater influence. The main reasons for this difference are as follows:

a) Differences in legal status. The status of civic organizations is clearly stipulated in PRC law. The Constitution of the People's Republic of China, the Organic Law on Villagers' Committees, the Organic Law on Neighborhood Committees and relevant documents of the Communist Party's Central Committee provide for the functions, status and nature of villagers' committees and neighborhood committees. However, ordinary civic organizations do not enjoy privileged legal status.

b) Differences in cultural tradition. The prestige of senior citizens' associations, for example, is based on a tradition of respect for senior citizens and of clan identification.

c) Differences in economic strength. It is difficult to attract members, handle village affairs and appeal to society without great economic strength. The main reason for the influence of the China Youth Development Foundation and All-China Society of Charity, is their success in raising a tremendous sum of funds, allocated to help the poor and disadvantaged children.

d) Differences in leadership prestige. Even if the above-mentioned conditions are met, it is hard for a civic organization to exert great influence without powerful leadership. The leading officers of most organizations or national associations often enjoy high personal prestige. They are either distinguished senior cadres who are retired from the corridors of power, capable experts or talented persons. From our survey of Dongsheng, we find that the three residents who enjoy the highest reputation in the village are the leading cadres of the three most influential organizations of the locality, namely the secretary of the Party branch, the villager's head and the president of the senior citizens' association (Yu Keping, 2000).

Existing Problems

In conclusion, China's civil society has a short history. There are many problems emanating from the political and economic environment, affecting its internal structure and functions. From this study, we find that China faces the following challenges:

> Most civic organizations are too dependent on Party and government, rendering them strongly official in nature. As stated, the distinctive features of China's civil society are government influence and official-civil duality. But with regard to many civic organizations, their official nature is too strong, their civil nature too weak. Citing concrete examples, the villagers'

committees, neighborhood committees, the Youth League, women's federations, militia's battalions, family planning associations, public security committees, mediation associations and other organizations in rural areas and streets are dependent on Party and government to an exceedingly large extent. Their statutes and internal activities are under the direct control of the latter, while they generally report to the Party branches or even request instructions. Most of their leading officers and senior members belong to the CCP and accept the leadership of the local Party branches. This is also true of professional associations and chambers of commerce, *inter alia*. A chamber of commerce in a city simply regards its task as the need to "heed what Deng Xiaoping said: follow the Party's Central Committee with Jiang Zemin at its core and take the path to socialism with Chinese characteristic" (Liu Junning, 2000).

There are many reasons for this. Historically, prior to the reforms, China knew but the single form of public ownership and economic state-planning. Politically, China implemented a highly centralized and integrated system, providing no basis for the existence of a relatively independent civil society. Following the reforms, the socialist certainties began to disintegrate, albeit without any end in sight. Until that time, China's civil society cannot enjoy high independence and a "non-official" nature. For practical reasons, China is adopting a socialist market economy featuring diversified ownership, with public ownership playing a dominant role, and emphasizing the right to government intervention. The focus of the political system is still the authority of the Party Central Committee and the leadership of the Party. A civil society which conforms to such political and economic realities inevitably becomes "official" in nature. In fact, it often becomes a tool of the Party and the government.

The functions which many civic organizations in theory adopt fall far short of their actual roles. According to the legal provisions, neighborhood committees and villagers' committees are autonomous civic organizations. In fact, their self-governance is greatly restricted by local Party and government organs in most rural and urban communities and often becomes a mere formality. For example, we pointed out the system for making village affairs known to the public, formulated by district and town governments as well as the villager's committees. However, much content seems to be of little substance. In Dongsheng, only a few items are recorded in the notebook entitled *The Work of Making Village Affairs Known to the Public and Exercising Democratic Management* every month. Only 100 Chinese characters could be counted during the first quarter of 1999. Obviously, this cannot account for the true budget of either village or village cadres (Yu Keping, 2000).

Members at time face mandatory obligations. Unlike other official bodies, civic organizations have a distinctive feature, namely that their members join organizations and participate in their activities on a voluntary basis. China's civic organizations have a long way to go in this respect. Professional associations, chambers of commerce, academic, charitable and professional organizations have many mandatory obligations which their members must perform. For example, all the members of civic organizations must play an active part in the major political activities of Party and state according to requirements, lest they face direct or indirect retributions. A few organizations impose so many obligations on their members, that they have virtually no room for any free choice. For example, citizens of child-bearing age must join family planning associations in their communities, or face the threat of sanctions. This contravenes the regulations by the villagers' committees and the very rules established by the family planning associations themselves. However, articles emphasizing members' rights have, in many rural areas, been made inaccessible. On the contrary, most articles state obligations and begin with "not allowed" or "prohibited."

From our study of China's civil society, we can conclude that as a market economy is gradually being established and the political and legal environment undergoes changes, all types of civic organizations are bound to emerge. This process will play a positive role in improving democratic governance, both in urban and in rural areas. This constitutes an important manifestation of political progress in China's society, in the footsteps of political and economic reform. However, on a whole, self-governance, independence and the voluntary nature of civic organizations are not highly developed, and often face problems. Effective countermeasures would result in the sound development of China's civic organizations, enabling the latter to play an even greater role in promoting political progress and good governance and furthering the twin aim of economic modernization and social development.

CHAPTER SEVEN

CHINA'S RURAL GOVERNANCE THEN AND NOW: A COMPARATIVE ANALYSIS OF DINGXIAN, ZOUPING AND JIANGNING COUNTIES[1]

Introduction: History, Reality and Methodology

Since China implemented the policy of reform and opening to the outside world, there have been two most conspicuous changes in China's rural areas: economically, the implementation of the household contract responsibility system with remuneration linked to output; politically, the institution of self-governance among villagers. Self-governance among villagers has been introduced to most of China's rural areas since the 1980s (hereinafter referred to as the Reforms). This has brought about a fundamental change in the entire rural political life, and a new model of governance is emerging in China's rural areas. Sociologists and political scientists have conducted a great deal of research and obtained many results. However, some difficulties concerning theory and practice arise in the reform of rural governance centring on self-governance among villagers. For example, what is the model for China's rural governance? What are its features? What is the status of self-governance among villagers in the political development of the whole country? What are the main difficulties and the future for the reform of rural democracy and governance? How about relations between self-governance and the Party's leadership? How can villagers be mobilized to take an active part in government and political affairs? Is it possible to make a shift from direct elections for village heads to direct elections for township and town heads?

---

[1] This article is the general report of the Project supported by the Ford Foundation—"China's Rural Governance in the 1920–1930s and 1980–1990s: A Comparative Analysis of the Cases of Dingxian County, Zouping County and Jiangning County," co-authored with Xu Xiuli. In addition to other relevant literature, the report is mainly based on the following sub-reports: "Rural Governance of Dingxian County during the Period of the Republic of China" by Li Defang, "Rural Governance of Zouping County during the Period of the Republic of China" by Zhuang Weimin, "Rural Governance of Jiangning County during the Period of the Republic of China" by Ma Junya, "Current Rural Governance of Dingxian County" by Wang Fengming, "Current Rural Governance of Zouping County" by Wang Zhenhai and "Current Rural Governance of Jiangning County" by Jin Taijun.

Historical inquiry often helps to solve such problems.

Reform of governance, namely the rural self-governance movement, was introduced to China's rural areas during the Republican period (1911–1949), originating from the self-governance of Zhaicheng Village, Dingxian County, Zhili Province (now Dingzhou City, Hebei Province). During the 1920s, Yan Xishan's village governance experiment in Shanxi would provide an example.[2] After the Nationalist Government had been established in Nanjing (1927), local self-governance was regarded as a central task of political construction, in accordance with Dr. Sun Yat-sen's Three People's Principles,[3] but the results were not gratifying. As of 1932, the Nanjing Government began to support counties experimenting with self-governance. After hostilities with Japan erupted in 1936, a new system was implemented in Nationalist (Guomindang)-controlled counties. The government tightened control over the grassroots units, so that the spirit of rural self-governance was distorted. Reform of rural governance became a mere formality in most areas and produced no permanent results, but it played a positive role in stabilizing rural society, promoting economic development and raising the quality of villagers, at least in some places. There is a keen scholarly interest in research on rural reform experiments.

Such early research is of great practical use but, regrettably, no systematic, in-depth study comparing reforms after and prior to 1949 has been carried out. Our research is designed to make up for this lacuna. Its purpose is thus to conduct a comparative analysis of the rural self-governance movements under the leadership of the Guomindang and of the Communist Party of China (CCP) respectively. In analyzing basic operating mechanisms, discovering similarities and differences, generalizations can be made through historical comparison, suggesting solutions concerning rural democracy and governance today.

We chose Dingxian, Zouping and Jiangning counties as case studies mainly because the three counties were influential model areas within the rural self-governance movement. Furthermore, most original docu-

---

[2] See *Studies of Problems Concerning Rural Self-governance during the Period of the Republic of China*, Li Defang, p. 17, People's Publishing House, 2001; *Introduction to Local Self-governance*, Leng Jun, p. 79, Zhengzhong Book Company, 1935; *Present-day Rural Movement in China*, Kong Xuexiong, p. 438, Zhongshan Cultural and Educational Center, 1934.

[3] See *Teachings about Local Self-governance by the Prime Minister, Words on Local Self-governance by the President*, County Management Draft Committee, Executive Yuan, Zhengzhong Book Company, 1941 and 1940.

ments (records, archives, research reports and publications) about rural reform in the three counties have been preserved. The availability of such source materials greatly facilitates historical research.

Research on rural governance has attained great popularity within China's academic circles. Especially young scholars are attracted, causing interest in government circles and by the public. Foundations are providing financial support, academic journals specializing in rural research have emerged, and research results on the subject have been legion.[4] There are three reasons why research on rural governance has become a hot issue. Firstly, problems concerning rural areas, agriculture and farmers constitute factors holding back China's social development. Secondly, government officials and intellectuals tend to regard rural governance reforms as a cornerstone of China's democracy and as a testing ground for political participation. Thirdly, scholars are experimenting with models of political development which are different from those in Western countries, suited to China's actual conditions.

Most of the academic literature are accounts of evidential materials. Although it furnishes important materials for further study, it lacks a theoretical framework. In some analytical literature, we notice efforts to try to develop such a framework. For the analysis of rural development, international scholars center on methodological approaches emphasizing economic, institutional, cultural and state-society analysis.[5] Albeit of great significance for our understanding of China's rural parts, these analytical approaches are in constant need of improvement.

Economic analysis, the core element of historical materialism, is our preferred approach. Proceeding from socio-economic relations and economic development, it is designed to analyze political reality in two ways. Firstly, by examining underlying economic factors and secondly, by deducing political development as a result of economic development. In the broadest sense, this represents an example of economic analysis, since economic factors are seen as the decisive variables for all political phenomena. Fundamentally speaking, all political phenomena,

---

[4] See *Indexes to Chinese and Foreign Literature on Research on the Issue of Governance in China's Rural Areas* (internal materials, December 2000), research group.

[5] For a comprehensive theoretical analysis of domestic research literature on rural governance in recent years, see "Elaboration of the Significance of Self-governance among Villagers and Theorized Experimentation," Jing Yuejin, *Research on China's Rural Areas*, China's Rural Problems Research Center, Central China Normal University (2001), pp. 87–117, China Social Sciences Publishing House, 2002.

including rural governance, have political causality and economic foundations. This is not to discount the inherent logic of sociopolitical development. Non-economic factors play an important role in political development as well.

Culture is one such non-economic factor. Cultural analysis is thus designed to gain an understanding of sociopolitical life through the analysis of people's traditions, customs, rites, psychology, attitudes and emotions. For the sake of analyzing rural political development, political scientists mainly employ the political cultural analysis approach, i.e., political culture as the model for political orientation. This includes people's political cognition, attitudes, faiths, emotions and values. In believing that political culture dominates people's (political) behavior, political cultural analysis can help us understand deep-rooted behavioral patterns, political models and systems, as well as the process of governance. But political culture is also affected by other factors. Obviously, it would be inappropriate to regard political cultural analysis as the main or even only analytical approach.

In fact, both economics and culture affect political life, mainly through the sociopolitical institutions. Political institutions are decisive factors influencing sociopolitical life and determining people's political behavior. As a condensation of political life, institutions represent political reality and development. Institutional analysis is thus the main approach of political analysis, traditionally focusing on national political systems. It has been said that "analysis of political science starts in the state and ends in the state," a typically institutionalist view. Although neo-institutionalism differs from traditional institutionalism with regard to the definition and analysis of institutions, both share the same basic assumption that sociopolitical life can be interpreted through an analysis of the political system and procedures. The fact that this analytical approach has predominated in political theory for such a long time shows its tremendous value: diverse political institutions directly standardize and restrain human political life and processes and political analysis cannot be separated from the analysis of political systems. Of course, this does not mean that institutional analysis has no defects, the greatest one being that it tends to favor static, superficially analytical approaches.

The "state-society" analysis, popular with younger scholars, is also a very useful approach. From the perspective of political analysis, we can divide society into political society (political state) and civil society. The former represents a public political sphere, the latter falling into private social and civil public spheres. In fact, every citizen in modern society lives simultaneously in both spheres. For example, when an official performs duties on behalf of the government, he is active in the political state. When he joins a civil organization for his own interests or interest, he acts within civil society. Political state and civil society are two quite different spheres, each with its own norms and behavioral approaches. In a sense, the process of modern political development is a process of interaction between state and society. Through studies on state building, nation building and the growth of civil society, we can acquire an understanding of changes in rural governance. This is of great help to our mastery of rural politics. But such a dichotomous approach is likely to separate state from society, and it is prone to a one-sided conclusion.[6]

Let us concentrate on two main analytical frameworks, namely the comparative historical and the governance approaches. The comparative historical approach combines vertical (historical and chronological) with horizontal (regional and spatial) comparison, combining general comparison with historical analysis. It presupposes that social and political developments follow the same global patterns and that political realities are constantly changing. In the present study, we will engage in a comparative historical analysis of similar localities in the three counties of Dingxian, Zouping and Jiangning and produce auxiliary studies of rural governance in different areas.

"Governance" and "good governance" are new theoretical frameworks within political analysis. Governance implies the exercising of public authority to maintain social order and further the public interest. At first glance it may appear that there are no great differences between governance and government, but the actual implications are quite different. One fundamental difference is that governance requires authority, but that authority does not necessarily come from government. The authority of a government must derive from government organizations. Governments are based on official public institutions, whereas governance can be derived from either official or civic roles, which at times coincide. Governance is hence a much wider concept. Secondly, the direction of exercising power differs. Governmental power is always exerted from above, managing social and public affairs by decree or by formulating and implementing policies. Governance, on the contrary, is a thoroughly interactive process, emphasizing cooperation and

---

[6] *Politics and Political Science*, pp. 16–24, Social Sciences Documentation Publishing House, 2003.

consultation, identification and recognition. The ultimate goal of governance is to achieve "good governance," a process of social management for the purpose of maximizing public interests. A central feature of good governance is to build up a new relationship between state and society, through cooperation between government and citizens. There are ten key elements of good governance: (1) legitimacy; (2) rule of law; (3) transparency; (4) civil engagement and civil participation; (5) accountability; (6) responsibility; (7) effectiveness; (8) stability; (9) justice; and (10) honesty.[7]

We chose the analytical framework of (good) governance mainly because it has clear advantages over any analysis of economic, institutional, cultural or state-civil society factors. Firstly, and innovatively, it offers a new analytical perspective by focusing on the synthesis between government and citizens. Secondly, it is more inclusive than other approaches, whilst emphasizing political development. It includes elements of institutional, economic and cultural analysis, while compensating for some of their defects. Also, it illustrates the orientation of political development, by emphasizing interaction between state and civil society and in stressing self-governance among citizens and non-governmental public authority. All this requires special attention in rural governance. Moreover, it avoids the false dichotomies prevalent in the social sciences, namely in segregating free markets from state planning, public from private sectors, political state from civil society, or national state from international community. Instead, it regards effective public management as a process of cooperation between the two. New techniques and its emphasis on cooperation question the role of the government as the only source of legitimate power. Rural governance, a complex sociopolitical phenomenon, focuses on government action and village self-governance. By analyzing legal systems, village regulations and popular conventions, rural governance combines state involvement and civil participation, helping us to gain a deeper understanding of complex processes.

In the following, we will compare the structure, essence, processes, means, contents, environment, significance, features, difficulties and orientations of rural governance in Dingxian, Zouping and Jiangning counties in different historical periods.

---

[7] Yu Keping, "Governance and Good Governance: A New Framework of Political Analysis," *Nanjing Social Sciences*, vol. 9 (2001).

Structure: Government, Political Party and Civil Organization

Rural governance aims at managing rural communities through rural public authority and at furthering the public good. Public authority in rural governance either rests with official or civil bodies or can be characterized by cooperation between official and civil organizations. During the twentieth century, the structure of rural governance has been determined by the government, political parties and civil organizations.

Reform of rural governance has its origins in the late Qing reforms, with local self-governance forming an important component. On December 27, 1908, during the thirty-fourth year of the Guangxu reign period, the imperial administration promulgated rules for local autonomy as well as for elections in smaller communities. Accordingly, all towns and townships were to establish councils and administrative boards as the sole authority of local autonomy. These councils and boards were to be constituted by general ballot among local residents. The late Qing reforms (1904–1911) can be characterized as political reforms initiated from above by the outgoing imperial government, under genuine political pressure. The Rules clearly stipulated that "local self-governance focus on the special handling of local public affairs and in assisting the official administration."[8] These early reforms hence bore the imprint of strong central government, the population playing but an auxiliary role.

A leading role for the government is also apparent in the self-governance of Zhaicheng Village, Dingxian County. This despite being referred to as a "path breaker in local self-governance," "a model of rural self-governance in all of Zhili province" by the Ministry of Internal Affairs of the early republican central administration (Le Defang, 2003). Initiated by government officials, self-governance in Zhaicheng was financially supported and supervised by the government. Early attempts at self-governance were inseparable from the name of Mr. Mi Digang, a village worthy, jointly with Sun Faxu, magistrate for Dingxian County. In 1914, Sun Faxu before long found that Zhaicheng Village was highly advanced in terms of education, and he hence proposed establishing a model village following the example of Japanese experiments. In the autumn of 1914, Mi Digang travelled to Suiyuan to reclaim wasteland,

---

[8] Article 1 of "Rules of Local Self-governance in Towns and Townships" (27 December 1908).

and preparatory work for the model village was initiated by Mi Xiao-zhou and Mi Jieping. In the following summer, the Ministry of Internal Affairs promulgated the "Regulations on Local Self-governance for Trial Implementation," together with "Detailed Rules for Implementation." After local self-governance had been implemented, Yuan Shikai—as the de facto ruler of the Republic of China—ordered the establishment of a "model area of self-governance" in Jingzhao, obliging the locality to follow the example of urban management in Western countries and to copy village regulations in Japan. Sun Faxu was encouraged. He immediately appropriated 300 yuan to Zhaicheng Village, which was specially spent on the construction of the model village. By September, a self-governance office for Zhaicheng was set up and in October, the village head, village assistant, district head and other staff assumed office. One month on, Sun Faxu designated Zhaicheng a model village, commending it to the governor of Zhili, the Ministry of Education and the Ministry of Internal Affairs as a model not only of local self-governance but of the reform of rural governance in the country as a whole. The success of the Zhaicheng experiment encouraged the government to introduce rural self-governance system more widely in Shanxi Province, imposed as central government policy from above.

The academic Liang Shuming realized his ideals of rural reform during the 1920s and 1930s in Zouping County, Shandong Province. Anxious to liberate villagers from the government's power and to permit self-governance, he advocated altering traditional rural governance, namely the combination of official with gentry governance, by integrating education with politics and by promoting the role of the local intelligentsia. Sceptical of central government authority in rural governance, he practised a policy of "utilizing the government." Alas, his efforts to free Zouping from government intervention did not bear fruit, leading to the failure in rural reform efforts in general. This included taxation and levies, land distribution, and political participation. Some lower-level administrative tasks, such as census, land surveying, taxes and levies, were actually passed on to the villages from the central government. Rural self-governance thus "remould peasants to suit the government, but did nothing to alter the government toward the peasantry." Rhetoric about social transformation thus conversely led to more dependence on the government.[9] Actually, without government

---

[9] *Theory of Rural Construction*, Liang Shuming, Chongqing, Rural Bookstore, 1939, Appendix: "Our Two Great Difficulties."

support, Liang Shuming's experiment could not even have begun. He chose a Shandong locality, because he had won the backing of Han Fuqu, military strongman and governor of Shandong. Han Fuqu supported rural self-governance, which he considered conducive to keeping the local political situation stable. Likewise, Liang Shuming needed the support of the powerful, because experimentation with self-governance required funding and funds came from the government. In October 1930, Henan Village College stopped operating because of civil strife. At that time, Han Fuqu was transferred to serve as Governor of Shandong Provincial Government. Soon after he took office, he invited Liang Shuming, backbone of the original college to Jinan City to discuss rural self-governance in Shandong, the establishment of institutions similar to Henan Village College and the designation of certain areas as experimental zones. In March 1931, Liang Shuming and others received 100,000 yuan of starting funds from the provincial government for the establishment of a Shandong Rural Construction Academy (Zhuang Weimin, 2003). The central government's support and a pursuant legal system were political preconditions for Liang Shuming's substantial social experiments. In December 1932, the central government in Nanjing passed reform motions for county administration and local self-governance, formulated the Regulations on the Establishment of County Political Experimental Zones in All Provinces, stipulating that provinces would be able to freely select experimental areas and retain 50% of local revenue. In February 1933, in accordance with the regulations of the Ministry of Internal Affairs, the Shandong Provincial Government formulated eleven articles on a research academy specializing in the establishment of such experimental zones in Shandong and twenty articles on implementation. Zouping and Heze were designated as county political construction experimental zones, the former referred to as "first experimental county," and placed under the tutelage of the Shandong Rural Construction Academy. Special laws and regulations promulgated by the central government and relevant implementation rules promulgated by the local administration furnished the legal framework for the reform of local self-governance. Thus, rural self-governance in Zouping was officially recognized by Nanjing, causing rural self-governance and governance to enter a new stage (Zhuang Weimin, 2003).

Rural self-governance in Jiangning was promoted by the National Government, which established a model county in local self-governance. In February 1933, the Jiangsu provincial government designated the experimental county on the grounds that "Jiangning is close to the capital and needs to be seen in a better light internationally." Its organizational regulations envisaged that the provincial government engage nine to thirteen persons to organize a Jiangning County Political Construction Committee, fully authorized to administer on behalf of the provincial government. The county government, subject to the county political construction committee appointed a county magistrate. The latter was subject to both the provincial government and the county political construction committee, but not to any other authorities. Mei Siping, magistrate of Jiangning County, was Dean of the Department of Politics of the Central Political Academy with Jiang Jieshi (Chiang Kai-shek) as its president.[10] The County enjoyed extensive autonomy. It was exempt from provincial taxes, allocating these for local developments.[11] In reforming local self-governance, delineating autonomous areas and electing village heads, excess numbers of qualified candidates volunteered for village head elections. In Jiangning, the village was no longer a one-level unit of self-governance, "township and town self-governance units did not have the right of independent self-governance and did not have democratic elections, but they were actually the administrative instruments of the government in the form of self-governance." This obviously ran counter to the spirit of local self-governance envisaged by Dr. Sun Yixian [Sun Yat-sen].[12] Reform of rural governance in Jiangning can thus be described as an *ab initio* attempt at central government manipulation. "This program obviously reflected government intentions in theory, motivation and legislation." Under the guidance of the government, Jiangning County engaged in tax reform, cleaning up police and administration, managing public security, controlling accommodation, education, hygiene, reforming customs and rural relief, as well as spreading agricultural technology and aspects of rural governance (Ma Junya, 2003).

Rural governance during the republican period was typified by a dual official-civil structure. Next to government and civil organizations, the governing political party played a major role in state governance. At the rural grassroots, the Nationalist GMD exerted hardly influence.[13]

----

[10] See Zheng Dahua, *Rural Construction Movement in the Republic of China*, p. 120.

[11] Government of Jiangning County Experimenting with Self-governance, *Introduction to Jiangning County Administration*, p. 1.

[12] Li Defang, *Studies of Problems Concerning Rural Self-governance during the Period of the Republic of China*, pp. 146–148.

[13] See Wang Qisheng, "Relations between Party and Government: Local Party Governance of the GuomindangGuomindang (1927–1937)," *Chinese Social Sciences*, 2001, no. 3.

Speaking of Zouping, there were only slightly thirty members of the GMD in the whole county. The power of the GMD generally did not penetrate the countryside. In 1935, the county's GMD headquarters was dissolved, as were organizations led by county GMD headquarters, the county thus effectively slipping out of GMD control. (Zhuang Weimin, 2003.) The situation in Dingxian County was similar. The Nanjing Government claimed to have the country under control, but the Dingxian GMD headquarters did not play a leading role in the County. Of its 208 county members in 1929, only twenty were peasants. Due to lack of funds, the GMD-controlled peasants' and women's associations were rather inactive and exerted little influence. When rural self-governance was implemented systematically, party work stopped completely. After it resumed in the county in 1931, the GMD membership count dropped drastically to 127, leaving almost no GMD members in the vast rural areas (Le Defang, 2003).

The situation since the 1980s differed substantially. Rural governance was characterized by a triple structure of authority, namely by the CCP, the government and villagers' organizations. The CCP, as the only ruling party, not only played a decisive role in macro-governance, but also at the grassroots level. The leading role of the local Party branches in rural self-governance was affirmed by the Organic Law on Villagers' Committees in the People's Republic of China, promulgated in 1998. "The rural primary organizations of the Chinese Communist Party (CCP) work according to the Constitution of the CCP, playing a leading and central role, thus supporting and guaranteeing self-governance by villagers according to the Constitution of the People's Republic of China and other state laws, and directly exercising democratic rights."[14] There are currently 65 million CCP members. Although the proportion of rural members has dropped to a historical low, they still account for about 32% and rural Party branches still play a core role in rural governance. As opposed to the scarcity of GMD members in Zouping during the 1930s, the CCP mustered a thousand times more members in the 1990s, totalling over 30,000. According to a recent survey about the current state of rural governance, 90% of villagers and 100% of village cadres think that the local CCP branches currently have a vital role to play (Wang Fengming, 2003). Only 8% of the villagers think

---

[14] Article 3 of the Organic Law on Villagers' Committees in the People's Republic of China (adopted at the Fifth Meeting of the Standing Committee of the Ninth National People's Congress on 4 November 1998).

that the villagers' committees should exert more influence than the Party. (Wang Zhenhai, 2003).

Within the current political framework, the CCP is the pivotal point of all political activities in state and society. Party organizations and government departments co-exist at all levels. Higher cadres enjoy the same material benefits as civil servants. Therefore, CCP organizations should not merely be regarded as political factor, but as a central public authority. Party organizations also rival government authorities in rural governance, at least in the broader sense. On the basis of this logic, the rural governance reforms since the 1980s have strengthened the role of government in rural governance. The government plays an almost unchallenged role in rural governance, manifested in the following aspects:

Firstly, in promoting the reform of rural governance, including rural self-governance. The theory that self-governance originated in the 1980s is correct in as much as after the demise of the people's communes, there was a power vacuum in rural society, resulting in a number of problems. "At the end of 1980, peasants established an entirely new primary power community—villagers' committees in place of production brigades and production teams, which were rapidly disintegrating in the rural areas of Qishan and Luoshan counties (Hechi Prefecture, Guangxi Zhuang Autonomous Region)."[15] Self-governance among villagers resulted from central government promotion. Already the PRC constitution of 1982 stipulated a system of self-governance of villagers' committees. Document no. 36 of the CCP Central Committee issued in the same year required experimentation with villagers' committees in specified rural areas, an example of the involvement of the government in promoting village autonomy. Case studies of Jiangning show that "construction of self-governance among villagers can be roughly divided into the three stages of start-up, development and climax. (1) Start-up: Establishment of the key villagers' self-governance organization—the villagers' committee. In 1985, Jiaocun Village (Chunhua township, Jiangning County) one of only two villages experimenting with villagers' committee elections in the whole province, elected its own villagers' committee. In the same year, all villages in the county completed the transition from centrally administered villages to autonomous ones,

---

[15] Bai Gang and Zhao Shouxing, *Election and Governance: Studies of Self-governance among Villagers in China.*

indicative of a more general shift from administrative management to self-governance. (2) Development: Self-governing model villages. In 1992, Jiangning County took the lead by nominating Dongwang Village, Moling Township as a model of self-governance, concentrating on the establishment of legal and customary autonomy. Its democratic elections, policy-making, management and supervision became an example to all townships and towns in the county. (3) Climax: Conveyance of rural autonomy to all administrative levels. In June 1998 the county's CCP committee and government decided to establish a model county, set up at the three levels of village, township (or town) and county. The former drew up schedules, targets and responsibilities and initiated practical demonstrations, thus disseminating the experience gained at selected units to a wider area and providing practical guidance. This invigorated the process of rural autonomy." (Jin Taijun, 2003)

Secondly, the government formulates rules and regulations, creating norms and control mechanisms for rural governance. With regard to the state, the constitution of 1982 clearly specified the legal status of rural self-governance. Furthermore, the central government promulgated the Organic Law on Villagers' Committees in the People's Republic of China (Trial Implementation) in 1987 and formally revised the Organic Law on Villagers' Committees in 1998. After 1982, the CCP Central Committee and its General Office issued a series of documents on self-governance and grassroots democracy. Accordingly, local governments formulated detailed rules and regulations on rural self-governance in light of actual local conditions The Hebei Province People's Congress, for instance, promulgated the Regulations on Organization of Villagers' Committees in Hebei Province in 1990, and the provincial Department of Civil Affairs formulated Regulations on the Elections of Villagers' Committees, following the end of the trial in 1993. According to these laws and regulations by central and provincial authorities, governments at all the levels within counties formulated detailed rules on the implementation of elections of villagers' committees and on the pursuant procedures. Also other aspects of rural governance, such as family planning, village affairs, financial management, rural stability or the awarding of contracts were addressed. The rules issued by the Zouping County CCP Committee and government contain a total of fifty articles on rural governance. (Wang Zhenhai, 2003)

Thirdly, the government determines the political elite in the countryside. According to the legal provisions and the constitution of the CCP, representatives of village Party branches and of villagers' committees must be directly elected. These elections, however, are sanctioned and organized by Party committees and governmental election guidance bodies at higher levels. In most cases, the outcome of such elections is controlled by electoral procedures and by the selection of candidates. As a consequence of greater grassroots democracy, the higher authorities find it more difficult to influence the appointment of villagers' committees. The authorities prefer to nominate Party members, sometimes directly appointing local Party secretaries. The government also plays a vitally decisive role in the elections for villagers' committees. To cite the example of Zouping County in 1999, the county authorities established a core group for elections to the villagers' committees and seventeen supervision, direction and liaison groups, comprising fifty-one county officials. The *Z.F.* [1999] No. 4 and with *Z.C.Zi*, [1999] No. 1 Documents were issued, and a clear requirement for elections at the end of the office term were set. On 29th January the county authorities held a working meeting attended by secretaries of all town and township Party committees, the director of the People's Congress and employees of the Office for Civil Affairs mobilized the above-mentioned candidates, giving them one-day training sessions. Other systems included the appointment of heads, deputy heads and members as well as the organizing of meetings. Leading county cadres of Party and Government frequently visited towns and townships to conduct investigations and research and provide on-site guidance. Towns and townships also established special leading bodies, held mobilization meetings, organized training at different levels and sent cadres from government departments to all villages for work. Cadres responsible for the respective work participated positively, influencing the outcome of local elections and highlighting the role of the rural Party elite (Wang Zhenhai, 2003).

Fourthly, government officials participate in village governance by virtue of living there. With regard to the current model of village governance, it is common practice for township and town governments to send Party and government officials to villages to gain practical experience in village governance. These so-called "cadres resident in villages" (*zhucun ganbu* or *baocun ganbu*) are responsible for the general governance of the village. As government representatives, their main responsibilities comprise the management, coordination and supervision of the villages which they are responsible for on behalf of higher level Party committees and administrations. In general, they eschew direct involvement in routine village affairs, but choose to take part in the management of elections of villagers' committees, as well as in the coordination of relations between villagers' committees and the local Party, supervision of village cadres, family planning, tax and fee collection and other major village affairs. In Dingzhou, the dispatch of liaison cadres to villages is considered a principal administrative method. "Quite a few township and town authorities transfer cadres directly under their authority, with experience in rural areas, knowledgeable in economic and management affairs and with a strong sense of responsibility from among cadres at all levels, to serve as deputy Party secretaries or acting deputy directors of villagers' committees. Leading cadres of township governments often go to villages to provide guidance by formulating and implementing legal documentation." They furthermore help villagers solve practical problems. In Dingzhou, "the working groups responsible for rural governance are assigned by the authorities at higher levels to different aspects of work and guidance in the countryside. The working groups of the Hebei Finance Department, for example, residing in Gedatou (Zhoucun Township), Suquan Village (Pangcun Town), Nanzhihe Village (Qingfengdian Town) and Caocun Village (Dongting Town) perform outstanding work in accomplishing projects such as the construction of village roads, upgrading of electric power, building of primary schools and the transformation of barren and unreclaimed land. This is much appreciated by the villagers." (Wang Fengming, 2003)

A fifth point is that the government provides subsidies to rural governance. During the republican period (1911–1949), China's rural economy was extremely backward, the countryside generally poor, without almost any public finance. The relative absence of such funds thus characterized the nature of village governance. After 1949, a collective system at three levels of ownership was implemented, with ownership by the production team as the basic norm. Since China implemented its reform policies, the productive forces of China's rural areas have been unleashed, with living standards rising quickly. Village finances have also improved, exonerating the government at least to a certain extent. However, when compared with the urban economy, China's countryside still lags behind, with low levels of income and public funds. Government subsidies thus remain an important factor. The main method which the government applies to influence village economics and governance is by means of welfare subsidies to village cadres. In Dingzhou, for example, the basic method of control in many localities is by institutional control of income, namely through subsidies to village cadres. Xingyi Town furnishes life and property insurance to cadres and grants subsidies to cadres who have left their posts (Wang Fengming, 2003).

Sixth, the government provides training and education to village cadres at regular intervals. Rural education for the elites was commonly practised in conjunction with rural self-governance during the republican period. One of the main purposes of Liang Shuming's Rural Construction Academy was to train self-governance personnel, a practice still extensively employed in current village governance. Practical training and more general education is routinely provided to all newly elected secretaries of the village Party branches and the villagers' committees. County or municipal CCP committees have established Party schools for the training of cadres. These are mainly designed to train cadres at and above township or town level, but they usually also hold short-term training courses for secretaries of village branches and directors of villagers' committees. Party committees of more developed townships and towns act likewise, with the emphasis on the training of key village cadres. For example, the Publicity Department of the Jiangning County Party Committee formulates and issues a *Theoretical Study Plan for Party Members and Cadres*, also a *Rotation Training Plan for Party Members* and *Suggestions on Implementation of Winter Training for Party Members and Cadres* on an annual basis. Party committees of townships and towns formulate corresponding plans for Party members and cadres. Over 95% of Party members and cadres in China's rural areas participate in the annual winter training programs, i.e., circa 25,000 persons, and Party schools in all townships and towns train about a dozen groups of cadres every year (Jin Taijun, 2003). Political education campaigns stress the need to study, develop political awareness, as well as honesty and uprightness. The "Three Represents" form the main vehicle of political education among rural cadres.

Although rural governance was promoted and directed by the central government during the republican period and in the People's Republic, local authorities have played a decisive role in rural governance. But formally and institutionally, the main public authority for rural governance rests with civil self-governance bodies and similar organizations. According to the Organic Counties Law promulgated by the republican government in Nanjing, all counties were divided into a small number of districts according to household registration and local conditions. Each district had an office with one sole head, responsible for the management of self-governance. District heads were publicly elected at auspicious moments. For all elections in townships and towns, public offices deposited the names of candidates to the county government for record. The same was true for the districts where public offices presented name lists to county magistrates for approval, all duly recorded by the Department of Civil Affairs. With regard to township and town residents, twenty-five households represented a *lü* and five households a *lin*. Heads of *lü* and *lin* were elected at respective residents' meetings, further recommended by the township and town leaderships to the county government.[16] According to the Resolution on the Bill for Completion of County-Level Self-governance, adopted at the Second Plenary Session of the Third GMD Central Executive Committee, preparatory organs for self-governance in all localities were established by the end of 1933, with complete local self-governance by 1934.[17] However, while most provinces had organized county governments, delimited districts of self-governance, as well as those of townships and towns, *lü* and *lin* by March 1934, few convened citizens' meetings, elections for senior offices towns or set up local offices.[18] Surveys and investigations show that actual results of rural self-governance were poor.

Institutional structure therefore did not match actual implementation, at least in most localities. In counties experimenting with self-governance, organs of governance could differ considerably. Liang Shuming's experimental vehicles in Zouping were private schools in townships and villages. Boards of school directors selected senior educationalists, usually persons of advanced age, moral integrity and popular support. They served chiefly as moral examples and mediators for disputes (Zhuang Weimin, 2003). While experimenting with self-governance, Jiangning implemented far-reaching changes in its administrative divisions. The former four-level system (county, district, township/town and *lü/lin*) was reduced to three levels (county, district, township/town). Villages were divided and the new rural components integrated into existing townships and towns. The latter were extended, while district and public offices were disbanded, with the effect that self-governance was implemented

---

[16] "Organic Law of Counties" (second revision, promulgated by the National Government on July 7, 1930).

[17] "Local Self-governance," Propaganda Department of the GMD Central Executive Committee, 1931, p. 46.

[18] Hu Ciwei, *The History of the County System in the Republic of China*, Dadong Book Company, 1948, p. 79.

at the two levels of county and township/town.[19] The National Chinese Association for Mass Education planned to abolish the original rural self-governance system in Dingxian County and implement a system of township and town construction committees, based on citizens' service corps under the county government (Li Defang, 2003).

Unlike the republican period, structures of self-governance in rural China today are the same throughout the country, with the villagers' committee and the village Party branch as the organs of self-governance in villages. The director of the villagers' committee (a.k.a. village head) and the secretary of the village Party branch are the supreme leaders of village affairs. The villagers' committee generally comprises groups or committees in charge of public order, social mediation, family planning and of the women's federation. Though the villagers' representatives' conference and the villagers' general meeting theoretically enjoy the highest authority within the village, the village Party branch or the joint conference of the village Party branch and the villagers' committee are the de facto leading institutions.

In addition to the legally prescribed rural self-governance authorities, other organizations established by villagers or the government also play an important role. These civil organizations fall under the following three categories. Firstly, offshoots of China's traditional culture, such as clan or family organizations or temple fairs. Secondly, mutual aid and public welfare organizations, for instance cooperatives, "green seedling" associations, as well as those for agriculture and forestry, halls for accumulation of good deeds, etc. Thirdly, there are auxiliary self-governance organizations, for example, public security associations, patrol parties, democratic financial groups, militia organizations, family planning associations and associations for the aged. Traditional culture exerts more influence in rural areas than in the cities. Clan or family organizations had a great impact on rural governance during the republican period, and this is true even now. In some fields, such influence even goes beyond that of the legal organs. Public welfare organizations are both active and popular. They also play an indispensable role in rural governance. During the republican period, the hall for accumulation of good deeds in Tangshan, Jiangning County and the Chinese National Association for Mass Education in Dingxian County, Hebei Province

---

[19] Xu Yinglian, Li Jingxi, Duan Jili and Bian Shushu, *Introduction to Nationwide Rural Construction Movement*, pp. 532–535.

often exerted greater influence than formal self-governance structures. Recent research into contemporary rural civic organizations has shown that China during the reform period has seen a rapid expansion of rural civic organizations, with ever greater political clout.[20]

In conclusion, rural governance was characterized by a division into official and civil structures during the republican period, in contrast to a triple structure (Party, government and civic organizations) during the reform period. In essence, however, the Party and the government retain all official authority. Although the structures of rural governance before 1949 differ from those during the reform period, government and authorities play the same leading role in rural governance. The government actively promotes the reform of rural governance, norms and balances the pace and orientation of rural governance reform through economic, political and legal means.

Subject: Villagers, Village Sages and Cadres

Rural governance naturally means different things to different people. If different roles are determined according to the status and role in governance, rural governance authority can be divided between common villagers, rural elite (generally referred to as "village sages," "gentlemen" or "the talented") and village cadres.

An active participation of the village population is at the heart of rural governance. Their education, ability and enthusiasm for political participation directly influence the quality of rural governance. Activists must meet at least three basic requirements: a moderately comfortable degree of wealth, solid cultural and educational foundations and enthusiasm for participating in local government work and political affairs. The reform of rural governance during the republican period was generally designed to raise civic awareness amongst villagers, an ideal which also holds true nowadays.

Liang Shuming's social experiment began with the establishment of Peasants' Schools (soon renamed into Schools for the Common People), as well as with agrarian cooperatives and innovation. Teachers for the Peasant Schools were being trained at Liang's Rural Construction

---

[20] Yu Keping, "China's Rural Civic Organizations and Changes in Governance," in Yu Keping et al., *Rise of China's Civil Society and Changes in Governance*, pp. 1–28, Social Sciences Literature Publishing House, 2002.

Academy. In January 1932, its Training Department dispatched over three hundred teachers and students into districts and townships in order to establish Peasants' Schools. By the end of the same year, ninety-one such schools had been established county-wide, with 3,996 participating villagers. Initially, schools were set up in big villages where conditions were more benign, with an average of five to eight per district. Later, smaller villages would pool resources in order to establish a Peasants' School. Under the guidance of the Rural Construction Academy, students of the Training Department served as instructors. Villagers would study for three months at a time. Courses included political theory (Sun Yat-sen's Three People's Principles), moral cultivation, literacy, history and geography, rural self-defense and agricultural science and technology. In addition to these more formal schools, some primary schools established evening schools, challenging both men and women, old and young to immerse themselves in literacy, current affairs, agricultural knowledge, for instance. By the end of 1933, 156 evening schools had been set up in the county, with 5,241 villagers enrolled. Furthermore, departments or schools for women were created, imparting knowledge on household affairs, health and childcare.[21]

Brandishing the banner of "education for the common people," Yan Yangchu of Dingxian County used the Chinese National Association for Mass Education in order to improve educational standards. Only education could unlock the vigour of the common people, improve their lives and consolidate the foundation of the state. Because peasants accounted for 80% of China's population and rural areas represented the country's economic and political foundation, popular education became a matter of foremost priority. Yan's social surveys established that the peasantry suffered from four shortcomings: ignorance, poverty, infirmity and egocentrism. He suggested corrective measures, which centered upon literary and artistic education. Economics lessons were designed to eliminate poverty and to boost productive forces. Health classes were to increase the peasants' physical resilience, while civic education was designed to eliminate selfishness and increase unity. Holistic education was thus to embrace aspects of schooling, society and family (Li Defang, 2003).

---

[21] Song Leyan, "Adult Education in Zouping County," in: *Rural Construction Semimonthly*, Vol. 6, issue 15, April 16, 1937.

To tackle illiteracy, the Tangshan Peasants' Education Hall in Jiangning County opened schools for the common people, employing a method of rotating, student-oriented teaching. Students were encouraged to impart what they learned to their family members as well as to their fellow villagers. Women's work-study classes were planned around the available leisure time of rural women, by providing basic literacy and general knowledge, such as in handicraft and economics (Ma Junya, 2003).

While village education in Republican China was based on solid theoretical foundations, exemplified by the education drive in Dingxian county, as well as in Zouping and Jiangning counties, illiteracy rates of up to 80% provided a formidable challenge. In this respect, the situation in China today has fundamentally changed. As a consequence of the government's enforcement of its nine-year universal and compulsory education policy in both urban and rural areas from the 1980s, literacy rates in the above localities among the young and middle-aged has approximated 100%. Against this new background, the educational imperative has changed from basic general knowledge to professional training in business skills and agricultural technology, as well as democratic and legal awareness.

The four educational priorities in Dingzhou prioritized peasants and cadres. Legal training stressed the need to perform official duties within the law and to eliminate illegal practices amongst cadres. Simultaneously, information campaigns helped spread awareness about laws and regulations, providing greater legal protection and a better understanding of rights and obligations. Insight into the mechanisms and legal framework of a market economy provides guidance into the production, processing and marketing. Classes in agricultural science and technology raise the scientific and technological awareness of cadres and peasants. Ideological and moral education increase awareness of social ethics and family values, raising the standard of social conduct. Furthermore, the municipal authorities carried out a project of training ten thousand young people for the new century. The "new countryside and new science and technology" campaign attracted vast numbers of rural residents eager to boost their incomes (Wang Fengming, 2003).

The County Communist Youth League (CYL) Committee of Zouping county has created technical and other professional training opportunities for youngsters. Between 1996 and 1998, the local CYL organizations designed pilot schemes and other wealth-creating projects.

In May 1996, for instance, information billboards for the latter were displayed in the county town. Furthermore, agrarian experts from the Provincial Academy of Agricultural Sciences offered training courses in Sunzhen Town, as well as the help of 140 "green fingers." In the same year in July, ten experts arrived in Zouping County to provide professional guidance to the rural young in Batian, Handian and other localities. In 1997, a campaign for leading "a fairly comfortable life" was launched, with 1,500 participating youth leaders assisting one poor Youth League member each to raise their standard of living. Primary CYL organizations also provided youth training, printing over 50,000 scientific and technical brochures. In November 1997, the county's CYL committee raised RMB 110,000 in funds, set up the Zouping County CYL Committee farm with rabbits of good breeds, while providing comprehensive services such as in animal breeding and disease prevention, selling relevant articles such as cages, issuing technical brochures and providing training (Wang Zhenhai, 2003).

The rural elite, namely those who enjoy high levels in education, management ability, wealth, judgement and public esteem, play a vitally important role in rural governance. Comparative studies reveal that historical perceptions of the elite can vary with time. Further to the above criteria, the rural elite ought to display integrity and ability. However, during the republican period, villagers particularly valued integrity in their village sages, whereas today managerial and financial prowess are appreciated. But now as well as then, the rural elite plays a major role in rural governance, exerting an even greater influence than the village officials.

Tang Qingjie, head of the Jishantang (House for Public Good) in republican Tangshan, Jiangning County, for instance enjoyed a degree of public esteem surpassing that of the town head. When problems emerged, people put their trust in Mr. Tang rather than go through the official channels. From interviews gathered during a recent field trip to Tangshan, an incident dating back to the autumn of 1931 was reported. Following an attack by several hundred villagers from locations in Liugangtou, Yan, Zhoujiabian, Wangjiazhuang, Xiaofuniushan and Jurong districts against a model forestry farm under the direction of Liu Zhiyin (Liu San), the Nanjing Metropolitan Garrison Command sent troops for quelling the disorder. Buildings were destroyed and so were the guns belonging to the forestry police. The clashes involving villagers, local government police and regular troops were diffused with the help of Tang Qingjie, who used his extensive network of contacts to come to the rescue of Liu San.[22]

The rural elite also plays an important role in present-day rural governance. Thrifty villagers enjoy high prestige if they are upright, handle matters fairly and contribute to the village's collective undertakings. Even if these choose not to become members of the villagers' committee or of the village Party branch, they still exert great influence. On the contrary, if a legally elected village head or Party secretary lacks in business skills, either for himself or on behalf of the village, his authority may be undermined. Recent research thus suggests that rural governance today is structured on personal talent. A case study based on findings from Guquan, Jiangning County, underlines the outstanding role of subjective factors. "Self-governance" is thus not an expression of collective autonomy, but of the leadership by the able and respected (Jin Taijun, 2003). It hence becomes necessary to encourage the rural elite to participate actively in the management of public affairs, to enable them to assume leadership by legal means, rather than form an "opposition" against the established rural authorities and the government. This is an essential precondition for good governance in rural areas.

Liang Shuming was fully aware of this key point when designing the rural self-governance system in Zouping County. He relied particularly on the rural gentry with natural prestige and status, putting them in charge of township schools as directors and heads of learning. Boards of directors were appointed before the local schools were established, exclusively consisting of leaders of public prestige ("For nothing can be done without rural elite's approval and help"). To secure their support and help, the Rural Construction Academy and the county government despatched instructors to all townships, visiting highly regarded local experts and asking these to take the lead by organizing boards of school directors. The latter could consist up to dozens of members depending on the size of the township. All directors of existing schools as well as village heads in locations without schools automatically became board members. Furthermore, the county government appointed one to three

---

[22] Based on the accounts by Sun Xiaoyun (chairman of the Tangshan Township People's Congress), Qin Enlu (80), Tang Qizhong (83, former merchant), Wang Benlie (76), Dai Zongyu (76, former teacher), Guo Shicai (84, former merchant), Han Zhenyou (70) and Wu Yumen (67, former head of the cultural center). Interviewed by Yu Keping, Jin Taijun and Ma Junya on 15 September 2001.

local persons who enjoyed prestige and were devoted to public welfare. Once established, one person of elevated age and moral integrity would be chosen as head. Another one to three talented persons devoted to public welfare were selected as executive members, one of whom serving as township director. The creation and structure of village schools resembled the above (Zhuang Weimin, 2003).

Between 1949 and the early 1980s, the ruling CCP regarded political qualities as the overriding criterion for cadres. Rural cadres were appointed along the same pattern. With the exception of the Cultural Revolution, when village revolutionary committees wielded power, the Party branch was in control. While its members monopolized rural politics, the traditional elite of gentry and sages became marginalized. For ideological reasons, the CCP absorbed workers, peasants and intellectuals, but not all members of the rural elite. Because of this political monopoly, Party members enjoyed considerable status and influence. Certain members or cadres therefore tried every means to prevent or control admission to the Party organization in order to safeguard their own interests. Since the introduction of the household responsibility system, with income linked to output, many talented persons have come to the fore, constituting a new generation of rural elite. The post-1949 village governance system, however, excludes them from public authority. Therefore, the political and the social elites have become two distinct forces in many rural areas. In the 1980s, the CCP Central Committee decided to implement rural self-governance based on villagers' committees across the country, with committee members, equal in authority to the village Party branch, universally elected. This system has of course been implemented in order to develop rural democracy, but in view of rural governance, it provides an opportunity for maximizing the use of the rural elite for the management of village affairs.

Self-governance is enabling a new generation of rural elite to become the legitimate source of village authority, with positive effects for China's rural governance on a whole. However, there is one problem which did not arise during the republican period, namely how to coordinate relations between the two chief organs of rural governance: the village Party branch and the villagers' committee, the sole legitimate authorities under the current system, The Party branch is anchored into the Organic Law on Villagers' Committees as the "leading nucleus," while the villagers' committee is protected as a pillar of rural authority in China's constitution and in the Organic Law. The villagers' committee is universally elected within the village, whereas the Party branch is voted in by the local Party members. Despite its reduced democratic mandate, the Party branch is unmistakably a leading institution in village affairs. This institutional arrangement and the replacement of the former elite by new members during the reform period inevitably create tensions. Recent studies have shown that this issue can seriously affect social stability and development in the countryside, causing financial chaos, negligence of village affairs and decaying social order. Sporadic violence can also occur, such as witnessed in 1993 in Dawangtuo, Tanliu, Muwang, Handian and Luoquan, all located in Zouping County (Wang Zhenhai, 2003).

Scholars have suggested three possible solutions for easing this tension. Firstly, there is a need to reduce the relative authority of the Party and raise that of the villagers' committee. Secondly, there is the need to make the Party branch more relevant in maintaining village governance, in close cooperation with the villagers' committee. And finally, the key members of both committee and Party need to become more integrated, in order to work toward harmonious relations. While for the time being, at least, the first solution seems unrealistic, the second and third ones have been put into practice in various ways throughout the country. In certain localities, senior Party authorities require that the village Party branch assume the chief responsibility in village governance ("Party secretary first, village head second"). Other suggestions point to making the Party branch into the village's policy-making organ, with the villagers' committee as the executive organ and the villagers' assembly as the highest organ of authority. For some localities, higher administrations have demanded that ultimate authority rest jointly in Party branch and villagers' committee and that major village affairs be examined and approved at joint meetings. The "dual vote system" imposed onto local branches by the CCP's Central Committee is, in essence, an institutional reform designed to increase the legitimacy and authority of the Party in the countryside. The system entails that all candidates be submitted to a vote of confidence before becoming eligible for Party branch elections. However, the first round of voting seems to be of greater importance. Members of the Party branch and those of the villagers' committee are encouraged to assume posts in both bodies simultaneously. Thus village Party secretaries often become directors in villagers' committees. The county Party Committee and County Government in Zouping, for instance, emphasize the leading role of Party organizations, supporting Party branches prepare for elections, and encouraging cross-membership between the two bodies, in particular of its local secretaries as directors of villagers' committees. Of a total of 2,592 village committee members and 1,095 Party branch members elected in 805 villages throughout the county in March 2002, 42% held posts concurrently, while 26% served conjointly as committee directors and Party branch secretaries.[23]

From the above we can see that informally chosen local leaders, such as village sages, the rural gentry and talented persons, have played a great role in village life. Despite the tremendous changes which occurred between the 1920s and the post-Mao reforms, the elite still plays an important role in rural governance. The transition from social to political leadership by formal institutional means and by reducing antagonisms and conflicts between the official and civil elites, is still a major challenge. The prevention of structural conflicts caused by simultaneous participation in the local committees and Party branches is of equal urgency.

Process: Election, Decision-making and Supervision

We have concluded that basic levels of wealth, the educational and ethical quality of the villagers, as well as their enthusiasm for participation in state and politics and the leadership qualities of the social elites are preconditions for good village governance. Ensuring that people of integrity and ability, who can handle affairs fairly while enjoying public respect become institutionalized authorities of governance is of vital importance to rural good governance. The same goes for the right of commoners to elect village cadres and have their say in local affairs. Elections, policy-making, management, supervision and similar activities thus constitute a basic process in contemporary rural governance.

One of the major, progressive features of rural governance reform was the introduction of a democratic electoral system. Elections had been part and parcel of the late Qing local governance reforms, during the first decade of the twentieth century. For example, the late-Qing Rules on Local Self-governance in Towns and Townships stipulated that residents of towns and townships had the right to elect representatives, albeit under stringent electoral conditions. Only men with a minimum age of twenty-five, who had lived in the same town or township for

---

[23] "Report on the Implementation of the Organic Law on Villagers' Committees and the Provincial Regulations on their Implementation in Zouping County."

more than three years and who paid two yuan in annual taxes or in donations for the public good could qualify. There were seven articles on disenfranchisement, which included opium smoking and illiteracy. Women only qualified if their tax payment surpassed those of the highest paying male voters.[24] The Organic Law on Counties promulgated by the central government in Nanjing in 1930 stipulated that district heads were to be elected within one year, to be confirmed by the provincial government in light of local conditions and with the approval of the Ministry of Internal Affairs. Deputy township and town heads were to be elected by local residents, following the appointment of candidates by the county magistrates. In the same vein, *lü* and *lin* heads were elected.[25] More voters were enfranchised than at the end of the Qing. Republican law thus stated that "citizens of the Republic of China, male or female, who have lived in townships or towns for more than one year or have owned property there in excess of two years, who are at least twenty years old and have become local residents through affidavit and registration have the right to attend the meetings of town or township residents and exercise the rights of election, dismissal, formulation and reconsideration."[26] According to the legal provisions, strict electoral procedures applied, with higher minimum requirements than today. However, since a democratic tradition was lacking and China was suffering tremendous upheaval, elections necessarily had great limitations. A lack of archival source materials makes academic research on the concrete conditions of rural self-governance rather difficult. We do, however, know that in localities where the electoral system was implemented, only the elections of *lü* and *lin* heads were authentic. Those of district heads never happened and that township and town heads continued to be chosen according to traditional methods, much as with today's village heads.

Zhaicheng Village, in early republican Dingxian County, copied the practices of model towns and villages in Japan, with village heads, assistants and other self-governance officials nominated and elected by villagers. Although this did not follow democratic criteria in the strictest

---

[24] Articles 16 and 17 of the Rules on Local Self-governance in Towns and Townships (promulgated on 27 December 1908).

[25] Articles 32, 42 and 45 of the Organic Law on Counties (revised and promulgated for the second time by the National Government on 7 July 1930).

[26] Article 7 of the Law on Implementation of Self-governance in Townships and Towns (promulgated by the National Government on 18 September 1929).

sense, it broadly reflected the collective will of the villagers as well as that of the gentry. Village governance in Zouping County rested on the authority of school directors, heads of learning and village directors (heads). Teachers would select candidates for the boards of school directors from within the village, who would then be scrutinized by the villagers' general meeting, eventually to be appointed by the county government. Villager's advice was taken into consideration with delegates mustering the support of at least half of all households. Decisions were taken following the principle of unanimous consent. If objections to a candidate were raised and supported by over one third of the delegates, a new candidate had to be nominated. If the required quorum could not be reached, the county government decided. Gerrymandering was not unheard of, such as in the case of Jiangning county, where electoral boundaries were redrawn in order to strengthen the government's influence. First-term village and *li* heads were appointed, not elected, and township and town heads were instructed to recommend twice the number of actual candidates for village and *li* elections, who the county government could provisionally appoint (Ma Junya, 2003).

The election of village cadres is of vital historical significance for rural democratic governance. This democratic process can be divided into two stages. Firstly, cadres of villagers' committees are indirectly elected during an initial, experimental period. Once elected by local residents, representatives formally elect village heads and other village cadres designated by the higher authorities by ballot. At the second stage, villagers directly elect village cadres, in what is generally referred to as a "sea election," first observed in Lishu County, Jilin.[27] "Sea election" means that the government does not designate candidates for villagers' committees and village heads prior to elections, but that voters nominate candidates according to Electoral Law and elect heads and other cadres directly into villagers' committees. After the 1990s, such direct "sea elections" were gradually introduced to rural areas across the country. At present, two electoral methods compete in rural China. In Dingzhou County, for instance, members of the villagers' committee were indirectly elected by village residents, who would also indirectly elect their cadres, since the latter are appointed by the representatives.

---

[27] See Yu Weiliang, "Electoral Procedures in the Hometown of 'Sea Elections,'" in Wang Zhenyao et al., *Cutting Edge of Self-governance Among China's Villagers*, Chinese Social Sciences Press, 2000, pp. 315–409.

Although "sea elections" were recently employed in rural parts of Jiang-ning County, there was a significant degree of red tape. A more per-fected version of the principle has been in force since 1999 in Zouping County. Due to the novelty of the concept, and also because of the complexity of the laws, policies and procedures, lack of attention to detail may cause conflicts, adversely affecting the overall situation. In this respect, Zouping County takes pride in grasping three key principles. Firstly, the villagers' electoral committees are strictly governed, with the villager representatives or associations recommending and electing committee members without government interference. Second, there is a guaranteed time frame. Electoral lists are published twenty days prior to polling day, final elections must be held within five days fol-lowing preliminary elections, and within a further ten days the village heads and representatives are to be nominated and elected. Thirdly, all must be advertised by public notice throughout the county, in six public notices. The "four musts and four prohibitions" are upheld in concrete operation. The elections are governed in strict accordance with PRC law, and any attempt to influence the designation, appointment or dismissal of villagers' electoral committees is strictly prohibited. Candidates for the villagers' committees must be directly elected by local residents. Public meetings open to the entire electorate must be convened, and not merely those open to household representatives or by means of "mobile ballot boxes." The names of candidates must be advertised to the public, ballots must be counted openly and the elec-tion results made known to the public. Any secret counting or failure to announce the results is prohibited. These regulations ensure that the legally prescribed procedures are implemented and all due rights are given to the people. After the public notices have been posted, detailing the time and locations of elections, written notices are sent by the electoral committees to all voters. This has led to a notable rise in electoral participation. Participation levels for the elections to the villagers' committees reached 93% in 2002. Direct elections, as demonstrated by comparative studies before and after the introduc-tion of "sea elections," have led to an increase in the quality of cadres (Wang Zhenhai, 2003).

As the highest authority in village life, the "rural self-governance authority" theoretically enjoys almost unchecked political and admin-istrative powers. In reality, however, the situation is much more complicated. During the republican period, the legal framework for self-governance underwent frequent changes. Lower administrative levels gradually assumed a greater degree of actual power, as did residents' participation. The Law on the Implementation of Self-governance in Townships and Towns (revised and promulgated in 1930) stipulated that rural or urban residents' representatives had rights to examine regulations, adopt budgets and final accounts, and decide on local matters, either at the request of the neighborhood, township or town authorities or as directly raised by citizens. Yet again, these laws did not match reality, and there were also great regional differences. In Zhaicheng Village, Dingxian County during the early republican period, the highest decision-making institution of the village was the village meeting attended by the village head and his assistants, the village district heads and all office holders. All important public village affairs were to be discussed and resolved at these meetings. Formal meetings were held every month. In case of an emergency, the head of the village meeting could call for a provisional meeting. When officers and district heads had pressing concerns to discuss, the head of the village meeting could be asked to hold a provisional meeting. A vote became legitimate if a simple majority could be achieved and if at least 50% of the adult village population participated. The implementation rested with the public office holders, who, mostly, also participated at village meetings. For this reason, the decisions reached at meetings could be implemented without much delay. In Zouping County the same mechanisms applied, with slight alterations. A board of village school directors was vested with the highest decision-making authority. Village heads would call meetings, which the school head, township instructors and teachers of the village's private school would attend as observers. Regular meetings were to be held at least three times per month, with extraordinary board meetings held when expedient. The village heads were responsible for implementing the board decisions.

Comparatively speaking, the equivalent mechanisms in rural China today are rather more complex. Decision-making rests with a web of institutions comprising the villagers' committee, the village Party branch, a joint committee of the former and the latter, and the meetings of village representatives and the village residents, respectively. According to the provisions of the Organic Law on Villagers' Committees, the general meeting enjoys the highest authority in the village. All adult villagers over eighteen years can participate. In certain cases, however, for instance in villages with large or scattered population numbers, the Organic Law on Villagers' Committees stipulates that representatives can hold meetings instead, in order to discuss matters addressed by the general meeting. Other legislation (Detailed Rules and Regulations on the Implementation of Elections of Villagers' Committees) in most provinces and municipalities stipulate a minimum of 400 to 500 villagers as the quorum for convening general meetings. The number of participating villagers can thus vary between twenty and seventy. Both village representatives meetings and general meetings are called by the director of the villagers' committee or secretary of the village Party branch. There is a number of issues which must first be discussed at the meetings before they can be implemented by the committee or the local Party. These include (1) local funding and taxation, (2) the allocation and rationale for subsidies, (3) the use of profits derived from collective enterprises, (4) fund raising for village-owned schools, roads and other infrastructure, (5) economic planning and contracting, (6) village contracts, (7) residential accommodation and (8) any other relevant matters deemed worthy of attention by the representative meeting.[28] Once examined and approved by the village representatives or the general meeting, the villagers' committee is responsible for implementing them. In reality, however, villages have their own specific power-sharing arrangements. Rather than relying on representatives' or general meetings, many localities entrust the joint working group consisting of the villagers' committee and the village Party branch as the highest decision-making organ. In others, the villagers' committee or the Party branch enjoy the highest authority. From the actual situation in Dingzhou, Zouping and Jiangning counties we can derive that the local Party is the real decision-making center, with the villagers' committee as its implementation organ.

Direct democratic supervision of the political institutions is an important component of modern rural governance. Village authority is thus subject to a threefold system of checks and balances comprising the higher authorities, local institutions and the population. Although the institutional mechanisms for ensuring the empowerment of villagers had been put in place during republican years, these could not be referred to as truly democratic, since there was no sufficient separation between legislative and executive powers. In Zouping, for example, the head of the village school enjoyed the highest status, though he was

---

[28] Article 19 of the Organic Law on Villagers' Committees in the People's Republic of China (adopted at the Fifth Meeting of the Standing Committee of the Ninth National People's Congress on 4 November 1998).

not responsible for any concrete administrative business. While village directors (heads) were responsible for governing the village, their actions were not directly supervised by the residents. Participation was, however, possible with the consent of the school director, whose chief responsibility was to "supervise the village directors and prevent their malpractices." Methods were flexible, including private admonition in cases of "arrogance," warnings for "shameful secrets" or pressure for directors to resign in case of internal conflict, at times with the assistance of the county magistrate (Zhuang Weimin, 2003). Supervision thus rested in the highest administrative authority.

Since the 1980s, a more democratic system of supervision of village powers has developed. The villagers' committee, Party branch, the villager representatives' and general meetings have inbuilt functions of mutual supervision and restraint. Direct elections constitute the most effective check of village powers. According to the Organic Law on Villagers' Committees, if over 20% of the electorate request the dismissal of village committee members, the committee is held to promptly hold a representatives' conference and put a request for dismissal to the vote. If over half of the villagers concur, dismissal will enter into effect. Furthermore, village cadres can be influenced by organizations such as the villagers' group for democratic handling of financial affairs. Despite such supervision mechanisms, the actual effect has been limited. The first reported case of dismissed village officials occurred in Jile village, on the outskirts of Harbin, Heilongjiang.[29] The most effective check on village powers is thus still the restraint mechanisms by the central government. Legally, the township and town governments cannot intervene in the work of the villagers' committee, and they have no right to dismiss cadres. But both Party and government can restrain village powers, firstly by having the right to appoint and dismiss members and secretaries of the village Party branch, the de facto power center in most of rural China, and secondly by controlling the election process. In a few extreme cases, the government has been known to parachute cadres into villages. In Dingzhou, for instance, the municipal Party committee emphasizes the need for channelling young cadres of high quality into village politics (Wang Fengming, 2003).

---

[29] Li Changping and Zhao Yan, "Story of the First Case of Dismissal of Village Officials by Villagers," *Yan Huang Chun Qiu*, vol. 4 (2003).

The villagers' participation in public affairs is at the heart of rural democratic governance. Through democratic elections, decision-making, supervision and administration, self-governance must aim at activating the majority of rural residents. Such a conclusion can not be reached for the republican period, when the most direct way of participating in rural governance was to join a self-governance organization. In Dingxian, Zouping and Jiangning counties, reformers of rural governance attached vital importance to the villagers' organizations, attempting to mobilize the rural masses. In Zhaicheng, Dingxian county, a Self-Governance Institute and a new school were established, in addition to associations for agrarian knowledge, legal aid, sanitation and pest prevention, agriculture and forestry, security and education. Political groups, such as for the ending of female foot binding, and for patriotic purposes, were also established, promoting self-governance with a broad civic basis. By the early 1920s, forty activists representing ten surname clans directly participated in the management of village affairs. More than ten qualified to represent the villagers at meetings.[30]

In terms of institutions, all adult villagers in China today have the opportunity to manage village affairs. This can take the shape of participating in direct elections to committees and people's congresses at county and township levels, and in rural districts in villagers' groups, at villager representatives' meetings or general meetings or of directly appraising Party branch members and villagers' committees. All this has greatly facilitated rural residents' political participation. Newer alternatives exist, such as single interest groups focusing on the proliferation of village affairs, of a democratic rural discourse or of the democratic handling of financial affairs in Dingzhou, Zouping and Jiangning counties. Members of such special groups are recommended or elected at villager representatives' conferences or at general meetings, participate in the management of village affairs and are responsible to all villagers. Villager representatives' conferences and general meetings have the right to dismiss members who neglect their duties. The women's association, Communist League and militias are mass organizations established in every village as required by the government. While the latter may have seen their apogee, the role of other organizations, such as the talented

---

[30] Mi Digang and Yin Zhongcai, "Zhaicheng Village," pp. 21–23.

persons' association, that for old age, the marriage and funeral association and one for the prohibiting of gambling are gradually rising.[31]

Participation of more poor peasants, rural women and other under-privileged groups is vital to rural democratic governance. In China's rural areas, which have a long tradition of male authority, the status of women is much lower than that of men. Rural women have been the most notable social underprivileged group. We can say that the status of rural women in rural governance indicates the depth and breadth of villagers' participation to a large extent. Our case study shows that during the Republican period, great attention was paid to women's participation in the reform of rural governance in Dingxian, Jiangning and Zouping counties. First, institutionally, women began enjoying the equal right to vote, although actual participation was still low. Laws on rural self-governance promulgated by the Nanjing government of the Republic of China gave women citizen's rights. "By attending the township and town residents' conferences and participating in elections for township and town heads, some women first exercised their democratic rights and began taking part in rural political activities" (Li Defang, 2003). Second, women began having the right to receive education like men. In addition to encouraging women to receive formal school education, rural women in counties experimented with the reform of rural self-governance. In 1929, the Tangshan Peasants' Education Center, Jiangning County, opened a women's work-study class in the people's school. Women between twelve and forty-five years of age and who were illiterate or partially literate were able to sign up for classes. The length of study for the junior class was four months, and that for the senior class was eight months. They did not pay tuition, and Tangshan Peasants' Education Center bore the labor and material costs. Once the finished products were sold, Tangshan Peasants' Education Center deducted their labor and material costs (they prepared other materials free of charge). Regardless of whether the students in the work-study class graduated, Tangshan Peasants' Education Center paid cash for their products and transported them to the county town for onward sale. To make things easier for the women engaged in work and study, the Center established a special provisional crèche to take care of

---

[31] Yu Keping, "China's Rural Civic Organizations and Changes in Governance," Yu Keping et al., *Rise of China's Civil Society and Changes in Governance*, pp. 1–28, Social Sciences Literature Publishing House, 2002.

students' children. Most of the students in the work-study class came from the lower strata of society. The first group of students in the work-study class, which ran from September 1929 to January 1930, mainly worked in agriculture, groceries, restaurants, firewood shops, bean curd shops, eateries and manual labor. Most were engaged in agricultural work, accounting for 62.79% of the total.[32] The professions of students recruited later were quite similar. In Dingxian County a special common women's school was set up, and a compilation of a Thousand Character Text for Women was planned to eliminate illiteracy among women. The traditional feudal ethics and customs which oppressed women physically and mentally, such as arranged marriages, foot binding and widowhood for women, were eliminated. To effectively eliminate these social ills, localities even took some compulsory measures. In Zouping County, the county government established a supervisory committee to ensure the removal of bandages from women's feet, and a supervision division to change these social ills. It sent a woman worker to every township who was responsible for promoting the removal of bandages used in binding women's feet in rural areas. These workers provided publicity and education in the townships and villages, were responsible for assisting rural organizations in verifying the removal of the bandages, and punishing those women who insisted on binding their feet (Zhuang Weimin, 2003). Women's rights and interests were protected and improved by establishing various types of specialized women's organizations, such as evening schools, work-study classes, associations, mothers' associations, housewives' associations, daughters' associations, committees for the removal of bandages used in binding women's feet, women's salons, health associations for women and babies, etc. These women's interest groups played an important role in cultivating and increasing their awareness of participation in government and political affairs and modern consciousness, as well as in promoting their emancipation, protecting their rights and interests and helping rural women overcome difficulties.

The circumstances and participation of women in China's rural areas during the Reform period have been quite different from those during the Republican period. During the Reform period, rural women's participation is no longer limited to the basic goals of women's

---

[32] "Process of Implementation of the Women's Work-Study Class in the Center," *Peasants' Education*, Volume 1, 6th Issue, 20 June 1931, pp. 4–10.

emancipation such as the right to education and the removal of social ills, because these goals were attained very soon after the CCP came to power in 1949. Women not only have their rights prescribed in law, but have also begun to enjoy participatory rights on the basis of equality of men and women. This is highlighted in three aspects. First, the rate of women's participation in election has greatly risen. Second, women play an increasingly important role in the management of village affairs. Third, the rights and interests of women are earnestly protected. A study of current rural governance conditions in Dingzhou, Jiangning and Zouping counties shows that women enjoy the same rights as men in the election of heads of villagers' groups, villagers' representatives, villagers' committees and township and town representatives. As with male villagers, over 90% of women participate in elections. The increasingly important role of women in rural governance is chiefly manifested in the steady increase in female villagers' direct participation in villagers' committees and Party branches. In Zouping County, the directors of women's conferences began to enter villagers' committees and village Party branches from 1996 onwards, and 99.3% of directors of women's conferences are now members of villagers' committees and village Party branches, having joined through direct elections and appointment at the village level. In recent elections, 121 persons joined the villagers' committee through direct election, accounting for 14.1% of the 858 villages (as below) in the county, 75 persons joined village Party branches through indirect election, accounting for 8.8%, and 691 persons were appointed to villagers' committees, accounting for 80.5%.[33] Although the status of rural women is quite different, they remain in an unfavorable position in comparison to male villagers. Effectively protecting the rights and interests of women is still an important task for present-day rural governance. Governments at all levels have adopted a range of administrative and non-administrative measures in this regard. For example, the plans for the development of women in all localities formulated according to the Program of the People's Republic of China for the Development of Women and the special collegiate benches for the legal rights and interests of women and children established in basic-level courts according to the Law of

---

[33] "Report on Primary Women's Organisations in Zouping County."

the People's Republic of China on the Protection of the Rights and Interests of Women, set clear requirements for the percentages of women cadres and offer training to them at regular intervals. Affirming the "half the sky" role of women and ensuring the equality of men and women are the basic goals of the CCP and the government. From the practice of rural governance, we can see that rural women play an increasingly important role in political activities. However, case studies also show that in comparison with male villagers, rural women still play a limited role in rural governance. For example, female members of villagers' committees and village Party branches are mainly directors of village women's conferences. Their role is also less important in village governance. A very small percentage of female villagers become directors of villagers' committees or secretaries of village Party branches. In 1999 there were only five women directors of villagers' committees and three women secretaries of village Party branches in Zouping County.[34]

To sum up, the process of developing rural democratic governance involves an ongoing increase in the participation of villagers, especially of participating in village elections, managing village affairs, deciding on major village affairs and supervising village cadres. Ensuring the participation of underprivileged groups including impoverished peasants, women and others in rural areas is an important measure to promote and protect the legal rights and interests of villagers. This has been effectively proved by reform during the Republican and Reform periods. Participation of women is a notable achievement of the reform of rural governance. In comparison with that during the Republican period, democratic governance in rural areas in present-day China has made breakthroughs in all major fields. For example, all-round implementation of direct elections of villagers, great increase in the rates of villagers' participation in election and the extensive practice of making village affairs known to the public, etc. But democratic election, decision-making, management and supervision and other basic aspects of village governance still fall far short of the ideals and goals of rural good governance.

---

[34] Talk by Pan Yulan, director of Zouping County Women's Federation at the seminar held by the research group on 25 August 2000.

Content: Public Welfare, Development and Administrative Affairs

The content of rural governance legislation is numerous and confusing. The relevant laws during the Republican period listed the following twenty-one items: census and personnel registration, land surveys, road, bridge, park and other public civil engineering, construction and repair, education and other cultural issues, security, national physical culture, health and rehabilitation, water conservancy, forest cultivation, planting and protection, reform and protection of agriculture and commerce, grain reserves and regulation, protection and prohibition of land reclamation, animal husbandry, fishery and hunting, organization of and guidance to cooperatives, reform of customs, raising children, taking care of the aged, poverty relief and disaster relief, and offering equipment, public issues, formulating joint pledges on self-governance, revenue and expenditure and management of public funds and property, budget formulation and final accounts, issues entrusted by the county government, district and public offices and other issues handled by townships and towns as prescribed by law.[35] The comparative principles in the relevant provisions of the Organic Law of Villagers' Committees of the People's Republic of China currently in effect include the following items: (1) "A villagers' committee shall handle the public affairs and undertakings of the village, mediate in civil disputes, help maintain social order and report the opinions and demands of villagers to the people's government, and make suggestions." (2) "A villagers' committee shall support and organize villagers to develop a cooperative economy and other sectors of the economy according to the law, take charge of services and coordination for village production and promote agricultural production and construction and the development of a socialist market economy." In accordance with legal provisions, a villagers' committee manages the land and other property of the village and those collectively owned by villagers and teaches villagers to use natural resources rationally and protects and improves the ecological environment. (3) "A villagers' committee shall publicise the Constitution of the People's Republic of China, its laws, regulations and state policies, teach and urge villagers to carry out their obligations as legally prescribed, take care of public property, protect the legal rights and interests of villagers,

---

[35] Article 30 of the Law on Implementation of Self-governance in Townships and Towns (revised and promulgated by the National Government on 7 July 1930).

develop cultural and educational initiatives, popularise scientific and technological knowledge, promote unity and mutual assistance between villages and conduct a variety of activities to promote socialist spiritual enrichment."[36] Some scholars divide management of public affairs in a rural community into seven aspects, i.e., public resources, public facilities, public culture, public security, public economy, public guarantee and public government affairs.[37] These are the main content of rural governance. If we make them more abstract, we can generalize the content of governance as the protection of public interests, the development of the politics, economy and culture of a community and the performance of administrative affairs.

Every village constitutes a small society. This was true during the republican period, and it is also true of the reform period. Rural governance covers almost all aspects, from the village's development plan through to family disputes. However, the concrete content and priorities of rural governance differ greatly from their historical background. For example, developing basic education was an essential task of rural governance during the Republican period. Now that nine-year compulsory education is being universalized, this is mainly a government task and no longer a primary task of village self-governance. The reform of rural governance during the Republican period did include family planning, but is now a major task of rural governance.

Developing rural education and raising the educational level of peasants were the most important focus of the rural self-governance movement during the republican period. From 1915 to 1916, when a self-governance model village was constructed, Zhaicheng Village, Dingxian County, used its public funds and financial subsidies from the provincial and county governments and made vigorous efforts to develop education. It requisitioned 3.3 acres of land, built and took ownership of a lower and higher primary school with 80 classrooms and nine teaching and administrative staff, the largest school in Dingxian County. With the rise of self-governance, the women's private school in Zhaicheng Village became a formal primary school (Li Defang, 2003). Once the Chinese National Mass Education Association began

---

[36] Articles 2, 5 and 6 of the Organic Law of Villagers' Committees of the People's Republic of China (adopted at the Fifth Meeting of the Standing Committee of the Ninth National People's Congress on 4 November 1998).

[37] *Patriarchal Clans in Village Governance—Survey and Research of Nine Villages*, Xiao Tangbiao and others, pp. 78–91, Shanghai Bookstore Publishing House, 2001.

its experiments in Dingxian County in the late 1920s, it based and focused all of its efforts on education.[38] A management model which integrated education with politics was used in experiments with rural construction in Zouping County. The township private school and the village private school were both political and educational organizations. Their main work included two aspects: school education and social education. With regard to school education, the village private school established a children's department (namely the primary school), an adult department and a women's department in light of actual conditions. The children's department was equivalent to the lower primary school of a national primary school. Pupils attended class in the daytime and took the same courses as those in national primary school. Pupils in the adult and women's departments attended class in the evening. The main courses included literacy, singing, philosophical talks, and military training. Other courses were organized based on actual requirements and specific local conditions. The township private school also then established a preparatory department for higher grade schooling and a vocational training department and provided instruction which the township needed, but which the village private school was not able to offer.[39] Local self-governance authorities in Jiangning County even took compulsory measures in schools and stipulated that every teacher had to teach no less than 50 children; if the number of children fell to less than 50, a sufficient number of children had to be recruited in the shortest time; severe punishments were drawn up for those who contravened the regulations or falsified student numbers. During the two years, the classes and grades in primary schools in Jiangning County experimenting with self-governance increased from 161 to 353 and the number of pupils rose to 13,976. In addition, the grades in public schools increased from 33 to 103, and the number of pupils rose from 965 to 4,570. The new secondary school had 92 students and 82 affiliated farms. There were also 112 offices enabling the population at large to inquire about Chinese characters; 185 qualified private schools with 5,465 pupils were assessed. "Increases in these numbers, stable allocation of educational funds and strict choice of teachers were higher than statistical figures in terms of actual progress."[40]

---

[38] *Historical Investigation of the Literacy Movement of the Chinese Popular Education Promotion Association*, Xu Xiuli, *Modern History Research*, 2002, 6th Issue.

[39] *Rural Construction Movement in the Republic of China*, Zheng Dahua, pp. 264–268.

[40] *Introduction to Jiangning County Administration*, the Government of Jiangning County Experimenting with Self-governance, Civil Affairs, p. 3.

Agricultural reform and rural economic development were further important rural self-governance aims in the Republic of China. In China's rural areas during the Republican period, agricultural productive forces were extremely backward, and peasants led a very poor life. Advocates of rural reform gradually realized that in comparison with the living pressure facing the population, literacy was of little importance. They therefore laid increased emphasis on measures to provide peasants with knowledge of modern agricultural science and technology, introduce improved crop strains, and establish agricultural technology experimentation bases as well as a center for spreading the use of agricultural products, so as to help them increase their productivity, increase their incomes and raise their living standards. From 1929 onwards, the Tangshan Peasants' Education Hall in Jiangning County provided peasants with cotton seeds supplied by the Agricultural School of the Central University free of charge, and purchased the cotton reaped from these seeds.[41] In 1929, about 500 kg of cotton seeds was given to 64 peasant households, which were planted in 23 acres of fields. The following year, 1,613.5 kg of cotton seeds were given to 211 peasant households, and were planted in 76 acres of fields. As well as providing cotton seeds, the Tangshan Peasants' Education Hall also gave peasants improved wheat seeds free of charge. Great efforts were made to disseminate the use of improved varieties of animals and plants and popularize modern agricultural technical knowledge and methods in Zouping and Dingxian counties, leading to substantial achievements.

Rural mutual assistance cooperatives were established, and peasants were encouraged to strengthen their capabilities by actively engaging in mutual assistance. The establishment of rural mutual assistance cooperatives was aimed at withstanding all risks by emphasizing collective strength and maximizing economic returns through cooperation. Mutual assistance and cooperation therefore often became important methods of rural governance in economically backward and threatened rural areas. After rural self-governance was introduced to Dingxian, Jiangning and Zouping counties, mutual assistance cooperatives expanded rapidly. For example, after township and village schools were set up in Zouping County, the number of cooperatives continued to increase. In 1934, there were 133 cooperatives with 4.446 cooperative members. By the end of 1935, there were 336 cooperatives, with an increased

---

[41] "Process of Spreading Improved Cotton in Tangshan and Future Design, Sun Fang," *Peasants' Education*, vol. 1, issue 3, 15 March 1931, p. 4.

membership of 14,939. By the end of 1936, there were 307 cooperatives with 8,828 members.[42] Cooperatives were significant in developing the rural economy and increasing peasants' interests. At that time, someone summed this up to four aspects. First, they spread the use of new technology and improved strains. In 1936, 7,700 acres of fields were planted with cotton across the whole county of Zouping, including 6,433 acres owned by cooperatives, accounting for 83.5%. Second, they increased peasants' incomes. Cooperative members who planted improved cotton generally saw an increase of 15–25 kg of unginned cotton per 0.165 acres. Third, they freed cotton peasants from exploitation by middlemen. Peasants solved the difficulties in selling their cotton through joint cooperative transport and sale. They increased their income by about 3 yuan for every 50 kg of ginned cotton. Fourth, as part of a cooperative, peasant households were able to more easily obtain loans, and the loan interest rate fell sharply.[43] In fact, rural cooperatives also played another very important role. Due to the lack of a social security system, they provided a form of social insurance for vast numbers of poor peasants and constituted a living guarantee mechanism.

Abolishing social ills and archaic customs and cultivating a wholesome environment were also a notable feature of rural governance reform during the Republican period. Backward rural areas were rife with the dross of Chinese feudal social culture, such as superstition, male superiority, harmful feudal ethics, gambling, drug use, etc. These evils seriously shackled people's thinking and concepts and hampered the development of rural productivity and the emancipation of peasants' personalities. Reform of social customs was regarded as an important aspect of the rural self-governance movement in Dingxian, Zouping and Jiangning counties during the Republican period. Village governance authorities advocated new customs in place of old social ills. For example, in Jiangning County furniture and seed exhibitions and a cattle competition replaced the original temple fair. Special movements were also initiated to eliminate evil habits, such as by prohibiting gambling

---

[42] "Report on Survey of 25 Years of Various Cooperatives in Zouping County," Luo Ziwei, *Rural Construction Semimonthly*, vol. 6, issue 17–18, June 1937.

[43] "Introduction to Cooperatives in Zouping County Experimenting with Self-governance," Que Ming, *Rural Construction Quarterly*, vol. 4, issue 10–11, 21 October 1934; *Rural Construction Semimonthly*, vol. 5, issue 16–17, March 1936; "Introduction to Shandong Rural Construction Research Academy and the Experimental Area in Zouping," Shandong Rural Construction Research Academy, Zouping, 1937, pp. 52–53, 118.

and drug use in Zouping County. Zhaicheng Village, Dingxian County also specially formulated Rules for Reforming Customs which clearly stipulated that "men may get married from the age of 20 onwards, and women from the age of 16 onwards. Women are prohibited from binding their feet. Girls younger than 16 years of age whose feet have been bound must have their feet unbound. During funeral rites, temple storytelling, the chanting of Buddhist scriptures, the preparation of paper persons and other activities are banned. The Gregorian calendar is stressed in wining during the Spring Festival, and the pasting of kitchen gods is prohibited. Except when complying with old feudal funeral ethics by the children of the deceased, bowing is practised at other celebrations, congratulations and condolences, while kowtowing is now prohibited. Other customs involving superstition must be changed" (Li Defang, 2003).

Because of the turbulent social conditions during the republican period, communal security work was very important. Preventive measures were taken not only against petty thieves in villages, but also against bandits and even foreign enemies. Villages in Zouping County formed self-defense groups, together with similar groups in townships. Village self-defense groups received training at regular intervals, attended township schools for monthly "township shooting" ceremonies and to conduct military training. In the summer and the autumn, the heads of township groups would patrol villages at night time, assisted by their colleagues in the villages, offering protection against bandits, robbers and thieves (Zhuang Weimin, 2003). A security group system was established throughout Jiangning county, whereby every village participated. Every administrative area would form groups, which all men under eighteen or over thirty-five could join, provided they had the necessary moral integrity. In the fallow season, they would receive group training. Usually focusing on capturing thieves, they would defend strategic passes in wartime (Ma Junya, 2003). Village security groups in Dingxian originally only "patrolled and sounded the watches at night, helped maintain public order and guarded against robbery and theft." Security became a paramount issue when Hebei became a pinnacle of resistance against the Japanese. Thus, the Chinese National Association for Mass Education designed the township and town construction committees, part of a citizens' service group, and prepared to resist the foreign enemy by making use of civilian forces (Li Defang, 2003). Vigorous, civilian resistance became a hallmark of Dingxian following Japanese invasion.

Today, some of the above criteria of rural governance are no longer important. Some have even been erased and new functions added, such as family planning, fee retention and payment, economic contracting, the examination and approval of housing sites, as well as transparency.

Family planning has been a basic national policy since the reforms began. In order to control population growth and even to effectively reduce the number of people in China, the Chinese government began implementing a "one couple, one child" policy in the 1980s. This policy is a great challenge in rural China, where the concept of male superiority and the need for male farmers refuses to recede. While impossible to implement this policy to the letter, the greatest task falls into the remit of the villagers' committees and the local Party. Even though levels of social, economic and cultural development have greatly risen and a flexible policy has been introduced to allow household with one girl to have the second child, it remains an arduous task for committee and Party members. Governments at higher levels have instituted a rigorous responsibility system for the implementation of the family planning policy, namely the "one-vote vetoing." Violation of this national policy is punished regardless of the offending official's political standing. Therefore, almost every village has formulated rules on family planning, which clearly stipulate the responsibilities and obligations of all villagers. Special committees and cadres, including directors, statisticians, press officers and drug testing volunteers, with responsibility for the implementation and examination of the family planning policy, take careful preventive measures, such as coaching rural women as soon as they reach child-bearing age.

The retention and collecting of fees refers to the villages' share in the public accumulation and welfare funds, as well as management fees. While a village is entitled to collect fees for running schools at township and village level, for family planning, special care to disabled servicemen and revolutionary martyrs and their families, as well as for militia training, road construction and health care, village retention and township collecting are actually a form of taxation. It thus directly affects the immediate interests of villagers and is politically sensitive. In circumstances when the collective economy is weak, peasants are poor and fees too high, fee collection becomes a difficult task. The villagers' committee and village Party branch make great efforts to collect all fees due, at times resorting to coercion. In rural Dingzhou, this process usually pursues the following path. At first township and village cadre meetings are held, the relevant laws and regulations expounded, cadres and policemen of the administrative tribunal of the Municipal People's Court convened to explain the administrative legislation, while raising awareness among township and village cadres and their ability of governing according to the law. Then, central and provincial regulations on fees and on labor management are being propagated by means of broadcasting, slogans or publicity trucks. Thirdly, households refusing to pay without good reason are named in every village, followed by a final written payment demand. If households still refuse to pay, without resorting to an appeal, the legal route remains the only option (Wang Fengming, 2003).

Family planning and village finances are government affairs of the highest order, managed by village self-governance organizations. Both demand a great degree of manpower and energy and form the principal tasks of the township and town government cadres resident in villages. Both also trigger antagonism and conflicts between village cadres and peasants. Villagers thus jokingly intimate that the officials "take both money and lives." Since both directly affect social and political stability in China's villages, the central government has tried to implement major improvements. The current rural tax and fee reforms are but one example. Initial results in the conversion of fees to taxes show that the reforms have notably reduced the burden of the peasantry, improving relations between villagers and cadres and promoting good governance.

At present, a collective land ownership system is in force, unlike during the Republic. Legally, peasants enjoy the right to cultivate family plots, obligatory fields and the use of housing sites, but their ownership is still vested in the collective. Therefore, the contracting of obligatory fields and the examination and approval of housing sites currently play a major role in rural areas and constitute important aspects of village politics. The astute handling of the above by village cadres is rewarded with increased power. In more developed villages which have their roots in the collective economy, the contracting of land, enterprises and other collective ventures are of particular importance. In Guquan (Jiangning County) for instance, the collective economy is very developed. In 2000, the total output value exceeded RMB 140 million (US$17 million), of which the local collective economy accounted for RMB 28.89 million. Village-owned Nanjing Guquan Group Corporation operates a plastics factory, a quarry, an ecological aquiculture plant, a filling plant and the local tea farm. Against this economic background, the management and contracting of enterprises becomes an important aspect of village administration (Jin Taijun, 2003).

Transparency of village politics is another major element of rural governance, since this empowers villagers by giving them insight into the public affairs of their village and by enabling them to supervise the administrative and economic actions of the local cadres. Transparency thus constitutes one of the key measures of good governance in the countryside. It has also become a legal requirement, with the adoption of the Organic Law on Villagers' Committees and through central government legislation. Most localities make their transparency policies known to the public, clearly stipulating the concrete implications, methods and punishments for those who violate transparency regulations. In Dingzhou, for instance, such public information policies include details on the economic and social development of the village and the annual agenda of the villagers' committee. Furthermore, it covers financial planning, receipts and expenditures, the collection, budgeting and use of fees and provisions for the use of labor. Transparency policies allow insight into the list of persons who enjoy village subsidies, as well as their criteria and amounts, into income from the village's collective economy, the collection and use of appropriations, compensatory fees and donations. Disaster relief, poverty alleviation and assistance to the disabled and water and electricity rates are covered, as are the collective economy, funds for public undertakings such as village-run schools and roads, culture and health, tender invitations and submissions, construction and contracting, collective property, land and industrial, commercial and contractual finances. Finally, all building applications, their approval and use for the current year, the name lists of persons entitled to get married and give birth, persons who give birth to children outside the approved system, the collection and use of fees for extra-plan births and similar matters of common concern must also be made known upon request. Dingzhou officials have formulated detailed regulations on how to implement the transparency legislation, how to measure its implementation, its supervision and reporting to higher government authorities and penalties concerning violations of the transparency system (Wang Fengming, 2003).

From the above research, we can see that the content and priorities of rural governance vary greatly in different historical periods. During the republican period, rural governance concentrated on solving problems such as developing education, providing adequate food and clothing, reforming outmoded customs and protecting against banditry. During the current reform years, new tasks have emerged, such as family planning, fee retention and collection or the advertising of village affairs to the public. Such tasks are entrusted to self-governance organizations by the state. The fact that the material and mental universe of villagers has changed beyond recognition and that the control of the state has become pervasive in the countryside means that completion of administrative tasks is now the most important task of self-governance organizations, using strong administrative techniques. Stability, of course, remains the overriding concern in both periods, as much as the increasing of public awareness and the promotion of public projects.

Methods: Mobilization, Cooperation and Compulsion

Just as at higher levels of administration, rural self-governance authorities need to rely on persuasion and education, administrative order and legal compulsion, political mobilization, voluntary cooperation, economic stimulation and moral encouragement to attain effective levels of governance. As in any rural acquaintance society,[44] however, social capital—defined as a network of trust, participation and cooperation—plays a particularly important role in the process of governance, stressing persuasion and cooperation rather than compulsion and coercion.

The main methods of rural governance during the republican period were persuasion and education. As outlined above, the rural governance movement in Dingxian, Zouping and Jiangning placed particular emphasis on peasant education, combining school knowledge with social education. The education of commoners in matters such as political awareness, new habits and social reforms could take many forms. Township and village schools in Zouping County, for instance, stipulated that all directors openly discuss matters of public concern with the people and to provide guidance in public affairs. They also asked to respect the opinions of the heads of schools, to represent their local constituencies in all discussions with the county government and, in return, convey the latter's intentions to the people. Finally, they were

---

[44] For the concept of social capital and its role in governance, see Robert Patnan (et al.), *Making Democracy Operate*, Jiangxi People's Publishing House, 2002, Foreword of the Chinese Version, Chapters 2, 5 and 6.

advised to mediate together with the other members of the board of directors in order to find solutions to local problems. This implied relying on persuasion and education, rather than pursuing the legal route. The popular education movement initiated by Yan Yangchu in Dingxian County set out to advance social awareness, persuade peasants to accept vaccinations, reject narcotics, resist gambling, build roads, plant trees, set up self-defense groups and improve sanitation. This was underlined through practical demonstrations and help toward finding a new lifestyle. The temple fair, teahouse, exhibitions and public meetings were used to mobilise the people and to promote reform. In sheer scale and effect, however, they did not match the political mass campaigns led by the CCP.

The ideological and political education applied in present-day China appears similar to the techniques applied during the Republic, although there are important differences. Today's method relies on political mobilization. In the countryside this means creating mass movements which influence the peasantry toward accepting authority and order. This method was often used by the CCP during the years of war with the GMD and with Japan, and it remained in common use after 1949. Party and government cadres at all levels are familiar with this method. Important activities in village life, such as family planning, the collection of taxes and fees and committee elections, are thus inaugurated by political mobilization initiated by government, committee and Party officials. This could be witnessed during recent elections to the villagers' committees in Zouping, Shandong, where much attention was focused on increasing political interest. The local media extensively publicized the Organic Law of Villagers' Committees and the Methods of Elections of Villagers' Committees in Shandong Province. The county's TV station established a special program on villagers' committees elections, broadcast daily. Towns and townships added to the momentum through meetings and public advertisements, in order to maximize public awareness (Wang Zhenhai, 2003).

Good village governance must be based on the full cooperation between those responsible for the management of village affairs and the villagers. Effective governance through cooperation and consultation was a goal during the Republic. This is also true for the current period. In his experiments in Zouping County, Liang Shuming did his utmost to oppose an implementation of rural reforms through "top-down" compulsory administrative means, stressing that all townships and villages should reform voluntarily in light of local needs and conditions.

To avoid direct conflict between township and village schools, as well as township residents and villagers and to reach a general consensus, he did not favor the introduction of democratic principles since he feared the resulting disputes and potential chaos. Hence, checks and balances of village powers were not in force, "to avoid rivalry" (Liang Shuming). With regard to the dismissal of leading grassroots cadres, Liang Shuming thought that this was not to be determined at villagers' meetings since such action was "too strict and ruthless." Instead he suggested that "all village affairs be handled through consultation" (Zhuang Weimin, 2003).

Cooperation and conflict resolution are also methods of governance used by the current administrators of Zouping County. When villagers are not content with government and/or village cadres, and conflicts cannot be resolved through normal channels, the former would seek consultations with the higher authorities. In case of an inconclusive outcome, contradictions may become more pronounced, giving rise to conflict. In view of this situation, before the village-level elections of 1999, the Zouping County Party committee despatched 1,843 cadres from 74 government departments, including the secretary of the county Party committee. Subdivided into seven groups, they visited 78,000 households, talked with 200,000 residents, gathered a total of 13,617 feedback forms, addressing 1,281 items matters, and provided 2,329 suggestions to the villagers' committee and the village Party branch, thus cementing ties between cadres and villagers.[45] The Party committee and the government of Xidong Town, Zouping County, formulated a system of popular consultations. In the first week of every month, town cadres would travel to the village to engage in honest consultations with members of the villagers' committee, the local Party, official representatives, heads of civic groups and some individuals. Prior to these consultations, the town Party committee and government would determine the nature of the actions needed during the month in accordance with the priorities of the town as a whole, as well as the actual conditions in the villages. They would prepare written documents, provide training to government cadres at routine meetings every Monday and establish priorities. All villages would notify Party members and villagers'

---

[45] Zouping County CCP Committee and Zouping County People's Government, "Examination and Rectification Help Ensure Stability, and Solidification of the Foundation Helps Long-term Peace."

representatives in writing, and inform villagers by means of posted and broadcast announcements. During the consultations, town and village cadres talked cordially with villagers, acquiring an understanding of pressing concerns, not forgetting to fill in the feedback form specifically produced for this consultation. These forms needed to be signed by the resident cadres, the local Party secretaries and the directors of villagers' committees before being collected. Following each consultation, a working group would analyze issues raised in all villages and organize the logistics necessary to find and implement solutions, which were to be fed back to the local residents at the following consultation. The result was that many issues addressed by local people could be solved in a timely manner, increasing popular appreciation for both Party and government (Wang Zhenhai, 2003).

Although cooperation is the foremost method of rural governance, administrative orders and a certain degree of compulsion are unavoidable. Administrative means are simple, fast, and usually very effective. They are hence favored by local governments and self-governance authorities. Reformers during both periods needed to ensure that infringements of state laws and government policies by villagers were rectified and punished rapidly. In the context of good governance, the thorniest problem must be the abuse of administrative and punitive means by rural cadres. In republican Jiangning, the government stipulated that if local residents violated laws or decrees, the township and town heads would be able to take them into custody or to pass the matter to the higher authorities for action. Some local officials of low moral quality abused these provisions and became local tyrants. "They reported all violations of the law to higher authorities. They had the authority to inspect and guide all villages, handle matters of self-governance, resolve disputes among the people, as well as to reform superstition and bad habits. They were true local tyrants."[46] Shortly after rural self-governance was promoted in Zouping, phenomena of undue reliance on administrative means and excessive use of strength became known. All reforms in rural areas were coerced, so township and village schools had to adopt a passive position. In the second half of 1934, the Rural Construction Academy began readjusting relations between the

---

[46] Wang Du, "General Report on the Experience of Jiangning County while Experimenting with Self-governance" (vol. 2) (manuscript), Practice Report of the Department of Administration of the Central Political School, September 1934, p. 199.

government and grassroots organizations and took measures against the tendency of undue reliance on administrative compulsion. According to the principle of "indirect use of strength," all rural matters were handled by township and village schools, and the county government did not resort to compulsion. However, great efforts had to be made to tackle the issue of public security and of rogue elements.[47] Such phenomena of abuse of bureaucratic competences and excessive use of strength in rural governance exist to varying degrees also in present-day China. Today administrative powers are used more than under the Republic, which makes it possible to abuse compulsion. Because of such abuse, violent conflicts between villagers and cadres are frequent and grave cases of administrations being in violation of the law do occur often. From the current practice it appears that the most effective method of overcoming abuse is to strengthen the rule of law in rural governance, improve the legal system, increase the awareness of cadres and villagers about the importance of the law and persist in governing village affairs according to the law (Wang Fengming, 2003).

Methods differed, and means of government administration as varied as administrative orders, persuasion and education, political mobilization, legal compulsion, voluntary cooperation, economic stimulation, moral encouragement among others apply. Political mobilization is often used today, while it played a minor role during the republican period. Education and cooperation figured in both reform periods, while reduced compulsion and increased cooperation are the very essence of rural governance. Cooperation between the government and villagers, between village cadres and villagers and in between villagers is the best way toward creating rural democratic governance.

Environment: Economy, Politics and Culture

From the above, it becomes clear that the rural governance reforms during the republican period resembled those of today in important aspects. However, there were also differences. The reasons and implications can be explained by looking at the environment determining both reform attempts. To start with, rural reform can be classified as political reform, and all political reform is closely related to economic

---

[47] Liang Shuming, "Concrete Practice of Village Private Schools and Township Private Schools," *Rural Construction Quarterly*, Volume 4, 4th Issue, September 20, 1934.

foundations. Changes in the social and economic spheres lead to changes in political life and vice versa. Political changes are not always matched by economic development, but they roughly coincide. To acquire an understanding of the reforms of rural governance, we need to analyze their socio-economic environment, especially the economic structure of ownership and the degree of economic development.

Private ownership of the means of production was the rule during the republican period, and most land was thus privately owned. In rural Dingxian, Zouping and Jiangning this was also the case. Village society could be divided into landed farmers, tenant farmers and landlords, the majority of villagers being landed farmers. Annexation or concentration of land were not obvious phenomena in these three counties. Peasant households in republican Jiangning, for instance, had 4.04 acres of fields on average, 95.3% being tilled by the farmers themselves, with only 4.7% on lease. According to a survey of eighty peasant households, all but one were tillers, there were no tenant farmers, and only one household tilled while leasing their field.[48] The situation was similar in Zouping County. According to a survey of 1,434 peasant households, landed farmers accounted for 86.36%, with an average of 3.83 acres of land per household or 0.8 acres per person. There were only twenty-six households of tenant farmers and laborers, accounting for 1.8%, sixteen landlord households, each household measuring 1.7 acres on average. Thus we arrive at a total of fifty landed farmers and landlords and an average of 6.86 acres of land per household, or 1.52 per person.[49] Because there were no production collectives, rural governance in this regard was absent. At present, however, collective ownership is pervasive, and all land is collectively owned. A major feature of China's reform policies is the contract responsibility system, with remuneration linked to output. This means that collectively-owned village land is distributed to farming households in accordance to their size. Peasants have the right to use and operate land, but do not have the right of ownership. The formerly entrenched differences between landlords, tenant farmers and

---

[48] Chinese Vocational Education Society, *Survey Report on the Livelihood of Peasants*, Chinese Vocational Education Society Publishing Section, June 1929, p. 13.

[49] Survey Department of Shandong Rural Construction Research Academy, "Survey on Current Conditions in the Distribution of Field Ownership of 434 Peasant Households in Zouping County and Arable Land," *Rural Construction Semimonthly*, vol. 5, no. 3, 15 September 1935.

landed farmers have thus all but disappeared. Land ownership has a direct impact on rural governance. Because today's village economy is collective in nature, the main concerns of rural governance are the management and distribution of the collective economic interests. This is why the contracting of land and of other collectively owned property, as well as the examination and approval of housing sites have become the chief tasks of rural governance.

In the fifty years between the 1930s and the 1980s, China's rural areas have experienced vicissitudes and tremendous change. Levels of production, economic development and living standards have risen considerably. During republican times, productivity was extremely low and peasants lived in dire poverty. Today, China's rural economy is expanding rapidly, while the proportion of agriculture in the rural economy has decreased drastically. Living standards have been rising in equal measure, with adequate food and clothing in ample supply. Compared to the republican period, ours are years of comfort. In Zouping during the 1930s, for instance, there was no modern industry, and all income was derived from agriculture and sideline production. The total income thus derived in 1935 was 4.3 million yuan, while the total expenses amounted to 4.2 million yuan. The average yearly net income per peasant was thus a mere 1.2 yuan. Under such conditions, "famine immediately appeared in times of poor harvests."[50] In 2002, by contrast, the gross domestic product of the whole county attained RMB 8.4 billion. Agricultural output value amounted to 1.36 billion, merely 16.2% of the total. By 2000, the per capita annual income had reached RMB 2,861 (Wang Zhenhai, 2003). However, in comparison with urban incomes, rural earnings limp behind. When comparing it with incomes in developed countries, the gap is even greater. This fact highlights that firstly, there is a paramount need for poverty eradication, particularly urgent during the republican period, and that secondly, also today, the developing of the rural economy and of living standards remain basic challenges of rural governance.

Also the political conditions of rural governance were different. During the republican period, the fundamental system implemented by the Guomindang was a variation of the Western three powers system, based on the existence of five separate powers. Since 1949,

---

[50] Zouping Rural Financial Circulation Division, "Introduction to Rural Economy of Zouping County," *Rural Construction Semimonthly*, vol. 6, no. 5, 16 October 1936.

the CCP has been implementing varying manifestations of a socialist political system with Chinese characteristics. Its main characteristic is the popular representation dominated by single-party rule and the combination of legislative and executive powers. These systemic differences led to discrepancies in terms of power structure, government functions, relations between Party and government, between central and local authorities, as well as between government and citizens. In our study we merely concentrate on the differences between Party and government, on political integration and the rule of law, as well as on the impact on rural governance.

Regarding relations between Party and government, the one similarity between both periods was that the Guomindang and the CCP acted as the ruling parties, albeit rather different in methods and abilities. The Guomindang's principle of centralized national rule was fully manifested at its top, whereas neither the GMD nor the central government exerted any palpable influence at sub-county level. Guomindang documents clearly stipulate that the party's methods of political work in townships and villages were meant to publicise its doctrines, to conduct social survey and to supervise local self-governance. With regard to GMD relations with the government, the party's headquarters played a supervisory, guiding and auxiliary role.[51] Overall, its status was weak. On the contrary, the CCP has the status of a nodal point in central and local political power at all levels and actually functions accordingly. The CCP and the government jointly exercise the political and administrative management of society. Local members of the Guomindang were generally few in number, its rural primary organizations being district branches without village organizations. The CCP, on the other hand, has many rural members, and its primary organizations are established in all counties. The same political background determines that there was only one authority of rural self-governance during the Republic, as opposed to today's two authoritative organizations, namely the village Party branch and the villagers' committee. Therefore, rural governance only involved relations between the government and the peasantry during the republican period, while relations between the

---

[51] "Concentrate on the Practical Work and Achieve the Party's Mission during the Period of Tutelage" (Notice to Party Headquarters at All Levels Sent by the Central Executive Committee of the Chinese Guomindang on 6 November 1929), *Local Self-governance*, pp. 55–65.

Party and the government today, and between the former and the peasantry remain fraught.

Political integration during the republican period remained an elusive ideal pursued by the Kuomintang government. Any effective integration between the central and local authorities and, horizontally, between local authorities was lacking. Warlords controlled the local organs of political power, while not few local forces were powerful enough to defy the central government. Government decrees were ineffective and the central authorities' reach barely permeated China's vast rural hinterland. The CCP, on the other hand, has an unrivalled capacity for political integration, with political integration vertically and on the same level high, and its political power stretching into the most remote locations. The political conditions of the day as well as an insufficient level of integration determined that different models of rural governance could coexist during the republican period, as opposed to the single, homogenous model we are witnessing today. Although national laws and regulations on local self-governance had been issued, three different models of rural governance existed in Dingxian, Jiangning and Zouping counties. The model of governance of Zhaicheng Village, Dingxian County copied Japanese rural governance, and the plan for rural governance designed by the Chinese National Association for Mass Education differed from the governance of Zhaicheng Village. Experimentation with rural self-governance in Jiangning County was directly promoted through administrative means. Political participation was tightly controlled, while civil forces were lacking. Zouping County experimented with Liang Shuming's theories on rural construction. There were great differences in many important aspects of rural governance between these three localities, and it would be no exaggeration to refer to them as the Dingxian, Jiangning and Zouping models, respectively, as some scholars have done. By contrast, rural governance reforms after the implementation of the reforms were homogeneous, i.e., virtually identical in structure, functions, procedures and processes of rural governance. Existing differences between localities were dictated by diverging levels of political and economic development and of governance techniques, while there are no fundamentally different models.

The Chinese political tradition is not based on the rule of law, but on rule by virtue, particularly ensconced in its vast rural areas. The legal basis for rural self-governance during the Republic reflected this. Republican laws went even farther than the current ones, but most existed in name only. Rural governance was not based on law, but on human domination, as typified by Liang Shuming's experiment in Zouping. In institutional design, he clearly opposed the supremacy of the law, upholding the rule of virtue, with village sages dictating the aims of rural policies. Accordingly, legal action was absent or being discouraged. Although rule by virtue is still deeply rooted in China today, the legalist alternative has been rising in importance. Rebuilding the country under the aegis of the law has become a clearly stated priority in China's current constitution. Lawfulness in political action, legal scrutiny of rural governance and the provision of regular legal education to cadres and peasants alike have become the main tenets of rural governance.

The cultural climate has a profound impact on rural governance. Cultural factors exert a strong influence on many aspects of people's behavior and on their political activities. Beneath, we shall analyze the combined aspect of culture and education and secondly of political culture, namely citizens' awareness of democracy and the law.

As a consequence of the absolute poverty reigning amongst the peasantry during the Republic, educational levels were low and illiteracy high. Due to the efforts of the Chinese National Association for Mass Education, literacy in Dingxian rose considerably, in fact above the national average, though nevertheless remaining high. According to a county-wide survey conducted by the association in the spring of 1927, of an overall population of about 400,000 (or rather of the 330,000 above seven years of age), illiterates accounted for about 270,000, or circa 83%. Male illiteracy measured some 69% and among women 98%.[52] Years of input by the association changed this situation greatly. In particular, literacy amongst the young increased notably. At the end of June 1934, literacy in the age group between fourteen and twenty-five years reached 61%, men accounting for 90% and women for 27.[53] This achievement can certainly be regarded as an outstanding example of the association's promotion of rural construction and above all its drive to eliminating illiteracy, although 10% of young men and 73% of young women were still illiterate, not mentioning those above

---

[52] Tang Maoru, "Peasants' Education in Dingxian County," School Education Department of the Chinese Common People Education Promotion Association, 1932.

[53] Yan Yangchu, "Summary of the Work in Experimental Areas in Dingxian County" (October 1935), in: *Collected Works of Yan Yangchu*, vol. 1, pp. 408–409, Hunan Education Publishing House, 1989.

their forties. Moreover, literacy alone does not amount to knowledge and to qualifications obtained through formal education. And the situation in two other counties was not as optimistic. According to a survey of 1935, the illiterate population of Zouping County amounted to 139,266, which is 84.2% of the total population, 70% for men and over 98% for women.[54] Jiangning County was educationally developed for its time, but male illiterates still accounted for 82.2% and illiterate women for 98.7%.[55] In sharp contrast to the republican situation, a law stipulating a nine-year period of compulsory universal education was implemented across the country during the reform period. Literacy rates among the rural young thus accounted for over 90%, on average. Because Dingzhou, Zouping and Jiangning were relatively developed counties, the nine-year compulsory education system was universally introduced with literacy rates reaching nearly 100%. Great differences in national education seriously affect the quality of rural governance. In contrast to the republican period, the development of a basic national education system is no longer an urgent task today. Great differences in national education seriously affect rural governance because the educational and cultural levels of villagers have a direct bearing on many aspects of self-governance among villagers, for instance on the election of local cadres, on supervision and decision-making, on transparency or on political participation.

Traditional political culture in China implies subordination to a ruler. Its basic political values are not freedom, democracy and equality, but hierarchy, order and unity. This produces a strong sense of subordination and collective identity, and is lacking in a sense of independence and participation.[56] Such traditional features are mainly manifested in the peasantry, distorting the reform of rural governance during both periods and giving rise to the "government control" approach. There are few differences between the two reform programs. Most villagers in republican years lack a sense of democracy, had no enthusiasm for and capacity of participating in political and government affairs and

---

[54] Wu Guyu, "Analysis of the Population Issue of Zouping County (Continued)," *Rural Construction Semimonthly*, Volume 5, no. 7, 15 November 1935.

[55] Government of Jiangning County (Self-Governance unit), *Introduction to Jiangning County Administration*, "Civil Administration," Table 6.

[56] Yu Keping, "Outline of the Chinese Traditional Political Culture," *Confucian Studies*, no. 3, 1989.

took a passive attitude toward self-governance. Dingxian County, for instance, despite having adopted rural self-governance early, suffered from political and administrative inertia, both from the part of government officials and of the rural residents. Therefore, in most cases, rural self-governance was all but formalistic. The Political Construction Research Center of Hebei concluded that in the vast majority of rural areas, residents lacked all understanding of self-governance and expressed no need for the latter. Township and village heads were generally elected by the people, but the electorate seemed hardly aware of its role, people not being interested. Many of the illiterate were easily manipulated, so that the gentry controlled the election. Under the democratic veneer of Dingxian County, therefore, lay an autocratic reality (Li Defang, 2003). Significantly, the greatest issue of rural governance in Dingzhou today remains political apathy. Some higher cadres lack enthusiasm for rural autonomy and in the collection of taxes and fees administrative measures are proving useless. Legal means are unexplored and self-governance appears absent. Grassroots cadres spend most of their energy trying to collect money and applying for government grants, while finding little or no time on encouraging development. Villagers respond by not complying with official work assignments and by harassing cadres for help and money, while being rude if proper service is not provided. In some villages, villagers have little interest in the election of village cadres. To stimulate enthusiasm, each voter is offered two yuan. If the general conference or the representatives' conference does not happen to address their immediate concerns, locals are unwilling to attend. If they do attend, they have to be given financial incentives (Wang Fengming, 2003).

In brief, the reform of rural governance is an important part of China's social reforms, and cannot be separated from the latter's political, economic and cultural determinants. All similarities and differences detected in rural governance reform can be ascribed to more general factors. During the republican period, "representative democracy" was implemented under the rule of the Guomindang, with a capitalist system based on private ownership. The political situation was turbulent, government orders were obstructed, and the level of social and economic development was very low. During the reform period, a socialist democracy under the leadership of the CCP has been implemented, its economy still dominated by a socialist market economy with public ownership. The political situation is stable, government orders are coherent, while China is witnessing rapid social and economic development. However, both periods also saw China's rural areas in a process of social transition. Traditional political culture is still deeply rooted, and some laws governing political development in modern China are proving resilient. Both elements determine the quality and results of rural governance, during both periods.

Conclusion: Models, Problems and Orientation

In the above chapters, we analyzed the structures, subjects, processes, contents, methods as well as social and historical backgrounds concerning the rural governance reform movements of the republican period and in the People's Republic today. The subsequent paragraphs will critically compare and analyze the similarities and differences, as well as the main difficulties both have encountered. Ways of overcoming these difficulties and of promoting good rural governance will also be discussed.

There are clearly many differences between rural governance during the republican period and that of the reform period. Nevertheless, the models of rural governance from both periods in modern Chinese history share some important common features, symbolizing the legal background as well as the future of China's rural governance.

China's rural governance is a governance model determined by the government. Reforms of rural governance, including village self-governance, have historically been initiated from top down. The government sets the parameters, checks and guides the structures, functions and orientations of rural governance by means of laws, institutions and policies. By various means, the government effectively controls the governing rural elite and even despatches officials to participate in village governance, if necessary. The supply of grants and subsidies, as well as by offering education and training opportunities to villagers and cadres strengthens the government's role. The real significance of "township administration and village governance" put forth by some scholars is merely a combination of township (government) and village (self-governance) in the process of village governance. Conflicts between higher and lower levels or between township administration and village governance are only auxiliary phenomena of a model led by the government. This government-centered governance model is deeply rooted in China's traditional political culture. It undoubtedly has its positive characteristics and historical value, however its critics may decry its methods.

China's rural governance follows a diverse model. Legally speaking, rural self-governance should be unitary (centralized) in nature. However, the results of the above study show that the structure of governance is pluralistic (diverse). Three different authorities directly participate in rural governance. Firstly, townships and town governments as the bearers of official authority.[57] Secondly, a type of purely civil, non-institutional, rural authority is represented by spontaneous civil organizations. Finally, there is a hybrid form of governmental-civil authority, e.g., village officials and public officials, private schools (Republic) and the present-day villagers' committee and village Party branch. These three authorities combined exert influence on the contents, processes, methods and results of rural governance. Generally speaking, government authority mainly affects the structure and orientation of rural governance, while a village's legal authority focuses on routine village affairs. The civil authorities deal with non-institutional village matters or those which cannot be handled by the institutions.

China's rural governance is an elite governance model. No matter what rural political system is implemented, the powerful social elite plays a decisive role in village governance. There are clear differences between the criteria defining local elites in each historical period. During republican times, the rural elite consisted of "country gentry" and "village sages," defined by moral integrity and prestige. During the reform period, the same class consists of "able persons," namely those capable of financial success. However, the roles played by both in rural governance are almost the same. The quality of rural governance hinges to a great extent on whether these elites were recruited into positions of authority by institutional means or informally. Once confirmed in their role, they often play a dual role of agents to and masters of the village. In a sense, the elites can be seen as representative of the imperial model which regarded commoners as the "root" of all imperial administration.

People generally assume that all reforms of rural governance in republican China ended in failure and that the basic reason for this lay in the ultimate collapse of the political and economic systems they

---

[57] Sub-county divisions were changeable and chaotic during the republican period. Generally speaking, the lowest administrative level in rural areas was the district.

relied on. Not all failures, however, can be attributed to the momentous problems faced by the Republic. The current round of rural reforms is on the contrary based on a strong and developing political and economic foundation. This does not mean that the current system is devoid of problems. The most common five lessons from history are referred to beneath.

1) The system of rural self-governance as legally dictated is by and large a mere formality. Both in republican and in contemporary China, central and local governments formulated laws and regulations on rural governance, making detailed provisions on villagers' rights, the mechanisms and procedures for self-governance and its aims. On a whole, however, the core elements of rural governance, such as the electoral system, decision-making and management procedures or supervision, become mere formalities and are not truly implemented. In some cases, matters are not handled according to the law. In others, formality prevails, at the expense of practical results. Occasionally, legal provisions are distorted in the process of their implementation. Such malfunctioning can partly be explained by imperfections within the system of self-governance. The main reason, however, remains the deficiencies of local government officials and village cadres in matters of law, democracy and responsibility. Villagers, on the other hand, lack an adequate understanding of democracy and of their rights, enthusiasm for participation and the capacity to take governance into their own hands.

2) The degree of self-governance among villagers is not high and there is too much government intervention. The core aspect of today's rural reforms is democratic self-governance and administrative autonomy. In practice, however, self-management is seriously impaired by the government's habit of meddling in village affairs. More often than not, legal village authorities become mere extensions of governments at higher levels. Rather than embodying the aspirations of the villagers, they execute the will of governments' institutions. Local governments furthermore directly intervene in governance by despatching officials to stay in villages, for instance. Such strong government interference seriously weakens the degree of self-governance.

3) The disparate structure of rural governance greatly reduces efficiency. Only when the triple structure of rural authorities displays a high degree of cooperation a positive role in promoting good governance is visible. Lack of coordination and open conflict, on the other hand, inevitably produce adverse effects. In republican years, structural

contradictions mainly occurred between autonomous institutions and local government. Such vertical contradictions persist into present-day rural governance. Moreover, as the central government's power expands, extending to ever lower levels, this structural contradiction is often more pronounced than during the Republic. Vertical conflicts mainly manifest themselves between individuals, villagers' committees, township and town governments and Party committees. The most important structural contradiction in contemporary China, however, is not vertical but horizontal, namely the contradiction between legal village authorities and between the villagers' committee and the local Party branch. The latter contradiction has a particular impact on village governance.

4) Social capital plays an important, often all too negative, role in China's rural governance, leading to a big discrepancy between rural reality and political ideals, both during the Republic and today. Objectively, social capital, as a network of reciprocity based on trust and participation, can influence rural governance either positively or to its detriment. The latter is the case, for instance, if a minority exploited their social capital in order to increase their interests against those of the majority, thus violating the law, conventions and institutions. The complex network of clan, family, friends, neighbors and school friends visible in the above case studies has had a profound impact on the democratic process and on village administration. Nepotism, an unfair distribution of public goods and legal failures can thus be a result of social capital.

5) Illegal forces can seriously disrupt democratic governance. Rural governance reforms during the Republic were imperilled by local, mainly clan, forces, as well as hostile landlords and gentry. By manipulating elections, controlling village affairs and lawsuits, they usually won over public opinion. Also today, in an era of reforms and openness, such localized opposition has begun to emerge, impairing rural democratic governance. In some localities, clan and family are still a vital factor, affecting self-governance among villagers. With the backing of powerful relatives, members can easily be elected as village cadres, affecting village politics. In certain localities, local strongmen and hooligans attempt to control the public through intimidation, deception, coercion and other illegal means. In some localities, well-off villagers have affected local elections and major decisions on village affairs through bribery.

Although the introduction of self-governance among villagers has encountered some serious challenges and even popular opposition, its advance remains on track. The causal relationship between societal reform and China's democratization ensures their stability. Rural governance reform is a great democratic undertaking affecting a majority of China's population. Historically, it heralds a major shift from traditional politics in the countryside. The above case studies show that democratic reforms benefit the peasantry in a number of ways. Legally, by enhancing democratic participation and management, as well as by furnishing institutional guarantees for civil rights. For underprivileged groups, including the poor and women, reforms have brought access to democratic privileges hitherto only enjoyed by higher rural strata. They are useful experiments in China's grassroots democracy, which can be applied to the political reform process on a national basis, thus anchoring democratic participation in a solid foundation. Reforms transform the traditional autocratic culture, broaden the peasants' awareness of democracy and law, cultivate their spirit of independence and autonomy, while fostering a democratic political culture. Furthermore, rural governance reforms are conducive to improving relations between the government and the rural population, thus maintaining social and political stability, raising cultural and educational levels, reforming rural customs, promoting public initiatives and benefiting the rural economy. The Report on Human Development for 2002 issued by the United Nations Development Program (UNDP) lauded the reforms, underlining that democracy in itself is a value, though there has not been a direct link to enhanced economic performance. However, "a democratic government never does worse than any other form of government in raising economic efficiency. Moreover, a democratic government obviously does better in meeting the more urgent social needs of its citizens. This is particularly true during critical moments when the destiny of most people is affected. What is equally important is that democratic participation is not only a means in human development, but its very goal."[58]

The development of a socialist market economy, progress in political democratization and the construction of a political culture require the promotion of a continuous reform process with regards to rural governance. Rural democratic governance should be oriented toward

---

[58] United Nations Development Program (UNDP), *Report on Human Development for 2002: Deepening Democracy in a Split World*, China Financial and Economic Publishing House, 2002, "Foreword."

"good governance," namely democracy, self-governance, rule of law, participation, justice, transparency, responsibility and stability. To attain this ideal, the following five aspects of reform and institutional improvement should be considered.

1) To improve laws and regulations on rural democratic governance, at all levels. Particular attention should be paid to rural self-governance, family planning, fair and reasonable taxation and levies, as well as to legal rights and the interests of the peasantry. In this context, the at present vastly differing conditions in China's countryside, need to be approached with a policy respecting the diversity of rights and concerns of the peasantry. In townships and towns, for instance, the principle of grassroots democracy should be enshrined, while full consideration should be given to local diversity. Furthermore, family planning policies should reflect the ever-changing actual conditions. The same goes for rural taxation.

2) To centralize contradictory structures of village governance with great urgency and to ensure that the authorities cooperate in a concerted and equitable way. Contradictions are most apparent between the villagers' committee and the village Party branch. The central government should explore all avenues to help settle such contradictions, for instance by advocating a "two-ballot system" in local Party elections. This system envisages joint meetings by the villagers' committee and by the village Party branch, cross-committee cooperation, and the general enhancement of village governance. One basic tenet is that village governance should be centered on one legal authority per administrative unit, elected through democratic procedures and reflecting the aspirations of both villagers and the framework of the law.

3) To gradually raise levels of rural self-governance and reduce direct government intervention. Rural democratic governance aims at ensuring that villagers manage their own village affairs pursuant to the laws, attaining good governance with the help of local officials. This necessitates a two-fold process, namely of voluntary government retraction from rural affairs which can be managed locally, and of active assistance if conditions for self-governance are not yet extant and in order to prevent rural unrest. Therefore, wherever educational and civic levels are high, the economy and culture developed, and where villagers are prepared to shoulder public responsibilities, the government should refrain from micro-managing rural life, boldly promote grassroots democracy and experiment with direct elections for local councils, thus raising the level of rural self-governance. In localities where economic

and cultural conditions lag behind desired levels, the government should not completely withdraw from village governance, while "good government" should remain the ideal of rural governance.

4) To do everything possible to protect and increase the legal rights and interests of the rural population, by reducing material pressure and by ensuring fair access to democratic governance. Good governance equals democratic governance, thus maximizing rural interests. If governance reforms merely aimed at preventing peasants from "making trouble," at efficiently collecting fees and taxes and at protecting family planning targets, while neglecting their legal, economic and political interests, that does not constitute good governance. The reform policies have brought a marked improvement in the material life of the peasantry, but there is still a significant gap between the latter and urban residents. Most subsist in terms of food and clothing, many live in poverty and the overall economic burden is still too heavy. Lifting the peasantry out of poverty and developing the countryside is still the government's golden rule and the solid foundation for developing rural democratic governance.

5) To develop positive social capital and to improve the informal institutions in order to encourage political participation. "Social capital," i.e., trust, reciprocity and participation, are essential for a functioning cooperation between villagers, rural elite and government officials. Such cooperation is vital for good rural governance. Social capital should be increased at all levels. Firstly, all possible steps should be taken to extend the trust, reciprocity and participation within the family circle up to a much broader rural community, allowing the vast majority of villagers to share this social capital. Secondly, the prevalence of the common good over individual interest should be enshrined through moral, legal and institutional means, in cases of conflict between private and public concerns. Lastly, penalties should be imposed for the inappropriate exploitation of social capital.

By improving democracy and the legal system, an autonomous and new political culture and legal system will prevail. China's political culture originates from the countryside, and the awareness of law and democracy among peasants and rural cadres is rather weak. Education in the legal system and in democratic principles reverse this situation and also improve the capacity of village cadres. The management of village affairs should be guided by both formal and traditional techniques, to ensure the rule of law to the maximum extent.

From our comparative case study of rural governance in historical and present-day China we can draw one basic conclusion. The republican experience of self-governance laid the actual foundation for the current reform policies. Rural democratic governance embodies the current trends toward democracy with Chinese characteristics in the countryside. Its reform constitutes a breakthrough in grassroots democracy and is also important for China's political restructuring. Given the current momentous changes in society, politics and the economy, rural democratic governance faces opportunities and challenges for another breakthrough. Prudently promoted rural governance reforms will invigorate China's rural society and the country as a whole.

References

1. Li Defang, "Rural Governance of Dingxian County during the Period of the Republic of China" (Research Report), 2003.

2. Wang Fengming, "Current Rural Governance of Dingxian County" (Case Study Report), 2003.

3. Zhuang Weimin, "Rural Governance of Zouping County during the Period of the Republic of China" (Case Study Report), 2003.

4. Wang Zhenhai, "Current Rural Governance of Zouping County" (Case Study Report), 2003.

5. Ma Junya, "Rural Governance of Jiangning County during the Period of the Republic of China" (Case Study Report), 2003.

6. Jin Taijun, "Rural Governance of Jiangning County" (Case Study Report), 2003.

CHAPTER EIGHT

THE PEOPLE'S CONGRESS SYSTEM IN REFORMING CHINA

The People's Congress System (PCS) is the basis of China's political system and is also the cornerstone of Chinese democracy. Modern democracies rely on different forms of representation, and PCS is one such representative system. Chinese representative democracy emerged as part of the country's process of modernization, and its origins can be traced back to the start of the twentieth century.

In the mid-nineteenth century, the Qing Dynasty was compelled to undergo certain reforms such as the Westernization Movement (*Yangwu Yundong*), which initiated China's modernization process. Economic modernization also forced political modernization, both directly and indirectly. The Qing Dynasty attempted to imitate Japan and Great Britain by introducing constitutional monarchy to China; on September 1, 1906, an imperial edict was issued to "prepare to draw up a constitution" and to establish democracy. In August of 1907, the Emperor Guangyu issued an order establishing the Consultative Assembly as the first step of a future Congress: "the constitutional government shall be dependent on public opinion, and require both an upper and lower chamber, which are the essence of the government. China is not presently able to establish both houses, but shall establish a Consultative Assembly as a first step toward this end."[1] On August 27, 1908, the Qing Dynasty issued a *Constitutional Outline Drawn up by Imperial Edict*, which set the term for preparing a constitutional monarchy at nine years. The Congress would be held at this time, and democracy would henceforth be practiced in China. The Qing Government formulated the *Regulations of the Consultative Assembly*, which specified its functions: 1) discussing the policies announced by the Emperor; 2) drawing up new laws; 3) setting the government budget; 4) setting taxes and government bond issues; and 5) handling citizens' petitions. The functions of the Consultative Assembly suggest that it was an embryonic form of modern congress.

---

[1] *The Records of the Emperor Guangyu's Life*, p. 5736.

However the Qing authorities' initiative was in fact an underhanded attempt to confuse and divide public opinion, as they were in essence opposed to modern democracy. As a result, the Qing Dynasty was overthrown by a new, progressive force at that time, the Nationalist Party.

Underpinning the legitimacy of the Nationalist Party—and the main weapon with which it came to power—was representative democracy. On November 29, 1911, the revolutionaries of the Nationalist Party held an Assembly of Representatives of All Governors, which acted as a temporary legislature. This Assembly passed a provisional constitution, the *Basic Organizational Law of the Temporary Government of the Republic of China*, and elected the President of State. On January 28, 1912, a temporary Congress was established, consisting of deputies from all of the provincial governments. This was China's first formal representative Congress in the modern democratic sense, and the Basic Organizational Law gave this temporary Congress the sovereign power of state. Basically, its powers included the abilities to 1) draft laws and review and pass bills governing the budget, taxes, the monetary system, bonds, etc., submitted by the temporary government or the President; 2) review and pass bills governing declarations of war, conclusion of treaties, as well as the administration, appointment and removal of leading officials of the central government, etc. On March 8, 1912, the *Provisional Constitution of the Republic of China*, the first formal constitution in Chinese history, was promulgated in the name of President Sun Yatsen. The Provisional Constitution established the basis for Chinese democracy by regulating fundamental democratic principles such as the sovereignty, freedom and equality of its citizens. This democratic framework saw no great change until the Nationalist regime was overthrown in 1949.

However, the Nationalist Party regime never wholeheartedly implemented US-style democracy in China, and was eventually forced to flee to Taiwan by a new standard-bearer for democracy and progress, the Chinese Communist Party (CCP). Ironically, the CCP's legitimacy and one of the main weapons it used to come to power came from the same source as the Nationalist Party when it overthrew the Qing Dynasty: from modern democracy, for as the CCP fought to remove the Nationalist regime, it gradually established a system of People's Congresses in areas that fell under its control.

The People's Congress System has its roots in the Chinese Soviet Representative Assembly. In November 1931, the CCP held the Chinese Soviet Representative Assembly's first plenary session in Ruijin, Jiangxi Province. The Assembly approved the *Draft Constitution of the Chinese*

Soviet Republic, which stipulated that the National Soviet Representative Assembly and its standing body, the Central Executive Committee, was the sovereign power of the Chinese Soviet Republic. It held fifteen different powers, including the abilities to: 1) approve and revise the Constitution; 2) conclude treaties with foreign powers and approve international agreements; 3) review and approve major domestic and foreign policies; 4) limit local government powers; 5) declare war and peace; 6) approve the budget and bond issues; 7) collect taxes; and 8) organize and lead the armed forces.

On October 14, 1945, the CCP decided to reform the political system in the Liberated Areas under their control and establish a people's representative congress system, which would be the sovereign power to which the government would be subject. Mao Zedong, the top leader of the CCP, strongly approved of such a system, and in April 1948, he reported that "people's representative congresses have now been able to develop in all Liberated Areas. These people's representative congresses should be the people's body of state power as soon as they are established. All power should belong to the representative congresses, instituted by government."[2] The people's representative congresses can thus be seen as both a portent of the post-1949 people's congress system, and as a transitional phase to it.

On September 21, 1949, the CCP held the first plenary session of the Chinese People's Political Consultative Conference (CPPCC); the session formulated and approved the *Common Program of the CPPCC* as a provisional constitution for the new regime governed by the CCP. The Common Program stipulated that "the state power of the People's Republic of China shall belong to the people. The organs through which the people exercise state power shall be the people's congresses and people's governments at different levels. The various people's congresses shall be instituted by popular general election."[3] The session also decided that the people's congress system should be implemented nationwide within the following few years once the necessary conditions had been reached. The first general election nationwide began not long after the Central Government, under the leadership of the CCP, had issued the *Election Law of the National People's Congress and Local People's*

---

[2] Mao Zedong, "Speech on the Cadres' Meeting in Shangxi and Shaanxi Provinces," *Selected Works of Mao Zedong*, People's Press, 1973, p. 1203.

[3] *Selected Constitutions At Home and Abroad*, ed. by the Department of Law of People's University, People's Press, 1981, p. 22.

Congresses at All Levels, as well as *Election Indications at the Grassroots Levels* in March and April of 1954. On September 15, 1954, the inaugural session of the first National People's Congress was held in Beijing; as a starting point it adopted fundamental laws of the new People's Republic of China such as the Constitution, the *Organizational Law of the National People's Congress*, and the *Organizational Law for Local People's Congresses and People's Governments at All Levels*. These laws all applied the principle of democratic centralism, affirming that the people's congresses were the organs of state power and were elected by the people. By this point, the people's congress system had been formally established and implemented across the country.

However, it was only after 1978 that the people's congress system was actually put into effect. From 1957 onwards, China's democratic development almost ceased because of the Anti-Rightist Movement. The people's congress system was undermined and congresses at different levels no longer functioned as prescribed by the Constitution. The system was finally destroyed in 1966 during the Cultural Revolution, and did not start to operate again until 1978, after the Third Plenary Session of the Eleventh National Congress of the CCP. In July 1979, the Second Plenary Session of the Fifth National Congress adopted a new *Election Law for the National People's Congress and the Local People's Congresses* as well as an *Organizational Law for Local People's Congresses and Governments at All Levels*, both of which were respectively substantially revised in December 1982 and December 1986. In December 1982, the Fifth Plenary Session of the Fifth National People's Congress formulated the *Organizational Law of the National People's Congress*; in March 1983, the Standing Committee of the Fifth National Congress approved *Regulations for the Direct Election of People's Deputies At and Below the County Level*; and, importantly, on December 4, 1982, the National Congress formulated the new *Constitution of the People's Republic of China*, which stipulated in detail the nature, status, functions, procedures and operating mechanisms of the people's congress system. This Constitution established the framework of representative democracy with Chinese characteristics.

According to the new Constitution, all power in the PRC belongs to the people. The organs through which the people exercise state power are the National People's Congress and the local People's Congresses at different levels. The NPC and the local people's congresses are constituted through democratic election, and are responsible to the people and subject to their supervision. All administrative, judicial, and procuratorial organs of the state are created by the people's congresses to which they are responsible and under whose supervision they operate. The NPC is furthermore the highest organ of state power, and has a permanent body, the Standing Committee of the NPC. The new Constitution vests the NPC and its Standing Committee with tremendous powers, including the powers of legislation, decision, supervision, and the approval and removal of leading government officials.

The new Constitution stipulates that people's congresses above the provincial level and their standing committees are the only legislatures permitted to exercise the legislative power of the state. China's legislative system operates at two levels. The NPC and its standing committee have the power to draft and formulate national laws with the following major legislative functions: to amend and interpret the Constitution; to supervise the enforcement of the Constitution and other laws; to enact, amend and interpret basic statutes governing criminal offences, civil affairs, state organs, etc. They also have the power to annul any government administrative rules and regulations, decisions or orders that contravene the Constitution or its statutes. The people's congresses and local governments established in provinces, municipalities directly under the Central Government, counties, cities, municipal districts, townships, ethnic nationality townships and towns are local organs of state power, but only those at and above the county level may establish standing committees. The people's congresses of provinces and municipalities directly under the Central Government, and their standing committees, may draft and pass local regulations, but these may not contravene the Constitution, any statutes or administrative rules and regulations. Any such local regulations must also be recorded with the NPC Standing Committee.

The Constitution stipulates that the people's congresses at various levels have major decision-making powers, including reviewing and approving plans for national and local economic and social development, and reporting on their implementation; reviewing and approving the state budget; as well as reporting on their implementation; the alteration or annulment of inappropriate decisions of local governments; and other functions and powers appropriate to an organ of state power.

The Constitution gives people's congresses and their standing committees many supervisory powers. They have the power to supervise the enforcement of the Constitution and other laws by governments at different levels; to supervise the operation of the governments, the people's courts and the people's procuratorates; to initiate inquiries through all organs of the state into specific questions and to adopt relevant resolutions; to hear the reports and obtain necessary information from all organs of state, which the latter are obliged to supply.

The Constitution also gives people's congresses the power to approve and remove leading government officials. The NPC has the power to elect the President and Vice-President of the PRC; to veto the choice of a Premier of the State Council nominated by the President, and to veto the choice of Vice-Premiers, State Councillors, Ministers in charge of ministries or commissions, the Auditor-General and the Secretary-General of the State Council nominated by the Premier; to elect the President of the Supreme People's Court and the Procurator-General of the Supreme People's Procuratorate; elect the Chairman of the Central Military Commission and, to veto the choice of all members of the Central Military Commission nominated by the Chairman. Meanwhile, the NPC also has the power to recall or remove all of the above from office. The local people's congresses have the power to both elect and recall or remove the chief officials of local governments, courts and procuratorates.

It is not difficult to see that from a legal perspective, the people's congress system in China has a modern democratic form. Firstly, the NPC is the only sovereign power of state and the highest organ of power of state in China; it has the exclusive right to exercise legislative and decisive power on important affairs. Moreover, the powers vested in it by the Constitution are greater than those of most Western Congresses. For example, in most Western democracies, the President or Premier is directly elected by citizens, and is responsible to the citizens who elected him/her; in China, the Constitution states that the President and Premier are elected by the NPC. In Western democracies, the Congress doesn't elect the chief judges of the Supreme Court, nor the general procurators of the procuratorate, and they, in turn, are not obliged to be responsible to the Congress. In China, however, the NPC has the power to create the Supreme Court and the supreme procuratorate, which in turn are directly responsible to the NPC. Secondly, like Western legislature members, the members of the people's congresses (i.e., the people's representatives) are elected by citizens along the democratic principles of equality and freedom. Deputies of people's congresses at and below the county level are selected by direct election, while those above the county level are selected by indirect election, i.e., they are selected by the lower congresses. All elections take the form of secret ballots. There has been a relative quantitative difference between the number of deputy positions and the number of candidates standing for election since the 1980s.

Moreover, from a theoretical legal perspective, the people's congress system is more democratic than Western systems. As mentioned above, the People's Congress is much more powerful than a Western congress in the sense that it has the power to select the President, Premier, the chief judges of the Supreme Court and the chief procurators. Furthermore, it is vested by the Constitution with a particular type of theoretically unlimited power, with "functions and powers appropriate to the highest organ of state power." The people's congresses, as the foundation of democracy, are elected by and responsible to the people; therefore, the more powerful they are, the more democratic they are. One sign of modern democracy is the extent to which citizens participate in general elections. China maintains one of the highest levels of political participation in the world. Whenever a general election of the deputies of the people's congresses at and below the county level is held, the CCP and its local governments do everything possible to ensure that all citizens participate in the election. For example, they conduct active election campaign broadcasts, provide a number of floating ballot boxes, and in some rural locations, pay the peasants to participate. As a result, voter turnout in general elections is often over 90% of the population. The principles of the "sovereignty of the people" requires a political system that is "of the people, by the people and for the people," in which citizens not only have the right to elect their own representatives to the legislature, but also have the right to recall or remove these when they fail in their duties. In this respect, the rights vested in citizens by the Constitution in China are different from the West. In most Western countries, the members of a legislature act independently and are not recalled or removed during their term of office unless a new general election is held; in China, however, the citizens have the right to recall or remove them. In accordance with the principle of "separating the three state powers among the legislative, the executive and the judicial branches," Western legislatures usually do not have the power to interfere directly in the activities of the executive and judicial branches; in China, by contrast, the people's congresses have the power to interfere in all government activities, including the activities of the people's courts and the people's procuratorates.

Nevertheless, from a different perspective, there are many important differences between the People's Congress System and Western democratic systems; these differences prevent the former from being classified as a modern democratic system, at least if one compares it by typical Western standards.

When comparing electoral procedures for members of legislatures, China holds general elections as in Western countries. However, in the United States, for example, all members of legislatures at different levels are directly elected by the citizens; in China, however, direct elections are limited to people's congresses at and below the county level. These congresses have no power to draft laws, and no legislative power. In other words, the legislatures in China are not constituted by way of a general and direct election by the people; the universal suffrage vested as a right in the people by the Constitution has not been fully implemented, to the extent that such a right is not available for the election of the members of legislatures.

The separation and balance of the three branches of power among the legislative, the executive and the judicial branches is one of the pillars of Western democracy; it follows that each of the three organs of state power is thus independent. Unlike in the Western system, China insists firmly on the principle of "the unity of the three branches among the legislative, the executive and the judicial," the result of the Marxist concept of "the union of the legislative and the executive." The people's congresses are the organs which provide real unity to the legislative, the executive and the judicial branches. State administrative, judicial and procuratorial organs are all constituted by the people's congresses, to which they are also responsible and by which they are supervised. State organs are instituted in this way in order to ensure that the people's congresses are able to exercise unified state power. Under this premise, the state's administrative, judicial and procuratorial powers, as well as its leadership over the armed forces, are clearly defined. In other words, the people's congresses can act in three possible ways: as a legislature that drafts or approves laws; as an executive that handles administrative affairs; and as a judicial power that has the right to interfere in judgements.

Thus, the essential difference between the people's congresses and Western congresses lies in the fact that while in Western countries the legislature is an independent sovereign organ which is effected and led indirectly by the political parties, including the ruling party, in China, by contrast, the people's congresses at and above the provincial level are not independent sovereign organs; they are effected and led directly by the CCP. In Western systems, no party has higher legal authority than the legislature as the sovereign power of state, although in effect, the majority party controls the legislature. In China, even though the Constitution has been changed several times since 1954, one article has remained constant, that which insists on the absolute leadership of the CCP. On the one hand, the Constitution stipulates that the people's congresses are the highest organs of state power; and on the other hand, it also stipulates that all organs in China must accept the leadership of the CCP. Indeed, one of the four fundamental principles is an insistence on the Party's leadership. Party committees at different levels have the power to direct the people's congresses; to instruct the congresses; and to interfere in the legislative work of the congresses. In short, the people's congresses must reflect the Party's leadership and their vital role is to implement the will of the Party in the will of state and to put the policies of Party into effect as the laws of state. This role is frankly and openly professed in documents, leader's speeches and in laws.

For instance, Peng Zhen, former President of the NPC, said that "all people's congresses at different levels must accept the political leadership of the Party. The NPC is led by the Party Central Committee, while the local people's congresses are led by the Party local committees. The Constitution clearly stipulates that our country is led by the Working Class, whose leadership is exercised through the CCP."[4] Jiang Zemin, General Secretary of the Party and President of China, has said that "our Party is the ruling party, and its dominance is ensured through Party leadership of the organs of state power. The Party would no longer rule without its leadership role. All organs of state power, including the people's congresses, local governments, courts, procuratorates and the army, must accept the leadership of the Party. Wrong ideas and behavior will weaken the leadership of the Party."[5]

The Constitution stipulates that the people's congress is the highest organ of state power on the one hand; and that, on the other hand, it must accept the leadership of the Party. A very complicated relationship between the sovereignty of the people's congress and the leadership of the Party is therefore apparent, and is one of the most important

---

[4] Peng Zhen, "Records of Talks to the Chiefs of Local People's Congresses" (March 7, 1981), in *Selected Literature on the People's Congress*, ed. by Yan Jiushi, Democracy and Law Publishing House, 1992, p. 140.

[5] Jiang Zeming, "Insistence on and Improvement of the People's Representative System," in *Selected Literature on the People's Congress*, ed. by Yan Jiushi, Democracy and Law Publishing House, 1992, pp. 205–206.

topics of contemporary Chinese politics. By definition, there should be no higher organ of power than the people's congress, in which the Constitution vests sovereign power; yet, the Constitution also specifies that the power of the Party is higher than that of the people's congress, which must accept the Party's leadership. As a rule, in political science, there can be only one sovereign national power in a country; where there is more than one such power, the country is inevitably split. Yet Mainland China has been without doubt highly unified since 1949. The implication of this relationship is whether the "will of the Party" represents the will of the state and people, or whether it denotes the people and the state themselves. In reality, this embodies the relationship between policy and law, or power and law. For the Party rules by political power, while the people's congresses rule by law. This relationship is so crucial to the development of Chinese democracy that every step taken toward democracy must consider how the country's leaders will react to it.

As mentioned above, the People's Congress System did not operate effectively until 1978, even though it was established as early as 1954. A major reason for this was that prior to 1978, national leaders held a simplistic attitude toward the complicated relationship between the people's congresses and the Party. The logic of senior leaders such as Mao Zedong was that the CCP represented the fundamental interests of all Chinese people, and that therefore the will of the Party denoted the will of the people. This being the case, given that the essence of democracy is the sovereign power of the people, it would naturally be most democratic to identify the will of the Party with that of the state. The people's congresses were consequently marginalised as political tools: the People's Congress System essentially ceased to function during the Cultural Revolution, and the majority were dissolved. Where they survived, they served merely as political decorations, as a rubber stamp for policy.

Obviously, the will of the Party cannot denote the will of the people, because the interests of the Party cannot thoroughly reflect the interests of the people, despite its claims to faithfully represent these. Therefore, the Party cannot either denote the people and the state, and both state and government must thus be separated from the Party. This was recognised after 1978 by a new generation of leaders, and openly voiced by Deng Xiaoping. With this new understanding of the complexity of the relationship between the Party and the people's congresses, the new political logic of these leaders is that the Party is no longer a higher organ of power than the people's congresses, and that the Party's leadership of the people should not occur through direct administration, but through indirect political leadership. This means that the Party now transforms its policies into national laws, its will into the national will, through the people's congresses. Once the Party's policies become the laws of state, the Party itself must act within the framework of the law, and the Party's policies must be in accordance with, and subject to, the law. As President Jiang Zemin pointed out, "the Party differs from the organs of state power in its nature, functions, organization and working style. The Party cannot be a substitute for the people's congresses to exercise state power. The leadership role that the Party plays in politics, thought and organization should take the form of political leadership in political principle, political guidance, political decision-making and political education as well as in its recommendation of major cadres to the government. We should do our best to enable the implementation of important Party decisions in the will of the state using legal procedures."[6]

Based on this new political line of thinking, the CCP has begun to emphasise the role and significance of the People's Congress System in political life and in Chinese democracy since 1978. There have since been great changes to the People's Congress System, including:

1) The quality of people's deputies has greatly improved. The modern legislative and decision-making process is extremely technical and increasingly professionalized, and requires people's congress members to possess a high level of knowledge and political skill. Previously, deputies had been popularly noted for their lack of independent will, their role as "robots" who voted exactly as Party leaders wished; they were not elected for their political ability or enthusiasm but rather for other attributes, such as because they were "advanced workers," or "model Party members," and so forth. These surveys indicate that this situation changed rapidly in the 1980s. For example, a survey of Beijing in 1987 showed that 55.6% of people's deputies held no particular "honours"; 46% expressed a deep interest in politics; 96.3% considered themselves to be deputies of the state and the people, rather than the Party; and

---

[6] Jiang Zeming, *ibid.*, p. 206.

82.9% believed that the Constitution was more important than the Party Constitution.[7]

2) The election procedures for deputies are much more democratic than in the past. Prior to the 1980s, the election process was manipulated by the Party, as they only fielded the exact number of candidates to fill the available positions. The new election law implemented in the 1980s brought about four significant reforms in this regard. i) Particular organs responsible for elections, which replace and are relatively independent from the Party, have been established; the Party now leads the elections indirectly, rather than by directly manipulating them. ii) A difference between the number of candidates standing for election and the number of positions available has emerged, sometimes double the number of candidates per position. This has created more significant elections, since there was barely any possibility for democratic selection with the previous one-to-one ratio of candidates per position. iii) The Party respects citizens' choices, even when Party-backed candidates are not selected. iv) The ratio of Party cadres among the deputies has been greatly reduced: prior to the 1980s, over 50% of deputies were the Party cadres; in Beijing in 1987, this rate had dropped to 43%.[8]

The most important change in the people's congress system in the 1980s was that the power vested in the people's congresses by the Constitution on paper has now been substantially implemented. The people's congresses are no longer merely decorative rubber stamps, but are now becoming "steel stamps." They have obtained certain fundamental powers in law-making, decision-making, in the appointment and removal of leading government officials, veto powers, and in governmental supervisory roles. In short, their previously theoretical legal power has been put into effect.

Prior to the 1980s, the congresses had virtually no legislative power, because they formulated or adopted very few laws. From 1954 to 1957, only forty laws were examined and approved by the NPC, while no local congresses drafted or approved any local law or regulation during this period. There were no major laws such as criminal law, criminal suit law or civil law; the importance of the role of policy in establish-

---

[7] Yu Keping and Wang Fuchen, "A Survey of the Quality of the Local People's Deputies in Beijing," in *Democracy and the Local People's Congresses*, ed. by Zhao Baoxu, Shaanxi Publishing House, 1988, p. 201.

[8] Yu Keping and Wang Fuchen, *ibid.*

ing legality in social life had stripped the congresses of their legislative power. In contrast, from 1988 to 1993, the NPC drafted or approved 252 laws and statutes, while local congresses drafted or approved over 3,000 local laws and regulations. The people's congresses are playing an increasingly important role in political life, as laws instead of policies have become the norm by which citizens and the government act. Furthermore, prior to the 1980s the congresses had no special organs responsible for drafting and initially proposing laws, and almost all laws were drafted by the ministries of the State Council. There are now wide-ranging departments in people's congresses at and above the provincial levels staffed by legal professionals who are specifically responsible for drafting or reviewing laws and regulations. Local governments no longer share legislative power with the people's congresses; instead, they are only authorised to draft statutes and regulations through the congresses.

The people's congresses' decision-making powers, vested in them by the Constitution, include the power to draft, review and approve major policies submitted to them by local governments; this power was never properly exercised before the 1980s. There has been a great improvement in this respect since the reforms. At least in form, all major local government policies have been subject to the review and approval of the people's congresses; there are also more and more recorded instances of people's congresses vetoing government bills. For example, in 1994, local congresses reported 120 cases to the NPC in which they actually exercised the power vested in them by the Constitution; of these cases, 18% were vetoes of bills submitted by local governments.[9]

In spite of the fact that legislative power is overall the most important function of the people's congresses at and above the provincial levels, most citizens see their power to appoint and remove leading government officials as the most impressive. There have been two areas of great progress in this regard since the 1980s. Firstly, all leading government, court and procuratorate officials are now appointed by congresses of the level which corresponds to the level of the position; secondly, there has been an increase in the number of vetoes exercised by the congresses to reject sole candidates put forward by the Party. In the latter cases, for the most part, the Party has been obliged to accept

---

[9] *Selections of Cases on How the Local People's Congresses Exercise Their Power by Law*, ed. by Yan Jiushi, China Democracy and Law Publishing House, 1996, pp. 46–103.

the veto and respect the congress' choice. For example, in one single year, 1988, candidates for Vice-Governor were vetoed by the respective congresses in six provinces; a further eighteen provinces vetoed forty-nine candidates for leading provincial official positions, 4% of the total 712 candidates.[10]

Since the 1980s, the legally prescribed supervisory powers of the people's congresses have also achieved practical significance. An increasing number of people's congresses have begun to effectively exercise their supervisory powers over local governments by questioning, investigating and correcting their inadequate performance, particularly with regard to unjust court judgements or prosecutions. The people's congresses appear to have become judiciary supervisory organs, and accept appeals from citizens against local government. In 1994, the NPC selected 140 typical cases in which local people's congresses effectively exercised their power, of which 57 cases concerned annulments of unjust judgements or prosecutions.

The People's Congress System has thus seen rapid changes, as the entire political, economic and cultural situation develops in Reforming China, and is moving toward a much more democratic orientation. More and more of the powers prescribed to it by the Constitution are being implemented in practice. Nevertheless, it is worth pointing out that there is still quite a gap between its legally prescribed powers and its powers in reality. Correspondingly, it will be a long time before Chinese democracy based on the People's Congress System is fully implemented. The people's congress is not the highest organ of state power, as prescribed by the Constitution; nor is it the sovereign power of the state—this power lies with the Politburo of the CCP; its function to elect, recall, or remove leading governments officials is still a decorative procedure rather than an essential power. In short, the truth remains that in practice the people's congresses are not higher than the Party, but instead remain subject to it. China's leaders are however clearly aware of and bluntly admit the problems in implementing the People's Congress System. As Qiao Shi, the President of the NPC, said, "Our People's Congress System is a good system, but there are still shortcomings in its democratic institutions, procedures and working methods due to our standing as a country at the primary

---

[10] Cui Dingjie, *The Chinese People's Congress System*, The Literature of Social Sciences Publishing House, 1992, p. 304.

stage of socialism, which constrains our politics, economics and culture. We must strengthen the construction of the people's congresses in accordance with the Constitution to enable them to take on the role of authoritative organs of state power which are able to carry out all of the functions vested in them by the Constitution."[11] These comments imply that the people's congresses have yet to be able to carry out all the functions prescribed to them by law, and have yet to become organs of state power with sufficient authority.

There are many reasons for the imbalance between the role of the people's congresses as described in law and their function in practice. The fundamental reasons for this imbalance are, basically, the following:

1) The particular status of the CCP in China's political life: as the founder of the PRC, the CCP has been the nucleus of political power in China and has established all the major aspects of its political system, including the people's congress system. An established political nucleus such as the Party is essentially contrary to the sovereign power of the people's congresses, and it will be very difficult for the people's congresses to become an independent sovereign power of state so long as the Party's position as the country's political nucleus remains.

2) The members of the people's congresses: China does not encourage Western-style political campaigns, and the CCP can easily control the election process if it chooses to do so, even though the citizens may freely recommend their own candidates according to the Law of Election. The leaders and deputies of the people's congresses at various levels are, for the most part, Party members. The Party Constitution requires all its members to, above all, absolutely obey all Party demands, with no exception made for members of the people's congresses. The deputies are thus obliged to vote approvingly of any bill already approved by the Party committee prior to its submission to the people's congresses.

3) Shortcomings in popular democratic habits and traditions: China has been led by despots for thousands of years, and the country's authoritarian political culture still strongly influences its people. A large percentage of the population does not care about democracy or the people's congresses as a possible path toward this, and accordingly

---

[11] Qiao Shi, "Speech on the Fortieth Anniversary of the Founding of the People's Congress," in *Writings for the Fortieth Anniversary of the Founding of the People's Congress*, ed. by Yan Jiushi, China Democracy and Law Publishing House, 1995, p. 58.

does not appreciate its rights either as electors or candidates. As President Qiao Shi recently said, "Because China has been a feudal society for several thousand years and because of the realities of our present social and economic development and other factors, it will take a long period of hard work to establish a complete and comprehensive legal system."[12]

In conclusion, first, from an idealistic democratic perspective, China's people's congress system is a form of modern democracy with characteristics which differentiate it quite obviously from Western democracies. It is a potential alternative to a capitalist democracy provided it is fully implemented according to its theoretical construction. As a relatively new form of democracy in spite of its over forty years' history, the people's congress system is still an idealistic system rather than a practically functioning one. Its legal functions and roles still remain mostly on paper and have yet to be completely implemented, and this gap between theory and practice is still quite wide. However, since China's reforms and opening-up, the People's Congress System has made great progress from being an idealistic system to a pragmatic, implemented system as China's society has undergone dramatic change. Chinese democracy is making steady forward progress, and the gap in the role of the people's congresses between how they are prescribed by law and how they function is becoming smaller. We can therefore be confident that as China's political and economic reforms extend and deepen, the idealistic goals of the People's Congress System can be implemented in reality.

---

[12] Qiao Shi, "A Talk With Journalists With China Information," December 28, 1996.

CHAPTER NINE

TOWARD AN INCREMENTAL DEMOCRACY AND GOVERNANCE: CHINESE THEORIES AND ASSESSMENT CRITERIA

Introduction

Any political discourse is bound by the political era in which it takes place. This is especially true in China, which has witnessed many political movements since 1949. Prevailing political terms are replaced by newer ones as an older political era gives way to a newer one. From 1949 to 1978, the most popular terms included "revolution," "dictatorship" and "class struggle," but their popularity has waned since 1978. Instead, new terms like "reform," "rule of law" and "stability" have since become well known. The term "democracy," however, is an exception to the vagaries of political fashion. Most Chinese scholars hold that democracy is a foreign word, and that "there was neither democracy nor science in traditional Chinese culture."[1] Nevertheless "democracy" is always on the list of popular terms in modern Chinese political history, regardless of the ruler or the regime. The Chinese Communist Party (CCP) used democracy as a basis of legitimacy for overthrowing the Guomindang (GMD) regime in the years leading up to 1949. Mao Zedong, the CCP's senior leader, even wrote a pamphlet entitled "New Democracy." "Democracy" remained one of the most effective slogans after the CCP came to power in 1949 and even during the "Cultural Revolution," though it was never actually implemented. China's politics and economy have undergone fundamental changes since the reform and opening up process began in 1978, and all formerly popular political terms have all but vanished—except for "democracy." There is no doubt that both the Chinese understanding and practice of democracy are undergoing great changes, but the term remains unchanged.

---

[1] Li Shenzhi, "Neither Democracy Nor Science in Traditional Chinese Culture," in: *Selections On Liberation* (1978–1998), ed. by Qiushi, Beijing, Jingjiribao Chubanshe, 1998, p. 1118.

Chinese Concepts of Democracy during the Mao Era

In the era of Mao Zedong, like other political terms, the concept of democracy was not open to discussion and was used exclusively by the authorities in a specific way. The only official view of democracy in that context was as follows: democracy was a superstructure built upon an economic foundation; in the final analysis, it was not an ultimate value and goal, but rather a means to achieve economic goals, and it therefore served economic development; all democracies in human history were by nature class democracies, for classless democracy does not exist. To date, there had been only two types of democracy: socialist and capitalist. Socialist democracy was the highest form of democracy while the capitalist version was false; democracy and dictatorship were complementary, in that democracy for the proletariat and dictatorship for the bourgeoisie were two sides of the same coin. As Mao wrote, "The combination of these two aspects, democracy for the people and dictatorship over the reactionaries, is the People's Democratic Dictatorship."[2] Democracy and centralization were combined into "democratic centralism," that is, centralization based on democracy, and democracy under centralized guidance. Such "democratic centralism" has been an underlying principle of both the Constitution of the Chinese Communist Party (CCP) and the Constitution of the People's Republic of China.[3]

There are many defects in such a view of democracy. First of all, it is an instrumentalist view that regards democracy as a means to attain economic goals, not as one of ultimate human value, so that democracy is devalued to the status of a simple instrument for human beings. As a result, democracy becomes inessential in practical politics. Furthermore, according to this instrumentalist view, democracy for the people and dictatorship over the enemy are indivisible. However with no legally prescribed way to differentiate between the people and the enemy, identifying the people and the enemy depended on the will of

---

[2] Mao Zedong, "On the People's Democratic Dictatorship," in: *Selected Works of Mao Zedong*, Vol. 3, Beijing, People's Publishing House, 1991, p. 1475.

[3] The General Provisions of *The Constitution of the Chinese Communist Party* stipulate that "we should abide by democratic centralism. This combines centralization on the basis of democracy and democracy under centralized guidance." Article 3 of the General Provisions of the *Constitution of the People's Republic of China* stipulates that "the state organs of the People's Republic of China should exercise democratic centralism."

the leaders with no objective criteria. As a result, those who fell into the category of people in the eyes of the leaders enjoyed democratic rights, while those who did not belong to the people were denied these rights. Such was the case during the Mao era. The scope of democracy was reduced while the scope of dictatorship was widened, due to the "magnification of class struggle." The object of dictatorship was initially identical to the "objects of revolution," i.e., landlords, capitalists, old bureaucrats, warlords, GMD reactionaries and criminals. But rightist intellectuals, dissidents, ordinary citizens and even the cadres of the Party and government later gradually became objects of dictatorship. The instrumentalist theory actually promoted centralization instead of democracy. Mao Zedong believed that democracy's only function was as a foundation for centralization, but the people had no say in this final, centralized power. Deng Xiaoping critisized this, saying "all power of the Party committee itself is often concentrated inappropriately and indiscriminately in the hands of a few secretaries, especially the first secretaries, who direct and decide everything."[4] Finally, the instrumentalist view of democracy also overlooked citizens' economic democratic rights. This view of democracy envisioned a "command" economy under which workers and peasants did not own their means of production because these belonged to the state or the collective. Ordinary citizens had no independent power over production. For example, peasants did not even have the right to decide what and how to plant in the fields, ceding this right to the cadres of the People's Communes.

Perhaps ironically, the worst outcome of instrumentalist democracy was the "ten years of chaos" of the "Cultural Revolution." During this "revolution," "democracy" became a tool which politicians such as the "Gang of Four" openly used to suppress their opponents. Ordinary citizens' rights were not guaranteed under the so-called "grand democracy" of "freely speaking out, fully airing views, holding great debates and writing big-character posters." In this way, even the President of the State and the Minister of Defense were arrested and died under arrest without trial. It was clear that Chinese politics would make scant progress if it did not abandon this instrumentalist theory of democracy,

---

[4] Deng Xiaoping, "On the Reform of the System of Party and State Leadership," in: *Selected Works of Deng Xiaoping*, Beijing, People's Publishing House, 1983, p. 329.

which in real life had led inexorably to political disaster. Therefore, an urgent demand arose from the people and CCP members alike to withdraw the legitimacy of Mao's democracy after his death.

Deng Xiaoping's View of Democracy

The Third Plenary Session of the Eleventh Party Central Committee in December 1978 is usually regarded as a milestone of China's reform and opening up process. The plenary session decided to put an end to the "Cultural Revolution," shift the principal work of the Party from class struggle to economic development, and elect Deng Xiaoping as the senior leader of the Party and the state. The main reason that the Session made so many important decisions within five days, according to some specialists on the history of the CCP, is that a thirty-six-day working conference was held prior to the Session at which its participants reached wide-reaching consensus on important issues, albeit after much heated argument and disagreement. The Session approved the decisions of the working conference, and Deng Xiaoping's keynote speech at the working conference was officially acknowledged as "the main speech of the Third Plenary Session."[5] As Yu Guangyuan, an authoritative CCP theoretician who attended both the Session and the working conference, proposed, one of the main topics of the working conference was to promote and discuss democracy. He indicated that almost all senior leaders of the Party were discussing democracy. All participants were deeply impressed by both Deng Xiaoping and Ye Jianying's remarks on democracy, and so were the cadres and the masses who read their remarks.[6]

It is now clear that Deng intentionally initiated a revision of Mao's view of democracy in his speech to the working conference. He particularly dwelled on democracy in his famous speech entitled "Emancipate the Mind; Seek Truth from Facts, and Unite as One to Look to the Future." Almost all points on democracy in his speech were designed

---

[5] The Editorial Committee for Party Literature under the Central Committee of the CCP, "Notes," in: *Selected Works of Deng Xiaoping*, Vol. 2, Beijing, People's Publishing House, p. 140.

[6] Yu Guangyuan, *The Great Historical Shift I Experienced: The Context of the Third Plenary Session of the Eleventh Party Central Committee*, Beijing, Central Translation and Compilation Press, 1998, p. 353.

to oppose and carefully revise Mao's view of democracy. Firstly, he talked about the relationship between democracy and centralism and indicated that Party leaders laid undue stress on centralism while "we must now lay particular stress on democracy, because for quite a long time democratic centralism has not been genuinely practiced: Centralism was divorced from democracy, and there was little democracy."[7] Secondly, he advocated economic democracy and producers' economic rights in terms of production and management. "We must take realistic measures to guarantee the individual democratic rights of workers and peasants, including democratic elections, democratic management and democratic supervision." Finally, Deng laid emphasis on democratic institutionalization, pointing out that "democracy should be gradually institutionalized and codified so that such institutions and laws will not change with changes of leadership or changes in the views or focus of attention of any leader."[8] Deng then further expounded his views on democracy and made a crucial revision to Mao's theory of democracy, in that he no longer regarded democracy simply as an instrument, but acknowledged that "democracy is our goal."[9]

Deng's theory of democracy is particularly noteworthy because it has been written into both the Party Constitution and the Constitution of the People's Republic of China as the guiding ideology which Chinese citizens and CCP members must adhere to, and as a guiding principle for China's political reform. Generally speaking, Deng's theory on democracy consists of four aspects: 1) Democracy is one of the basic goals of Chinese political reform. He stated that democracy is a goal of the CCP and that there can be no socialism without democracy. He summarized his most important policies: "We must both develop democracy politically, and also reform the economy and other social fields."[10] 2) China will not practice Western democracy. Deng held that Western democracy, with its multi-party representative system, the checks and balances of the legislature, executive and judiciary were a democracy of the monopolistic capitalist class, whereas Chinese democracy consisted solely of the People's Congress System. 3) Democracy

---

[7] Deng Xiaoping, "Emancipate the Mind; Seek Truth from Facts, and Uniting as One in Looking to the Future," in: *Selected Works of Deng Xiaoping*, Beijing, People's Publishing House, 1983, pp. 144–146.

[8] Deng Xiaoping, *ibid*.

[9] Deng Xiaoping, "Stability Overrides All," *ibid*., p. 285.

[10] Deng Xiaoping, "Develop Political Democracy and Carry Out Economic Reforms," *ibid*., p. 116.

must be combined with law. China would get nowhere without extensive democracy and a sound legal system. 4) Democracy must be practiced under the leadership of the CCP and presupposes political stability. China would be reduced to chaos, according to his logic, if democracy were not instituted under the leadership of the CCP and there could be no democracy in a politically unstable situation.

In essence, Deng's theory of democracy corresponds with that of Mao. Both of them lay particular stress on the class nature of democracy, reject the Western multi-party system and advocate the sole leadership of the CCP and the system of People's Congresses under the leadership of the CCP. Deng, however, made a crucial revision to Mao's theory of democracy, in that he regarded democracy as a goal of the CCP, and stressed the institutionalization of democracy, economic democracy and the development of a legal framework. As a result, great changes have taken place in terms of Chinese democracy in theory and practice since the reform and opening up process began.

Democratization and Chinese Economic Growth

There is no doubt that the major result of the reform process has been rapid economic growth. The speed of China's economic development is so high that many have called it "a miracle." The average annual growth rate of China's GDP in the twenty years from 1978 to 1998 exceeded 9.8%. In 1998 China's GDP reached RMB 7,955.3 billion, compared to a mere RMB 358.8 billion in 1978. This rapid economic growth resulted in an enormous rise in the standard of living of China's population. The rural average per capita income increased from RMB 133.6 in 1978 to RMB 2,160 in 1998, 4.3 times the 1978 figure. The urban average per capita income reached RMB 5,425 in 1998, 3.5 times the 1978 figure.[11]

The rapid growth of China's economy is a direct outcome of economic diversification which, in turn, is one result of the reform of the traditional socialist economic system. As a first step, China reformed the structure of ownership and introduced a diversified economy. The output of state-owned enterprises (SOEs) generated a dominant portion of GNP until the 1980s, but nowadays this is gradually giving way to

---

[11] See *China Statistical Yearbook* (1998), Beijing, China Statistical Publishing House, 1999.

non-state owned output. Although the investment proportion of SOEs in terms of total fixed assets remains at over 70%, 60% or more of the increase in recent years' GNP has come from non-state enterprises, because over 70% of SOEs operate at a loss. Secondly, China has reformed its management and operational systems. The rural People's Commune system was abolished and replaced by a variety of contract or subcontract systems. In urban areas, the previous egalitarian production and distribution systems were replaced by a new structure of work responsibilities with different levels of pay. Thirdly, the planned economy was replaced by a market system, and the mandatory centralized economic mechanism yielded to a market price mechanism. Furthermore, important economic sectors including finance, insurance, logistics, employment, housing and so forth were significantly reformed and new structures put in place.

The above-mentioned economic achievements of China's reforms are widely acknowledged. However, some argue that progress and change in China has affected everything except politics. Some even attribute the success of China's economic reform to the policy of primarily reforming the economic system, followed by political reform, while they associate the failed economic reforms of the former Soviet Union with radical political change. This argument may be correct by Western standards of a multi-party system and the separation of powers into the legislative, executive and judiciary. However, it is not true by Chinese political standards. In Chinese society, of the three fundamental variables of politics, economy and culture, politics has always been the most important and decisive in the final analysis. Mao Zedong expressed this quite clearly when he stated that politics was in command and was the soul for all work, "especially in a transitional society."[12] In China, it is probable that there can be no social reform—including economic reform—without political reform. The decisions of the Third Plenary Session of the Eleventh Party Central Committee can be considered as political reforms which stimulated the above-mentioned economic transformation. The process of China's economic diversification was initiated by political reform, which in turn is accelerating the process of political change.

---

[12] Mao Zedong, *Quotations from Chairman Mao*, Beijing, Capital Printing House, 1968, p. 118.

Political reform has been both independent of, and dependent on, Chinese reform over the last two decades. Political reform initiated the process of economic diversification which, in turn, has accelerated political change and brought about relative political pluralization. The events in Chinese politics over the last two decades can therefore be characterized as an about-turn from absolute centralism toward incremental democracy. By "incremental democracy," I mean the following: firstly, that the previous centralist system has been weakened and a pluralization of political life is emerging. However, political pluralization is conditional. In other words, China's politics is in a transitional phase from traditional totalism[13] toward conditional democracy. Secondly, when comparing economic and political liberalization, the extent and degree of the latter is much lower. In this author's view, such a process of relative or conditional pluralization will be found in political changes described below.

Separating the Party from the State

One of the outstanding features of traditional Chinese socialism has been to identify the Party with the state, a structure acclaimed by Mao Zedong as a political system under the "absolute centralist leadership of the Party." This was a typical centralist political model, under which the CCP, as the only ruling party, monopolized all legislative, executive and judicial powers, including all economic, ideological and management powers, national as well as local. The Party was identified with the government and vice-versa. At the very beginning of the reform process, reformists within the Party placed the separation of Party and state on the agenda, and even considered this to be a major breakthrough in traditional politics. After twenty years, China has made significant progress in the separation of Party and state, although the ideal of a complete separation of Party and state has yet to be realized, and will in fact be impossible to realize under a one-party system. Two aspects of progress are worth mentioning. First of all, the CCP has for the first time announced that it can no longer be considered as above the law, and has to act within the framework of the law—it has acknowledged

---

[13] The term "totalism" is different from "totalitarianism." This was originally put forward by American China expert Tang Tsou of Chicago University. It refers to a particular state whose essential feature is identification of the state with society. It is related to totalitarianism and authoritarianism, but also differs from those concepts.

that "it is an extremely important principle that the new Party Constitution stipulates that 'all activities of the Party (must be performed) within the framework of the law.'" From the central level right down to the local echelons, no activities of Party organizations or members may violate the national Constitution and laws. Moreover, "they must abide by the Constitution and other laws, and not hold privileges which place them above the national Constitution and other laws."[14] Secondly, the Party may not replace the government in exercising executive and administrative power. The Political Report of the Thirteenth National Party Congress includes an extra section on the separation of Party and state, which reiterates that this separation of functions is the key to political reform. "It is the Party that has led the people to establish the state bodies, public associations and various economic and cultural organizations; and the Party should guarantee that state bodies exercise their functions in full. It should however respect these and not take over the function of the public organizations." The Political Report emphasized that the Party's leadership should not be identified with administration and execution duties, defining political leadership as "leadership of political principles, important decision-making and recommendation of cadres to state bodies."[15]

Emergence of a Civil Society

During the Mao era, due to the overlapping of Party, state and society, there was no independent civil society. It is only since the reform process began that a relatively independent civil society gradually emerged. The number and diversity of civil organizations has increased significantly, with much greater legitimacy and autonomy. Prior to the reform process, only a few public and social organizations such as trade unions, the Youth League and the Women's Federation existed. Strictly speaking, however, they were not organizations of civil society, as all of them were in fact part of the Party and government hierarchy, with no independence. They were also auxiliary departments of the Party-State. Civil

<hr>

[14] Central Committee of the CCP, "Notes of the Central Committee of the CCP in terms of Safeguarding Socialist Law" (July 10, 1986), in: *Selected Documents of the National People's Congress*, ed. by the Research Office of the General Office of the Standing Committee of the NPC, Beijing Democracy and Law Press, 1992, p. 166.

[15] Zhao Ziyang, "Marching along the Socialist Road with Chinese Characteristics," Political Report of the Thirteenth National Party Congress, *ibid.*, p. 185.

society organizations (CSOs) have started to grow rapidly in the wake of market-oriented economic reforms. From the 1950s to the 1970s, only a few civil organizations existed, which were officially defined as "social associations" under the rigorous control of the Party-State. In the early 1950s, there were forty-four national social associations, and fewer than 100 had emerged by 1965; there were 6,000 local social associations during this period. By 1989, the number of national CSOs had increased to over 1,600, and local CSOs exceeded 200,000. By 1997, the number of CSOs at and above the county level nationwide had swelled to 181,318. There are no accurate statistics for CSOs below the county level, but according to conservative estimates, there are over 3 million.[16] Of these 739,500 are villagers' committees for self-governance and 510,000 are local trade unions.[17] Besides social associations, certain new CSOs emerged in the 1990s. Officially titled "civil non-enterprise units," there are approximately 700,000 such units across the country, according to civil affairs department estimates.[18] These all function, providing a foundation for democracy and creating a significant impact on democracy and good governance.[19]

Taking the Rule of Law as a Goal of China's Political Development

One of the major factors which led to the great tragedy of the "Cultural Revolution" was that there was no "rule of law," but rather, the "rule of men." This is the reason why the new generation of leaders and intellectuals laid considerable emphasis on the "rule of law" as soon as the reform process began, and why they prefer a state where the "rule of law" prevails as an overarching goal. The Fifteenth National Party Congress held in September 1997 formally endorsed national rule by the "rule of law." The "rule of law" was also inserted into the Political Report as one of the CCP's political goals. The National People's Congress later amended the Constitution by inserting the phrase "practicing the rule of law in the state" and constructing a socialist state where the "rule of law" applies, to establish "the rule of the state by the rule

---

[16] *China Civil Affairs Yearbook* 1998, Beijing, China Social Press, 1999.
[17] *China Statistical Yearbook* 1998, Beijing, China Statistical Publishing House, 1998.
[18] *China Civil Affairs Yearbook* 1998, *ibid.*
[19] For Chinese civil society and governance, see Yu Keping, "The Emergence of Civil Society and the Changes of Governance in Reforming China," in: *Social Science Quarterly* (Hong Kong), Autumn issue, 1999.

of law" as a constitutional principle. It is estimated that the National People's Congress (NPC) and its Standing Committee adopted 351 laws and statutes, the State Council drafted 800 regulations and the local People's Congresses more than 6,000 local laws and regulations in the twenty years between 1979 and 1999.[20] From 1994 until 1996, the NPC and its Standing Committee drafted a law or statute every thirteen days, while the State Council issued a regulation every six days. The authorities intend to establish a comprehensive system of Chinese law by the year 2010. This legal system is considered one of the basic goals if China is to establish national rule by the rule of law instead of the "rule of men."[21]

Broadening the Scope of Direct Elections and Local Self-Governance

Deng Xiaoping and other post-Mao Chinese leaders paid particular attention to local democracy and encouraged grassroots democracy. In line with this democratic logic, the *Election Law of the Representatives of the National People's Congress and the Local People's Congresses at All Levels* adopted in July 1979 stipulates that all representatives at and below the county level must be elected directly by voters. Although no leading Party and government cadres are appointed by direct election, experimental direct elections for town and township leaders were conducted in Sichuan Province and Shenzhen Special Economic Zone in 1998 and 1999, suggesting that this process may be expanded in the near future. The outstanding development in terms of grassroots democracy was the issue of self-governance of villagers. According to the *Organic Law of the Village Administration Committees of the People's Republic of China* adopted in December 1989, villagers' self-governance should be rolled out gradually across the country, so that upper government echelons no longer run village affairs, and the administrative body of the villages is not appointed by the Party Committee or higher government bodies, but is elected directly and freely by villagers. By the end of 1997, approximately 60% of villages had started with self-governance and over 900,000 village committees had been elected with 90% of voters participating in elections.

---

²⁰ Renmin Ribao, April 14, 1999.
²¹ Jiang Zemin, "Holding High the Banner of Deng Xiaoping Theory and Push the Cause of Building Socialism with Chinese Characteristics into the 21st Century," in: *Selected Documents of the Fifteenth Party Congress*, Beijing, People's Publishing House, 1999, p. 33.

There are four elements to the villagers' self-governance process. 1) Election of villagers. The head of the village and the members of the village committee must be elected through free, direct and secret vote. 2) Village assembly. All major decisions, including plans and projects related to the development of the village economy, public goods and other important issues, should be approved and decided on by the village assembly or representative assembly. 3) Dissemination of the village's political and financial affairs. All matters involving the village's public interests must be made known to the villagers. 4) Village rules and regulations. Routine village matters are managed according to village rules and regulations. The implication of village self-governance is immense, specifically in democratic terms, as of China's 1.3 billion people, over 800 million live in rural areas.

Separating Government Functions from Enterprise Management

It is a feature of traditional socialism that the government owns and runs enterprises. Under this system, the state monopolized and managed all major enterprises. Directors were appointed by the Party and the government, enterprises had a similar hierarchy to government bureaucracy, and enterprise directors held official cadre ranks. For example, a director of a minister-level enterprise enjoyed the same privileges as a government minister. The integration of enterprises and government was a product of the planned and "command" economy, and is incompatible with a modern enterprise system and market economy, which requires all enterprises to operate as independent corporations. The twenty-year process of economic reform, in a sense, has been a process of separating government functions from enterprise management. This was seen by Mao's successors as one of the main tasks of reform, so the central topic of the Fourth Plenary Session of the Fifteenth Party Central Committee Congress held in Beijing in 1997 was furthering the reform of state-owned enterprises (SOE) and the establishment of modern corporate structures. China has made much headway in this regard, although this is a difficult process and the country still has a long way to go. So far all enterprises—including SOEs—have been relatively separated from government and the government no longer run enterprises directly. SOEs are for the most part transforming their ownership and management. Meanwhile, SOE directors no longer serve as officials of Party and government. Absolute centralist politics have been shaken to their roots as their basis, the unity of government and enterprises, is gradually disappearing.

Recent Chinese Discourses on Democracy

Further evidence that traditional absolute centralist politics are giving way to incremental democracy can be seen in the changes in the relationship between the central and local levels, between the government and its citizens, the more liberal political climate and other political changes. The more liberal climate has initiated a wider discourse on democracy among Chinese intellectuals. During the Mao era, free discussion of political issues, especially democracy, was never permitted and none dared to do so. Since the implementation of reforms, political issues still remain sensitive and even a little risky, but the climate is liberalizing to the extent that an ever fewer number of intellectuals who participate in political discourse on democracy are subject to persecution. All issues are carefully divided into two categories: the first, the political ones, may still not be discussed freely, and the second, the academic ones, which can be freely discussed. This pattern of thought has been fiercely attacked: "Reserving free speech to academic issues and not allowing political issues to be discussed deprives vast numbers of citizens of their rights to political participation and provides only a few people with access to politics."[22] Under this more liberal political climate, Chinese intellectuals now dare to face "sensitive" political issues: "The reform of the socialist political system is a sensitive issue. Why is it sensitive? It is sensitive because of interference from the 'Left' and the 'Right.' How can we solve major problems? And how can we advance if we cannot discuss and study these problems because of their sensitivity?"[23]

Although there are still various pressures and obstructions, Chinese intellectuals are taking advantage of the relatively liberal climate to launch a major discourse on politics, especially on democracy, which has been a favorite topic over the last twenty years. A multitude of essays, books and articles about democracy published over the last two decades provide a variety of views on democracy, which can be categorized into three groups: orthodox Marxism, Liberalism and Incremental Democracy.

---

[22] Zhang Xianyang and Wang Guixiu, "On Free Speech," in: *Reading*, No. 9, 1979.

[23] Liu Ji, "Actively Explore Realistic Paths to Socialist Democracy," in: *Reports of Problems in China's Political System* (1978–1998), ed. Liu Zhifeng, Beijing, Chinese Movies Publishing House, 1999, pp. 1–2.

Orthodox Marxism

Orthodox Marxism believes that democracy means that people are the masters of their own country, and is a superstructure based upon and serving the economic foundation. Democracy has a distinctive class nature and there is no democracy outside of class: "It is the historical nature of democracy and of the state that the ruling class enjoys democratic rights while the ruled do not, or only enjoy very few, incomplete formalized democratic rights."[24] According to this logic, only socialist democracy is the true and highest form of democracy serving the majority of the people, while the capitalist version is a false democracy serving only a minority of people. Orthodox Marxism draws a natural conclusion from this theoretical logic: China can never practice Western democracy in the sense of a multi-party system and the separation of the legislature, the executive and the judiciary. Otherwise, in its advocates' eyes, Chinese history will regress. Only the people's representative system is suited to China's reality. This has priority over any capitalist democracy and is the sole realistic way toward Chinese democracy which "can guarantee that people rule the state by law and become the masters of the state."[25]

Liberalism

Liberalism emphasizes the universality of Western democracy. According to this theory, China has embraced the market economy, which is a liberal economy requiring liberal politics. The elements of liberal democracy are representative democracy, a multi-party system and a separation of the three legislative, executive and judiciary powers. The theory requires China to allow the existence of opposition parties to the CCP, and all other parties must be allowed the right to be in power by the Constitution. The powers of the legislative, the executive and the judiciary must also be separated. Chinese liberals rarely express their views on democracy directly, because the Constitution stipulates that the CCP is the only ruling party in China—one of "four principles" which it is politically risky to oppose. However, they openly

---

[24] Feng Wenbin, "On Problems in Socialist Democracy," in: *Practical Selections for 20th-Century China*, ed. by Li Bingqing, Beijing, Chinese Peace Publishing House, 1998, p. 61.

[25] Du Gan, "An Analysis of Political Pluralisation," in: *Social Sciences Studies*, No. 2, 1992.

praise liberal economic and political values: "We are in a transition to a market economy. The market economy will impel economic liberalism, which is the basis of all other liberalism.... We are entering a global age. The market economy has become a global trend, and liberty and liberalism are becoming increasingly global values, too.... After 300 years of comparison and choice worldwide, and especially after over a century of social experimentation on the largest scale in China, we have ample evidence to hand that liberalism is the best and most universal value."[26]

The Chinese orthodox Marxist view of democracy is reduced so that it has an impact on actual political life because it stresses centralism rather than freedom, the Chinese characteristics of democracy rather than its universality, and its substantial importance rather than its procedural importance. The liberal view of democracy is only to be noticed in a small intellectual circle due to the lack of a necessary legitimate basis and feasible conditions. In comparison, China's political development is being greatly influenced by Incremental Democracy, since it reflects the reality of reform pretty well.

Incremental Democracy

Incremental Democracy's pragmatic attitude distinguishes it from orthodox Marxism and liberalism. It emphasises the *effects* of democracy rather than its theory; it is not preoccupied with a particular theory or doctrine of democracy but embraces the useful elements from various theories and doctrines; it fully agrees with the universality of democracy while retaining a clear understanding of China's specific situation and traditional culture; it doesn't emphasize the role of intellectuals, but instead that of people from all ranks and classes; it advocates the full use of existing conditions to push Chinese democracy forward incrementally by path-dependence.[27] Incremental Democracy in China may boil down to the following aspects.

---

[26] Li Shenzhi, "Carry forward the Liberal Tradition of Peking University," in: *Traditions of Peking University and Modern China*, Beijing, China Personnel Publishing House, 1998, pp. 4–5.

[27] The term "path-dependence" is borrowed from biology by social scientists such as the renowned US economist Ronald Coase. It means that a social organism, like a biological one, will expend too much if it changes so fundamentally that it deviates completely from its previous condition or traditions.

Highlighting Democratic Procedures and Institutions
Incremental Democracy holds that democracy is above all a set of institutions and procedures guaranteeing the freedom, equality and other political rights of citizens. The essence of democracy is popular political participation, and a popular participation process is a fundamental path to democracy—participation is a manifestation of democratic rights. It is also essential that a democratic constitution enjoins the sovereignty of the people, and all modern states have their own "democratic" constitutions. However, democracy would have no meaning if a constitution on paper specifying citizens' rights lacked the practical ways and means to implement these rights. In a pragmatic democracy, practical procedures for implementing constitutional democratic rights are no less important than the articles of the constitution themselves. Incremental Democracy insists that it is critical that Chinese democracy is equipped with feasible procedures enabling citizens to have a say in final decision-making and participate in the planning of the political agenda. On the one hand, Chinese laws must be improved and on the other hand, even more importantly, citizens' legal rights provided by the constitution and laws must be guaranteed and implemented.[28]

Accepting Civil Society as a Precondition for Democracy
Incremental Democracy believes that civil society is an intermediate associational layer between the state on the one side and the basic building blocks of society on the other, inhabited by social and civil organizations named "the third sector," "NGO" and "Civil Society Organizations." CSOs are relatively independent of the state, enjoy some autonomy in their relations with the state, and are formed voluntarily by members of society to protect or extend their interests, values or identities. The major reasons that civil society is essential to democracy are as follow: "Firstly, one of the main features of civil society is its autonomy, which is also one of the ultimate goals of democracy. In this sense, the democratic development process means a process of expanding civil society and withdrawing the state. Secondly, the essential meaning of democracy is popular sovereignty. In all modern states, popular sovereignty is always indirect, while governments exercise direct power. Thus, from a feasible and pragmatic perspective, the

---

[28] See Yu Keping, "Substantial Democracy or Procedural Democracy," in: *Way*, No. 12, 1997.

essential meaning of democracy is popular supervision and control of the government, which can only be effective if civil society is sufficiently strong and powerful. In other words, popular supervision and control of government does not work without a strong civil society."[29]

Respect for the Rule of Law

Incremental Democracy believes that it is only by the rule of law, instead of the rule of men, that personal autocracy can be prevented and citizens' rights can be protected. China has been traditionally under the rule of men for thousands of years, so implementing the rule of law is relatively difficult. No democracy, no rule of law. The most important task for Chinese democracy is to transform the rule of men into the rule of law and to establish a state where the rule of law prevails. Nowadays, progress in implementing the rule of law can even be regarded as progress in Chinese democracy. China has declared its aim to establish a socialist state under the "rule of law," and has drafted thousands of laws and statutes at both the central and local levels. A Chinese legal system based on the Constitution is forming, enabling China's political, economic and social life, for the most part, to have a legal foundation. There is a long way to go, however, until the "rule of law" is established, and an even longer way to go to establishing the bare necessities for implementing "rule by law." A majority of officials and civil servants act according to policies rather than law. As one law professional put it, "Firstly, officials and civil servants often don't abide by the Constitution and laws, but implement policies. For the sake of their own local or departmental interests, there are instances where local or departmental authorities draft local or departmental policies in violation of central government laws and policies, and act illegally to serve their private interests. Secondly, certain judges, procurators, policemen and lawyers do not abide by legal procedures and even abuse the law at will according to their own individual interests. Thirdly, ordinary people do not have an understanding of the law but prefer the traditional idea that "handling legal affairs relies on personal connections."[30]

---

[29] Yu Keping, "Socialist Civil Society: A New Subject," in: *Tianjin Social Sciences Bimonthly*, No. 4, 1993.

[30] Li Shuguang, "The Legal Orientation of Political Reform," in: *Political China*, ed. by Dong Yuyu, Beijing, Today's China Press, 1998, p. 81.

Affirming the Critical Role of Government in Promoting Democracy
Incremental Democracy argues that East Asia's political and cultural traditions differ from those of the West, in the more important role that the state or government in social development and civil life plays. In China, grassroots democracy and local self-government is motivated by government, civil society is led by government, and the market economy is initiated by the government. Furthermore, "the process of the rule of law is led by the government, not by citizens' spontaneous endeavours, which was exemplified by the government campaign in support of the popularization of laws."[31] In accordance with this logic, Incremental Democracy neither suits the libertarian desire to minimize the functions of the state, nor the desire that firm or gentle use of government powers should depend on the specific situation. Instead, it encourages government to play a more active and initiatory role in the development process of Chinese democracy. For "a government violates human rights if it does what it shouldn't as much as if it doesn't do what it should."[32]

Advocacy of Cooperative Democracy
Incremental Democracy aims to build democracy on the basis of cooperation between the government and its citizens, and to encourage constructive collaboration between the government and its citizens in all aspects of political, economic and social life. In the Mao era, there prevailed a philosophy of struggle that urged people to clash and struggle against each other. It was against the democratic spirit that the model of political interaction between the government and its citizens was a zero-sum game, i.e., conflict, and that the main means of resolving conflict was coercion. On the contrary, an increasing number of intellectuals want to develop "a democratic system of cooperation" by which "the government is subject to popular democratic supervision. People handle their own affairs and local authorities deal with their own affairs, such that there is cooperation between the government and the people and between the central and local authorities." To be specific, the democratic system of cooperation has three outstanding features: firstly, "the pressure and motive power of local governments at all levels

---

[31] Li Shuguang, *ibid.*, p. 80.
[32] Yu Keping, "What Government Should and Should Not Do," in: *Political Science Studies*, No. 1, 1998.

to promote economic development and social progress in their localities comes both from the government at the higher level and from the local people"; secondly, "it is designed to divide work appropriately between the central and local authorities and between political and economic organizations, define their responsibilities, rights and obligations, and then create the conditions needed for their cooperation"; and thirdly, "all participating parties share the benefits of cooperation."[33]

Recent Chinese Discourse on Governance

The concepts of governance and good governance have only appeared in Chinese academic circles in recent years, not least due to the World Bank's Annual Report of 1992 which was entitled "Governance and Development." Once the report was translated and published in China, a number of Chinese economists and political scientists began to pay attention to the issues of governance and good governance. Around the mid-1990s, Chinese economists began to research corporate governance, while some political scientists studied good governance in Chinese political life. Generally speaking, the concepts of "governance" and "good governance" are strange to Chinese scholars, so no uniform Chinese version of these two concepts has yet appeared.[34]

The terms "government" and "governance" have been used alternately in the field of public management related to political affairs. This was for example the case in the English-speaking world. Since the 1990s, Western theories of governance and good governance have been introduced in China, and some Chinese scholars have thus tried to distinguish governance from government by limiting "government" to the activities of the central and local authorities, while they refer to "governance" for all public management activities, including corporate management. The views of certain Western specialists and professional institutions on governance like N.N. Rosenau, R. Rhodes, Bob Jessop

---

[33] Rong Jingben et al., *Reform of the Political System at the County and Township Levels*, Beijing, Central Compilation & Translation Press, 1998, pp. 371–384.

[34] We have so far found four special articles on governance and good governance from a political science perspective in China. From 1997 onwards, six Chinese scholars and I have been engaged in a research project on "Civil Society and Governance in Reforming China," which will be finished at the end of this year.

and the Commission on Global Governance appear to be particularly influential in China. Chinese scholars widely regard governance as "governing without government," a process of interaction between the state and civil society; a new cooperation between the government and the civil, public and private sectors; a management and coordination mechanism with consensus and identity, a social self-organizational network, and so on.

Basically, governance stands for a synthesis of management of public and private affairs and a sustainable coordination process to maximize the common good. It steps beyond the dichotomy of the state and civil society, the public and private, the governmental and non-governmental, and coercion and voluntariness. Like government, governance requires the authority and power necessary to maintain public order and maximize the common good. However, governance must be distinguished from government by two main differences. Firstly, although both governance and government require authority, the authority for governance is not necessarily based upon specific government bodies, while that of government is always based upon certain state apparatus. The scope of governance is therefore much broader than that of government. Governance, rather than government, is necessary for all communities from universities, corporations and interest groups to small clubs, schools and voluntary organizations as long as they work properly. Second, power is implemented differently. Government power always operates from the top down, primarily through orders, statutes, bureaucracy and coercion, while the power of governance is mutual, interacting both from the top to bottom, and from the bottom to the top, primarily through collaboration, coordination, negotiation, social networking, neighborhood, identity or consensus.[35]

The concept of good government is an element of traditional Chinese political culture, and good government has been perceived as an ideal political model for thousands of years since government first came into being. From the perspective of traditional Chinese political culture, the assessment criteria for good government include justice, high efficiency, honest officials, good service, and rule of law. These criteria can be of course used to evaluate any government, and a good government which meets these criteria will be the popular political expectation as long

---

[35] Yu Keping, "Introduction to Governance and Good Governance," in: *Marxism and Reality* (Bimonthly), No. 5, 1999.

as governments exist. The dominant concept of good government in Chinese political culture has been shaken and gradually given way to good governance as China has embarked on the modernization process, especially in the global age. We suggest that a set of assessment criteria for good governance be developed on the basis of the traditional good government as below: 1) legitimacy; 2) transparency; 3) accountability; 4) the rule of law; 5) responsiveness; 6) effectiveness; 7) order; 8) stability (see the appendix for details).[36]

Essentially, good governance is a political model for the global age. It is the return of political power to society from the state and is thus a process of popular participation in political life. Good governance means good cooperation between the state and civil society or between the government and its citizens. Good governance is more concerned with the citizens rather than the government in the sense that it is possible for certain small communities to progress without government but it is impossible for them to progress without good public management. Good government is possible without citizens' active and voluntary participation and their identification with the tasks of public authorities, but not so with good governance. In short, good governance is based upon the citizens or civil society, rather than upon the state or the government; good governance without a strong civil society appears to be impossible.

Furthermore, it is critical for good governance that people have sufficient power and rights to participate in elections, decision-making and government supervision. Obviously, only under democratic conditions can people be entitled to such power and rights. Good governance and democracy thus coincide here: good governance is unfeasible without democracy, and vice-versa. Good government may be possible under an authoritarian regime, but good governance would never be possible without functioning democratic mechanisms. The objective of our political development should be good governance on the basis of democratic governance. Hence we conclude this paper with an attempt to develop a set of analytical criteria and indicators of Chinese democratic governance that combine a synthesis of universal principles of democracy and good governance and specifically Chinese features (see appendix).

---

[36] See Yu Keping, "Good Governance: A Political Model in the Global Age," in: *Way*, No. 1, 1999.

Appendix

Principal Assessment Criteria and Indicators for Research on Chinese
Democracy and Governance

Assessment criteria	Specific Indicators or area of concern
Rule of Law	• Status of laws and law-making • Official and citizens' understanding of and respect for law • Actual role of law in reality • Autonomy and authority of legislative and judicial activities • Universal application of law across the country and different sections and departments
Political Participation	• Election laws and regulations • Scope of direct elections • Methods and measures of elections • Access to secret vote • Selection method of candidates • Proportion of candidates to positions • Percentage of citizens registered to vote • Voting percentage of citizens • Extent of participation by socially disadvantaged groups
Plurality	• Extent of participation by women • Extent of participation by ethnic groups • Participation by democratic parties • Participation by private owners • Professional representation of Party and government officials • Regional representation of the Party and government • Ages of the Party and the government officials
Transparency	• Quantity and quality of political channels and media, including media restrictions and publication laws, independence of media, government censorship, acts of violence against journalists • Promotion of decision-making process • Promotion of activities of government organs including the public security organs, procuratorial organs and people's courts • Provision of information about official procedures • Publication of budgets and expenditure plans • Citizens' knowledge of political affairs • Citizens' rights of access to political information

Table (*cont.*)

Assessment criteria	Specific Indicators or area of concern
Human rights and citizenship	• Constitutional provisions and laws concerning civil and political rights • Implementation of legal provisions related to civil rights • Respect for and protection of rights of minorities and dissidents by law and by the government • Popular awareness of human rights • Official awareness of human rights • Popular capacity to protect their own rights • Respect for and protection of rights of the disabled, the weak and the poor
Supervision of the Party and the government	• Legal rights of citizens against injustice and improper behavior of government • Check and balance of powers • Popular checks on government powers • Supervision by mass media of the Party and government • Role of public opinion in checking Party and government power • Self-disciplinary regulations and practice of the Party and government
Internal Party democracy and cooperation between the CCP and democratic parties	• Elections within the Party • Procedure and mechanism for selecting Party leaders at various levels • Decision-making institutions within the Party Committees • Relationship between the Party and the government • Relationship between the Party and ordinary people • Relationship between the CCP and the democratic parties
Grassroots Democracy	• Percentage of villagers' self-governance in the countryside • Percentage of inhabitants' self-governance in towns and cities • Self-governance of local communities • Popular participation in local government proceedings • Operation and role of labor representative assemblies • Extent of participation by trade unions • Extent of participation by women's federations • Direct elections of leadership at township level

Table (*cont.*)

Assessment criteria	Specific Indicators or area of concern
Civil Organizations	• Number and diversity of civil society organizations • Involvement of membership in key government decisions • Extent of participation by civil organizations • Impact on political, social and economic life • Legal, economic, political and cultural environments
Legitimacy	• Fairness and regularity of government's behavior and policies • Popular identification with the Party and government • Justice of authoritative allocation of social values • Extent of legitimization of Party activities • Percentage of corrupt officials • Access to legal system for wider constituencies
Accountability	• Official honesty • Responsibility of officials for their behavior • Punishment of officials due to illegal activities • Communication between officials and citizens • Official respect for citizens' opinions • Official mechanisms for accepting and dealing with public opinion • Frequency of election and alternation of officials • Highlighted incidence of corrupt practices • Public awareness of government procedures and regulations
Responsiveness	• Consultative mechanisms for the Party and government • Mechanisms for redress against restrictive legislations, regulations, administration, judgements, and other legal action. • Changes to government policy as a result of popular advocacy • Party and government initiatives due to societal deliberation • Government innovations • Use of alternative dispute resolution mechanisms • Frequency of interaction between the government and citizens • Government debates as part of decision-making process attended by citizens • Extent of citizens' involvement in the ruling groups of the Party and the government

Table (*cont.*)

Assessment criteria	Specific Indicators or area of concern
Effectiveness	• Cost of government • Frequency of government policy failures • Efficiency of policies • Length of time required to make key decisions • Government capacity to deal with eventualities • Popular satisfaction with government policies • Quantity and quality of public goods provided by the government
Social Order	• Hierarchy of the Party and the government • Adaptability and authority of law • Authority of the Party and the government • Popular confidence in the government • Sustainability of existing social norms • Popular political identity • Challenges to the existing order
Social stability	• Crime rates • Ethnic conflicts • Regional differentiation • Polarization of the rich and poor • Relationship between the center and local levels • Relationship between cadres and masses • Popular sensitivity to social crisis • Growth of anti-government activities such as petitions, protests, demonstrations, etc.